John F. Kennedy

Other Titles in the
People Who Made History Series

Charles Darwin
Adolf Hitler
Martin Luther King Jr.

John F. Kennedy

Clarice Swisher, *Book Editor*

David L. Bender, *Publisher*
Bruno Leone, *Executive Editor*
Bonnie Szumski, *Editorial Director*
David M. Haugen, *Managing Editor*
Scott Barbour, *Series Editor*

Greenhaven Press, San Diego, CA

Library of Congress Cataloging-in-Publication Data

Kennedy, John F. (John Fitzgerald), 1917–1963.
    John F. Kennedy / Clarice Swisher, book editor.
        p.   cm. — (People who made history)
    Includes bibliographical references (p.   ) and index.
    ISBN 0-7377-0225-7 (lib. bdg. : alk. paper). —
    ISBN 0-7377-0224-9 (pbk. : alk. paper)
    1. United States—Politics and government—
    1961–1963. 2. Presidents—United States—Biography.
    I. Series.
    E841.K36   2000
    973.922'092—dc21   99-17692
                                                                CIP

Every effort has been made to trace the owners of copyrighted material. The articles in this volume may have been edited for content, length, and/or reading level. The titles have been changed to enhance the editorial purpose of the Opposing Viewpoints® concept. Those interested in locating the original source will find the complete citation on the first page of each article.

Cover photo: Corbis-Bettmann
John F. Kennedy Library, 24
NASA, 25
National Archives, 19, 30, 32

Copyright ©2000 by Greenhaven Press, Inc.
PO Box 289009
San Diego, CA 92198-9009
Printed in the U.S.A.

CONTENTS

Foreword   10

John F. Kennedy: A Hero for His Time   12

Chapter 1: The Major Influences on John F. Kennedy's Development: The Fitzgerald and Kennedy Traditions

1. **The Fitzgerald Influence: Charm, Energy, and Hard Work** *by Gail Cameron*   36

    The son of an Irish immigrant, John F. Kennedy's maternal grandfather, John F. Fitzgerald became the popular mayor of Boston, winning Irish voters with his charm and "Fitz-blarney." At his side was his favorite child, Rose, who learned to campaign and work crowds with the Fitzgerald energy and confidence. As a mother, Rose instilled a love of politics and the desire to win in her children, including John F. Kennedy.

2. **Toughness Propels the Kennedys' Survival and Success** *by Richard J. Whalen*   45

    A spirit of toughness threads through generations of Kennedys—from John Kennedy's great-grandfather and great-grandmother Patrick and Bridget, to his grandfather Patrick Joseph, to his father Joseph. All of the Kennedys worked hard and took advantage of opportunities to move by generations from the status of impoverished immigrants to that of a wealthy family.

3. **The Influence of Joseph Kennedy, the President's Father** *by James MacGregor Burns*   54

    Determined to overcome the prejudice he experienced as an Irishman, Joseph Kennedy built a huge fortune; and once at the top economically, he turned to politics to augment his financial power. Because he wanted his children to be prepared for a harsh world, he encouraged them to compete with one another and demanded high standards in their schoolwork.

Chapter 2: The Kennedy Style of Politics

1. The Nixon-Kennedy Debate
by Christopher Matthews   63
Richard Nixon, who had recently been in the hospital and had campaigned up to the last minute before the first 1960 presidential debate, was no match for his suntanned, well-groomed, and well-prepared opponent, John Kennedy. For the first time, television images were a deciding factor in a presidential race.

2. The New Frontier *by Arthur Schlesinger Jr.*   71
Kennedy introduced the phrase "The New Frontier" in his acceptance speech at the Democratic convention in Los Angeles as a set of new challenges for the 1960s. To work on them, Kennedy assembled a host of intelligent, enthusiastic people from government, universities, public service, and business.

3. Kennedy: Master of the Art of Power
by Gore Vidal   79
Kennedy used his personal attractiveness and charm, his individuality, his quick wit, and his ease in conversation to create a powerful persona early in his presidency. His energy, style, and youth set a tone markedly different from that of his predecessor, President Dwight Eisenhower.

Chapter 3: Kennedy's Domestic Agenda

1. The President Versus the Steel Industry
by Irving Bernstein   87
After two decades of disruptive strikes in the steel industry, President Kennedy was determined to have the 1962 contract between management and labor settled peaceably with an outcome beneficial to the economy. When U.S. Steel raised prices after a negotiated settlement, Kennedy fought back, and U.S. Steel backed down.

2. Kennedy's Failure to Work for Civil Rights
by Henry Fairlie   95
Though Kennedy made a campaign commitment to introduce civil rights legislation, he procrastinated for two years and then offered only tokenism. Pushed by civil rights leaders and forced to respond to the violence surrounding civil rights protests, Kennedy developed a strategy of moral consensus, hoping to avoid political confrontation that might defeat legislation altogether.

3. Kennedy's Civil Rights Legislation Becomes Law
by Allen J. Matusow   102
In the spring and summer of 1963, violence in Birmingham, Alabama, protest marches in cities throughout Amer-

ica, and defiance of federal orders to allow black students to enroll in universities led President Kennedy to the conclusion that the time was right for a civil rights stand. He addressed the nation and sent civil rights legislation to Congress. After Kennedy's assassination, Robert Kennedy worked with Congress to pass the bill, and President Johnson signed it into law.

Chapter 4: Kennedy and Foreign Policy

1. **The Bay of Pigs Disaster** by *Thomas G. Paterson*   115
Having inherited problems with Cuba from the Eisenhower administration, Kennedy approved a plan for a covert invasion of the island to topple Fidel Castro. Though advisers tried to warn Kennedy of potential risks, the plan went forward and subsequently failed, creating doubts about Kennedy's ability to lead.

2. **The Peace Corps**
   by *Charles Lam Markmann and Mark Sherwin*   123
Within three months of his inauguration, President Kennedy proposed the creation of a Peace Corps, an organization of volunteers to work on projects in underdeveloped countries. The program was so popular nationally and internationally that it began sending volunteers before the year was out.

3. **The Alliance for Progress** by *Bruce Miroff*   132
Kennedy, who sympathized with the plight of the poor in Latin America and feared that their conditions might cause a revolution, developed the Alliance for Progress to promote democracy and stability. After a decade, social conditions had not improved, but American corporations had profited by exploiting poor countries.

Chapter 5: Confronting Khrushchev and Waging the Cold War

1. **The Kennedy-Khrushchev Meeting in Vienna**
   by *Kenneth P. O'Donnell and David F. Powers with Joe McCarthy*   142
Determined to convey to Khrushchev that the United States insisted on maintaining a western presence in Berlin, Kennedy wanted to meet his Russian opponent early in his presidency. The talks had a share of banter and humor, but the two leaders primarily focused on testing each other's strength and on disagreements and threats over the West's presence in Berlin.

2. **The Berlin Crisis** by *Theodore C. Sorensen*   151
President Kennedy decided that the western allies had to stand up to Khrushchev when he threatened to eliminate

their presence in West Berlin by signing a treaty with East Germany. Kennedy both increased military strength and expanded talks. Though Khrushchev put up the Berlin Wall, the western presence was preserved, and tensions lessened.

3. **An Overview of the Cuban Missile Crisis**
   by Raymond L. Garthoff   162
   The Soviet-American conflict over Cuba escalated during the fall of 1962. To counter American covert actions, the Soviets planned to install troops and missiles in Cuba. When intelligence detected the plan, Kennedy resisted firmly. In the face of possible nuclear strikes, the two sides settled without catastrophe.

4. **The Russian View of the Cuban Missile Crisis, and Kennedy's Response**
   by Nikita Khrushchev and John F. Kennedy   171
   From the Russian perspective, American plans for action against Cuba were aggressive and threatening to a small island that had freely chosen communism. At the request of Cubans, the Russians had planned to place missiles in Cuba for use in the event of an American attack. Kennedy responded that the attempt to install missiles in Cuba was a deliberate effort to alter the balance of power.

Chapter 6: Assessing John F. Kennedy

1. **An Assessment of Kennedy's Policies and Programs** *by William G. Carleton*   179
   Though Kennedy changed the style of presidential campaigns, he achieved few of his domestic campaign promises, in part because he failed to court Congress. In a Cold War with the Soviet Union and in competition with Nikita Khrushchev for political advantage, Kennedy searched for clear direction during his first two years, but he achieved world acclaim for his handling of the Cuban missile crisis in October 1962.

2. **An Assessment of Kennedy's Character**
   by Thomas C. Reeves   188
   John Kennedy developed a pragmatic approach to life and created a popular image that sometimes obscured the fact that he engaged in inappropriate behavior and associated with people involved in immoral and illegal activities. His character was influenced by his father, who urged him to strive for the top and win at any cost and who willingly used his money to promote J.F.K.'s progress.

3. **Kennedy's Liberal Legacy** *by David Burner*   196
   By filling the positions in his administration with intellectuals, academicians, and liberals, Kennedy shifted the

American political climate to the left. This administration formulated Cold War policies characterized by confrontation blended with caution and restraint and developed humanitarian opportunities to counter communism.

Discussion Questions and Research Projects   209

Appendix: Excerpts from Original Documents
Pertaining to John F. Kennedy   211

Chronology   228

For Further Research   231

Index   233

FOREWORD

In the vast and colorful pageant of human history, a handful of individuals stand out. They are the men and women who have come variously to be called "great," "leading," "brilliant," "pivotal," or "infamous" because they and their deeds forever changed their own society or the world as a whole. Some were political or military leaders–kings, queens, presidents, generals, and the like–whose policies, conquests, or innovations reshaped the maps and futures of countries and entire continents. Among those falling into this category were the formidable Roman statesman/general Julius Caesar, who extended Rome's power into Gaul (what is now France); Caesar's lover and ally, the notorious Egyptian queen Cleopatra, who challenged the strongest male rulers of her day; and England's stalwart Queen Elizabeth I, whose defeat of the mighty Spanish Armada saved England from subjugation.

Some of history's other movers and shakers were scientists or other thinkers whose ideas and discoveries altered the way people conduct their everyday lives or view themselves and their place in nature. The electric light and other remarkable inventions of Thomas Edison, for example, revolutionized almost every aspect of home-life and the workplace; and the theories of naturalist Charles Darwin lit the way for biologists and other scientists in their ongoing efforts to understand the origins of living things, including human beings.

Still other people who made history were religious leaders and social reformers. The struggles of the Arabic prophet Muhammad more than a thousand years ago led to the establishment of one of the world's great religions–Islam; and the efforts and personal sacrifices of an American reverend named Martin Luther King Jr. brought about major improvements in race relations and the justice system in the United States.

Each anthology in the People Who Made History series begins with an introductory essay that provides a general overview of the individual's life, times, and contributions. The group of essays that follow are chosen for their accessibility to a young adult audience and carefully edited in consideration of the reading and comprehension levels of that audience. Some of the essays are by noted historians, professors, and other experts. Others are excerpts from contemporary writings by or about the pivotal individual in question. To aid the reader in choosing the material of immediate interest or need, an annotated table of contents summarizes the article's main themes and insights.

Each volume also contains extensive research tools, including a collection of excerpts from primary source documents pertaining to the individual under discussion. The volumes are rounded out with an extensive bibliography and a comprehensive index.

Plutarch, the renowned first-century Greek biographer and moralist, crystallized the idea behind Greenhaven's People Who Made History when he said, "To be ignorant of the lives of the most celebrated men of past ages is to continue in a state of childhood all our days." Indeed, since it is people who make history, every modern nation, organization, institution, invention, artifact, and idea is the result of the diligent efforts of one or more individuals, living or dead; and it is therefore impossible to understand how the world we live in came to be without examining the contributions of these individuals.

JOHN F. KENNEDY: A HERO FOR HIS TIME

John F. Kennedy's life, though only forty-six years long, spanned major American historical events. Born at the beginning of World War I, he lived during World War II, the Korean War, the Cold War, and died at the beginning of the Vietnam War. As a boy, he lived during the Roaring Twenties and the stock market crash, the dust bowl, and the Great Depression. As an adult he experienced the chagrin other Americans felt as the Soviet Union launched Sputnik and moved ahead in space exploration; he suffered with all Americans as the police attacked children during the civil rights movement; and he saw the dawn of the television age and the start of the sixties revolt. Historical events, personal experiences, and his own personal qualities came together to make him a congressional representative, a senator, and the thirty-fifth president of the United States.

John Fitzgerald Kennedy was born in Boston on May 29, 1917, the second child born to Rose and Joseph Kennedy, who were descendants of Irish immigrants. Their oldest child was Joseph Jr., born in 1915, and the other seven children, Rosemary, Kathleen, Eunice, Patricia, Robert, Jean, and Edward, called Ted, followed John, who was called Jack. The Kennedy parents reared their children with discipline and guidance, and the children, like other children with strict parents, sometimes resented the demands but responded with respect. Joseph Kennedy repeatedly said, "My business is my family and my family is my business."[1] The children were expected to participate actively in sports and develop a desire to win; they were expected at the dinner table to ask questions, discuss issues, express disagreement, and develop agile minds. All of the children had to read for one hour a day during the summer, from a book list approved by the parents. A Boston friend, Norman McDonald, said that Joe Kennedy "disciplined Jack like a Jesuit. When the father was around, Jack could not invite any friends he wanted to their summer home in Hyannis Port. He had to submit a guest list and schedule to his father, and would invite only people who were useful."[2] Rose Kennedy supported her husband's insistence that the children finish in first place, but she was also the major teacher of proper conduct and manners. At times Jack thought he had a model mother, but at others he said she lacked affection and was either at a Paris fashion house or on her knees in church.

Throughout his life Kennedy suffered from poor health and lived with pain. He had had four childhood illnesses by age three, and in 1920 he had a case of scarlet fever so severe the priest administered last rites. He was routinely afflicted with colds, infections, and periodic back pain, made worst by a football injury at Harvard. His brother Bobby, joking about his brother's illnesses, said, "If a mosquito bit Jack, the mosquito would die."[3] As an adult he was diagnosed with Addison's disease, a fault in the secretion of the adrenal glands, characterized by weakness, loss of weight, and low blood pressure. During his entire life Kennedy took great pains to cover up his poor health and to exert unusual effort to compensate for his physical limitations.

EDUCATION AND MILITARY SERVICE

After elementary school, Jack Kennedy was educated in private schools. In 1930, at thirteen, he attended Canterbury School in Melford, Connecticut, but an appendicitis attack caused him to drop out. In the fall, he went to Choate, a prestigious college preparatory school in Wallingford, Connecticut, that was attended by many children of Boston's elite society. Describing himself as a drifter at Choate, he made only average grades and graduated in 1935. After part of a year at Princeton, he went to Harvard, his father's choice of schools, and became a more stable student during his sophomore year. When he spent six months in England, his interest in history, which had begun during childhood, was strengthened. He studied England's efforts during the 1930s to make concessions in the hope of avoiding a war in response to the aggression of Adolf Hitler. Based on this research, he wrote an essay entitled "Appeasement at Munich: The Inevitable Result of the Slowness of the British Democracy to Change from a Disarmament Policy," and submitted it as a senior thesis required for graduation with honors. He graduated from Harvard in 1940, and later that year *Why England Slept,* based on his senior thesis, was published.

Kennedy was personally untouched by America's major historical events during the first two decades of his life. He was a small boy during World War I, and no one from his family was involved in the conflict. Joseph Kennedy's growing wealth allowed the family to live as usual through the twenties, the stock market crash, and the Great Depression, which Kennedy said he knew about only from reading history books. World War II, however, was different. Jack Kennedy enlisted in the navy in September 1941, worked for a time in naval intelligence in Washington, D.C., and then trained as an operator of PT (patrol torpedo) boats before taking command of PT 109 in the Solomon Islands in April 1943. In August, on a routine mission, his boat collided with a Japanese ship and was sliced in half; two of the thirteen crewmen were killed. Nine crewmen swam more than three miles to an island, as Kennedy towed one of the wounded. Robert Donovan, who wrote a book about PT boats, said, "I talked to everyone in his crew and those men would do anything for Kennedy. There is no question that Kennedy was brave, that he saved that crewman's life."[4] From another island, Kennedy carved a message on a coconut, which was delivered by a native, and the eleven survivors were rescued. In 1960, while campaigning in Wisconsin, a high school student asked Kennedy how he became a hero; he answered with a smile, "It was easy—they sank my boat."[5]

After the PT incident, Kennedy spent nearly a year in Chelsea Naval Hospital, from June 1944 to early 1945, recovering from surgery designed to repair a disk problem in his back. Doctors put a metal plate in his spine, but the operation failed to stop the pain. While in the hospital, he received the Navy and Marine Medal for his action with PT 109. During July his brother Joe, who had been flying hazardous missions in Europe, died when his plane blew up. The death of his brother and his long hospital stay changed his life. He started thinking about politics and knew his father expected him to run for office now that he was the oldest living son; he said, "It was like being drafted."[6]

THE HOUSE OF REPRESENTATIVES AND THE SENATE

Kennedy's career in politics began in the fall of 1945, when he decided to run as a representative from the eleventh congressional district in Boston for a seat vacated by Jim Curley, a veteran Boston politician. The eleventh district was composed mostly of Irish, Italian, and other immigrant working-class poor. In 1946, at twenty-eight, Kennedy rented space in the Bellevue Hotel and started campaigning months before the other nine candidates running in the Democratic primary. Shy and unsure of himself, he found campaigning hard, but he worked the streets and shops and held dozens of house parties to meet constituents. Biographer James MacGregor Burns explains: "He disliked the blarney, the exuberant backslapping and handshaking, the exaggerated claims and denunciations that went with politics, especially Boston politics. Nor was he convinced of his own talents as a speaker, or as a mixer."[7] Nonetheless, he campaigned diligently and won the primary by a vote almost double his nearest rival's, and he went on to win the November election easily in a solidly Democratic district—he had established a political base.

His second bid for this House seat in 1948 was hardly a contest because he had no serious rivals, but his youth still caused others to doubt his credibility. One afternoon in Medford, Massachusetts, a high school football player yelled to him, "Hey, kid, come on over and snag some passes." After a few, Kennedy left, and the coach told the student that the "new kid" was the U.S. Representative from the Eleventh Massachusetts District.[8] In Washington, D.C., Kennedy shared a town house with his sister Eunice in Georgetown, an old-fashioned neighborhood with trees, bright flowers, small shops, and a quiet, tasteful atmosphere. He developed friends in Congress, lived an active social life, and became very popular. Three hundred Washington correspondents voted him "the handsomest member of the House." His saddest experience while living in Georgetown came in 1948, when his sister Kathleen was killed in an airplane crash in England.

After spending three terms in the House of Representatives, Kennedy ran for the U.S. Senate. In 1952, Joseph Kennedy persuaded Jack to run against Senator Henry Cabot Lodge, a popular senator from the Boston Brahmins, the social elite who had never accepted the Kennedys; Joe said, "When you've beaten him, you've beaten the best. Why try for something less?"[9] Jack's brother Bobby was in charge of the campaign, and the whole family worked. His mother Rose spoke to a dozen or more groups each night for six to eight weeks. The Kennedy women organized thirty-eight tea parties, sent engraved invitations, and developed a system to identify each guest's name. "It was those damn tea parties that beat me," Lodge complained after the election.[10] Kennedy beat Lodge in the November election by seventy thousand votes.

During his first term as a senator, Kennedy met and married Jacqueline Bouvier. Born on July 28, 1929, and twelve years younger than Kennedy, she came from a wealthy family, had been educated at Miss Porter's, a prestigious finishing school, and had had all the benefits of social status. After spending her freshman year at Vassar, she studied at the Sorbonne in Paris for a year and finished college at George Washington University in Washington, D.C. She worked in her first job as a receptionist at the *Washington Times-Herald* before becoming a photographer, the job she held when she met Jack. Joseph Kennedy thought Jack needed a wife and family for his political career and preferred Jackie, as did Jack. He proposed, and the wedding took place on September 12, 1953, at St. Mary's Roman Catholic Church in Newport, Rhode Island, in a ceremony performed by Archbishop Richard Cushing. Three thousand people gathered on the streets around the church hoping to see the famous couple. Twelve hundred guests gathered for the reception at the estate of Jackie's mother and stepfather, Janet and Hugh Auchincloss, as the couple stood in a receiving line for more than two hours.

For Jackie the first years of marriage held many unfamiliar and unexpected experiences. Fitting into the Kennedy family, with their competitive sports and high-speed activities, overwhelmed her until she broke her ankle in touch football and felt free to withdraw. In 1954, after a fall that further injured his already bad back, Kennedy underwent two operations to try to fuse shattered disks; he nearly died during both of them, but he rallied, and the second was successful. During his long recuperation, with Jackie constantly at his side, he worked on *Profiles in Courage*, helped by Jackie and his speech-writer and friend Ted Sorensen, who found materials for his research. The book, a study of famous men who had the courage to take moral and personal stands in the face of defeat, was published in 1956 and won the Pulitzer Prize for biography the following year. In 1956 Kennedy decided, against his father's advice, to try for the vice presidential nomination on the ticket with Adlai Stevenson. When it was clear that the Democratic convention would decide the vice presidential candidate, Jack spent his time working for votes. Jackie went through an unhappy period: She was seven months pregnant at the time of the convention and alone much of the time, she knew her husband saw other women, she hated politics, and she lost the baby soon after the convention. Though Kennedy had lost the vice presidential bid, he did gain national attention by running, and major magazines started putting his picture on their covers.

During the next two years, things improved for the Kennedys. They moved into a house in Georgetown, which Jackie furnished in the style she liked. In November 1957 Caroline was born. In 1958 Kennedy ran for reelection to the Senate, winning by the largest plurality ever in Massachusetts. Before his second Senate term, Kennedy had been bored with most legislation and with the slow pace of congressional activities. After the 1958 election, however, he took legislation seriously and became a leader with a new purpose.

ISSUES BREWING DURING THE FIFTIES

The decade of the 1950s seemed like a quiet period of peace and prosperity for America, but issues brewing beneath the surface turned out to be significant for Jack Kennedy later on. Republican Dwight Eisenhower, elected in 1952, was a popular president whose two terms were a quiet time with few controversies. As the decade came to a close, Americans were tiring of Eisenhower's presidential inaction and beginning to long for new issues and action. Without much notice, the civil rights issue was changing. The appointment of Chief Justice Earl Warren in 1953 brought Supreme Court decisions that undermined the practice of treating blacks as separate-but-equal. Black leaders were becoming more active, and northern politicians were becoming conscious of the potential for black votes.

In Latin America social conditions were worsening: In country after country, populations grew and the gap between rich and poor widened, threatening revolution. Eisenhower rejected a comprehensive plan to help the poor in Latin America. In the 1950s Americans feared that the masses of poor had Communist leanings. Americans so feared communism that they sided with military dictators at the expense of the poor. In 1958 Senator Kennedy argued unsuccessfully for funds to alleviate the conditions that might lead to the infiltration of countries by Communists.

Significant events were also occurring in Cuba. In 1958 Fidel Castro ousted the right-wing dictator Fulgencio Batista and set up a dictatorial left-wing regime. Denied help from the United States, Cuba soon received aid from the Soviet Union and formed a close alliance with the Soviet Communists. In 1959 thousands of refugees fled to Florida and there plotted to return and overthrow Castro. The Central Intelligence Agency (CIA) of the Eisenhower administration under Allen Dulles secretly armed and trained large numbers of these refugees, a practice that went against American and international law.

The Far East had been an American concern since the Korean War, which began in 1950. Americans were fearful of China and the spread of communism, and American leaders subscribed to the domino theory, which held "that if one country in Southeast Asia fell to the Communists, all others would topple over like dominoes."[11] The French had tried to defend local autonomy in French Indochina, but ultimately failed; when the French left in 1954, America moved in to strengthen non-Communist governments. The Geneva agreement of 1954 divided Vietnam, making the northern half Communist and leaving the south to President Ngo Dinh Diem as long as he could survive. Eisenhower pledged his support to Diem, a policy Kennedy later inherited.

Finally, there was the issue of the space race. The Soviets launched Sputnik, the first satellite in space, on October 4, 1957. Already worried about Soviet power and Communist expansion, Americans became even more nervous thinking that the Soviets were ahead in space exploration. All of these issues of the 1950s—civil rights, Latin America, Cuba, Vietnam, and the space race—would later affect the tenor and policies of the Kennedy presidency.

RUNNING IN THE 1960 PRIMARIES

As the 1950s drew to a close, Kennedy wanted to run for president. His friends advised against his running, as did his father, who wondered if his son realized the problems and crises that he would face. Jack said, "Dad, for two thousand years every generation has thought that its problems were insurmountable. And yet these problems were solved, and solved by human beings. So why shouldn't I try?"[12] As with

In the Presidential campaign of 1960, John F. Kennedy won voter support by recognizing the changing face of American society.

previous campaigns, Kennedy started early; Joseph Kennedy supplied the funds for the campaign, Bobby Kennedy organized it, and friends and the whole Kennedy family worked on it. In West Virginia, Kennedy saw poverty in the coal-mining area that he had never seen before. "I won't forget it. I can't forget it," he said.[13] For a TV commercial Kennedy was thrown in with a bunch of coal miners—no script, no instructions—and he just talked with them, able to listen and convey his concern as the camera rolled. He won West Virginia by a landslide. By May 1960, he had swept seven primaries. Campaign columnist Rowland Evans Jr. said, "The Kennedy organization doesn't run, it purrs. It has the smooth rhythm of a delicate watch."[14] Kennedy went into the 1960 Democratic Convention in Los Angeles uncertain he had enough delegates to win, and he could not convince Adlai Stevenson to support him. When the Wisconsin delegation voted, Kennedy had 748 of the 761 votes he needed. Kennedy people persuaded the Wyoming delegation to cast its fifteen votes for Kennedy, giving him the nomination. After much debating and meeting, Kennedy chose Lyndon Johnson as his running mate, and Johnson accepted.

Kennedy delivered his acceptance speech before eighty thousand people at the Los Angeles Coliseum. "We stand on the edge of a New Frontier, the frontier of the 1960s, a frontier of unknown opportunities and paths, a frontier of unfulfilled hopes and threats."[15] He had introduced the phrase—"new frontier"—that was to identify his presidency. After the convention, Jackie, pregnant with her second child, was asked to hold a news conference at the family compound in Hyannis Port; three hundred reporters and TV people attended. This shy woman who had hated politics charmed them.

> To French reporters, she talked in French; to Spanish reporters, in Spanish. She had everybody at ease, everybody in the palm of her hand, and she seemed in no hurry to leave. She was there for an hour and a half, talking about Jack and showing them the family pictures on the wall. Her self-possession was complete.[16]

THE 1960 PRESIDENTIAL CAMPAIGN

After the Democratic and Republican conventions had determined the two candidates, Kennedy launched his campaign to defeat the current vice president Richard Nixon. "For millions of Americans, the end of the fifties and the rush of the sixties began with the presidential campaign of 1960."[17] Again Kennedy's campaign was well planned and involved the whole family: Bobby was campaign manager and Kennedy's adviser; Jack made Ted coordinator for eleven western states plus Alaska and Hawaii; and the Kennedy women traveled to make speeches and meet with groups of potential supporters. But Kennedy was his own best campaigner. A strategist who had worked for many presidents thought Kennedy was the best natural politician since Franklin Roosevelt—and perhaps better than Roosevelt. Laura Bergquist, a reporter from *Look* magazine, described his skill: "What this man could do that was so extraordinary was to reach out to people—anybody—and give them the feeling, 'I'm for you!' He made you feel you were a real *person,* you were someone who counted. He made you feel important."[18]

The 1960 presidential campaign initiated television as the most important medium for reaching voters. Kennedy was

> well suited to the incredible political possibilities of both television mass marketing and the maturing national culture in which the electronic media played such a crucial role. He was movie star handsome, comfortable before the cameras, and he intuitively understood how to speak in a low-key, familiar style suited to television's living-room intimacy.[19]

Nowhere were Kennedy's television advantages more evident than in the live Nixon-Kennedy debates. Kennedy came to them rested, tanned, and impeccably dressed; Nixon had recently been released from the hospital and had campaigned the night before. Kennedy was handsome without makeup; Nixon's beard made him look shadowy and his makeup pasty. Interestingly, those who heard the debate on radio thought Nixon had won, but those who saw it on television thought Kennedy had won. As the campaign wore on, Kennedy wondered to Bobby, "What would we do without television?"

Enthusiastic supporters multiplied and the bank of volunteers mounted; women loved Kennedy and men wanted to be his friend. Relentlessly he campaigned from city to city, shaking hands, listening to people's concerns, and looking into their faces as he did so, but the job was grueling. Ralph G. Martin reflects:

> Handshaking is friendly until your hands bleed. Confetti looks festive until you're forced to spit out mouthfuls hurled directly into your face. Applause is wonderful until you can hardly hear yourself speak. A crush of screaming women is flattering until they tear your clothes. A campaign is a drama of fixed time into which an impossible schedule gets squeezed.[20]

During this fast-paced campaign, Ted Sorensen was a mental resource. Kennedy called Sorensen his "intellectual blood bank" and his conscience on social issues, including civil and human rights.

Kennedy faced one challenge that most presidential candidates do not have to face—he was Catholic. In 1928 Catholic Al Smith's candidacy had raised tensions between Protestants and Catholics. None of Smith's statements that he was committed to the Constitution and public schools had quieted the rhetoric of anti-Catholic bigots, and he was defeated. In 1960 Kennedy was prepared to face the same prejudice and had decided to confront the issue directly when reporters' questions came. He had contrasting opportunities to respond. After Kennedy's speech at the Los Angeles Press Club, a reporter asked him, amid laughter, "Do you think a Protestant can be elected President in 1960?" Kennedy grinned and told the audience, "If he's prepared to answer how he stands on the issue of the separation of church and state, I see no reason why we should discriminate against him!" And there was a roar of applause.[21] He had another opportunity to declare his views and answer questions when he addressed a convocation of Protestant ministers in Houston, Texas; his speech may not have persuaded skeptics, but his answers to questions disarmed the bigots.

Kennedy's humor, good will, and concern for others helped him turn many campaigning situations to his advantage. He was often poor at public speaking, talking too fast, making poorly timed pauses, nasal in tone, and slipping into a Boston accent. He had particular difficulty talking to farmers and understanding their problems. Arriving an hour late for a farm rally in Sioux City, Iowa, he asked farmers in his best Harvard accent, "'So I ahsk what's wrong with the American fahmah today!' While he paused for effect, a farmer yelled, 'He's stahving!' Kennedy almost collapsed with laughter as the audience joined in."[22] In October, a Georgia judge sentenced civil rights leader Martin Luther King Jr. to four months of hard labor for driving with a license from another state. When Kennedy was told about King's plight, he called King's wife Coretta to offer his sympathy. Bobby called the judge, not as a politician but as a lawyer, and told the judge that all defendants have a right to make bond and King should be out of jail by the end of the day. The judge complied. Following these actions, the senior Martin Luther King announced that he had changed his mind and decided to vote for Kennedy because Kennedy had the courage to do what is right. In the last two days of the campaign, Kennedy wanted Jackie to join him in New York, a pivotal state, even though Jackie's doctor had warned her against travel in the last weeks of her pregnancy. She went anyway and made speeches in Spanish, Italian, and French. After one of her speeches, Kennedy followed up with, "I assure you that my wife can also speak English."[23]

THE ELECTION AND THE INAUGURATION

On election night neither Kennedy nor Nixon took an early lead and held it; until well after midnight the election was too close to call. The Kennedy people felt demoralized as they saw many western states go to Nixon. When the final count was in early the following morning, Kennedy had received 34,321,349 votes, only 112,803 votes more than Nixon had; of the electoral college vote he had won 303 votes to Nixon's 219. "Kennedy accomplished the almost unprecedented feat of turning the ruling party out of office at a time of peace and prosperity," overcoming anti-Catholic sentiment and defeating a party that had enjoyed wide popularity under Eisenhower.[24]

In the interim between the election and inauguration Kennedy's son was born. Shortly after Thanksgiving, Jackie was rushed to the hospital while Kennedy was on his way to Palm Beach for rest. He arrived and turned around immediately, learning of the birth of his son John Fitzgerald Kennedy Jr. midway between Florida and Washington. A few days later the baby was baptized.

During this same period, Kennedy planned for his presidency. Before the election, Kennedy had already instructed his adviser Clark Clifford to suggest people for his staff and a plan for their operation. The plan called for a system like a wheel with Kennedy at the center and a collection of experts drawn from business, public service, and universities fanning outward, each available to the president and each free to interact with one another. This staff of cabinet officers and advisers became known as the New Frontiersmen. By inauguration day Kennedy was ready to move into the White House with Jackie, Caroline, and his new son John John, as he came to be known.

Inauguration Day, January 20, 1960, was cold and windy. Richard Cardinal Cushing gave the invocation. Poet Robert Frost was to read a poem for the ceremony, but the wind blew his papers and the sun shone in his eyes making it impossible for him to read, so he recited one from memory instead. Kennedy took the oath and delivered his address slowly and dramatically. "Let the word go forth from this time and place, to friend and foe alike, that the torch has been passed to a new generation of Americans." Kennedy continued, "Ask not what your country can do for you—ask what you can do for your country." After the ceremony, House Speaker Sam Rayburn said, "That speech he made out there was better than anything Franklin Roosevelt said at his best—it was better than Lincoln. I think—really think—that is a man of destiny."[25] Historian David Farber suggests that Kennedy recast the national image, from Eisenhower, "a simple, tough, small-town man doing his neighborly best to maintain old virtues of freedom and liberty," to the image of America with "global missions and commitments."[26]

THE UPS AND DOWNS OF THE PRESIDENCY, 1961

President Kennedy's first year in office was a mixture of success and failure. In March he issued an executive order forming the Peace Corps, making it possible for Americans to volunteer their skills and services to developing countries around the world. Under the direction of his brother-in-law Sargent Shriver, this program attracted many young people and became very successful. Also in March he proposed the Alliance for Progress, a program to help Latin American countries; later he would discover that help was difficult to deliver to needy people who were governed by a military dictatorship. His domestic legislation made little progress in Congress. Though the Democrats held the majority, many were southern Democrats who formed a coalition with conservative Republicans to block Kennedy's progressive legislation, such as federal aid for school construction and teachers' salaries and the creation of a Department of Urban Affairs. His worst disaster was the Bay of Pigs, the invasion of Cuba planned by the CIA during the Eisenhower administration. The rebels who landed had expected to be joined by

John F. Kennedy issued forth a new era of bold determination at his inauguration ceremony in 1961.

At a joint session of Congress President John F. Kennedy delivers his historic speech in which he proposes to put a man on the moon by the end of the decade.

forces revolting against Castro, but those troops failed to materialize and the rebels were caught unprotected. According to Ralph G. Martin, Kennedy told his adviser David Powers,

> "I must have been out of my goddamn mind to listen to those people [advisers and experts]. How could I have been so far off base? All my life I've known better than to depend on experts. How could I have been so stupid to let them go ahead?" And at a press conference he said, "Victory has a hundred fathers and defeat is an orphan."[27]

Kennedy made a second state of the union speech in May 1961 in which he addressed the space issue. The Soviets had launched Sputnik, the first manned space flight, and had launched a second flight in which a man orbited the earth. Kennedy directed budget adviser Ed Walsh to report on needs and a budget for a space program and told Congress that he believed Americans should put a man on the moon before the end of the sixties.

Kennedy's 1961 dealings in Europe were also a mixture of success and failure. In June, he went to France for talks with French president Charles DeGaulle about the Soviet Union, a nuclear test-ban treaty, and the relations between the

United States and France. The talks were polite, but resulted in no significant outcomes. This trip belonged to Jackie, whom the French adored for her beauty and her ability to speak French. After days of attention given to his wife, Kennedy concluded his visit by referring to himself as the man who accompanied Jacqueline Kennedy to Paris.

The Kennedys went on to Vienna, where Kennedy met with Soviet leader Nikita Khrushchev. The meetings turned out to be a forum for the leaders to size up one another. They discussed Berlin, small wars around the world, and nuclear disarmament—but not seriously. Khrushchev saw Kennedy as young and weak; he belittled Kennedy for not winning the Cuban invasion and boasted about his power in Berlin and about the success of Communist advancements in the world. Kennedy stood up to Khrushchev on a number of issues, all the time analyzing this opponent. Asked by his secretary Evelyn Lincoln how the talks had gone, the president replied that they had not gone well. Again Jackie drew attention from the crowds in the city. She also impressed Khrushchev. At the banquet given in the Kennedys' honor, he moved his chair close to hers and talked almost exclusively with her through dinner. The headline in the *New York Herald Tribune* read, "Smitten Khrushchev is Jackie's Happy Escort."[28] The final stop on this trip was London for the baptism of the daughter of Jackie's sister Princess Lee Radziwill. For a third time on this trip crowds gathered to see Jackie and to hear about her gowns and her glamour. An editorialist of the British paper the *Evening Standard* wrote, "Jacqueline Kennedy has given the American people from this day on one thing they have always lacked—majesty."[29]

In August 1961 Khrushchev built the Berlin Wall dividing East and West Berlin, another test of Kennedy's will. Soviet and American troops stood face to face at the border of East and West Germany, and both sides made nuclear threats, but Kennedy held firm, refusing to back down or to attack. His courageous stance proved to be a successful tactic because Khrushchev never took over West Berlin or hampered western travel there.

During this first year as president, Kennedy developed a special relationship with the press and made press conferences popular television viewing. Reporters liked him because he gave rational, thoughtful answers and showed humor at his own expense. Veteran journalist James Reston wondered at Kennedy's ability to recall facts, like the precise drop in milk consumption in 1960. Reston said, "He either overwhelmed you with decimal points or disarmed you with a smile and a wisecrack."[50]

THE PRESIDENCY, 1962

From the beginning, the Kennedys wanted to emphasize the arts and intellectual endeavors. By 1962 Americans were becoming increasingly fascinated with the White House guests and activities that promoted this goal. Jackie was undoubtedly the major player in planning and successfully carrying out the events. Among the guests invited to formal dinners and entertainment were Spanish cellist Pablo Casals, Russian-born composer Igor Stravinsky, a group of artists and writers, and the year's Nobel Prize winners. The highlight of 1962 was Jackie's tour of the White House. She had begun when she first moved in to locate historic pieces of furniture and works of art to replace tasteless and meaningless additions made over the years. She thought that the White House should reflect the country's history and be furnished only with fine pieces, some of which she found in basement storage rooms. When she had finished, CBS Television filmed a tour in which she moved from room to room explaining notable pieces and offering anecdotes:

> CBS researchers had spent two months checking every piece of White House furniture, but Jacqueline Kennedy insisted, "I don't need any research. I don't need any script. I can do it right now." . . . She herself supplied the show's opening, a letter to Congress from Theodore Roosevelt that she had found in a book. Working without a script and wearing a "bosom mike," she wandered through the White House rooms, never once fluffing her lines. She seemed so relaxed and did it so well that the film shooting took only one day instead of the budgeted two.[51]

Jack Kennedy was proud of his wife.

From the beginning of his presidency, Kennedy claimed he had no desire to get America more deeply involved in Southeast Asia, but at the same time he was stepping up military and economic aid to South Vietnam in a counterinsurgency program designed to avoid the need for American ground troops. This program included sending experts skilled in sabotage and terrorism, technical aid, advisers to train South Vietnamese troops, and money, which, it turned out, got into the hands of corrupt officials. Kennedy secretly sent five hundred Green Berets—an elite counterinsurgency strike force—and more military advisers, the euphemism for troops. In February 1962 Kennedy admitted the troops were firing back in self-defense. By October 1963 America had sixteen thousand troops in Vietnam, helicopters were flying combat support missions, and pilots were strafing enemy targets. Kennedy doubted the wisdom of the policy, but he feared a loss to communism and knew withdrawing troops would be seen as a political defeat. He vowed to withdraw Americans from Vietnam right after the 1964 election, which he expected to win.

The major event of 1962 was the missile crisis in Cuba. Even after Kennedy's resolve over the Berlin Wall, Khrushchev apparently still believed he could bully Kennedy. On October 16, Kennedy learned that the Soviets had installed nuclear warheads in Cuba, just ninety miles from the Florida coast, a violation of the 1823 Monroe Doctrine, which declared that any extension of foreign power to any part of the Western Hemisphere endangered American peace and safety. After intense discussion, the decision was made to stop all Soviet ships bound for Cuba and to demand the removal of missiles already installed there. After Kennedy spoke to the people on television on October 22 explaining the grave situation, America waited. When Soviet ships approached the sixty American ships surrounding Cuba, the tension was high until the Soviet ships turned back without provocation. Subsequently, the installed missiles were removed, and the thirteen-day trauma was over. "The President's firm stand had taught the Soviet Union a new respect for the strength and determination of the United States, and at the same time it had cleared the air and improved chances for peace. As a result there came a slight thaw in the cold war."[32] That thaw resulted in a treaty signed by Great Britain, the Soviet Union, and the United States in August 1963 to end all above-ground nuclear tests.

ENCOURAGING BERLINERS AND CONFRONTING AMERICAN SOUTHERNERS

Kennedy thought that he should go to Europe in June 1963. His advisers thought it a bad idea since American popularity in Europe was questionable and there might be lingering resentment in Germany left over from German defeat in World War II. Kennedy argued that people can be stirred to change; former World War II enemies were becoming friends, and Kennedy wanted to cement those friendly feelings. The trip took him to Germany, Ireland, and Italy. In Berlin, Kennedy toured the Wall before going to the city hall, where the square was packed with people shouting his name. When in his speech he said, *Ich bin ein Berliner* (I am a Berliner), the crowd roared. Then he challenged anyone who doubted the city's spirit and its resolve to resist communism to come to Berlin. At the end the "roar was so intense and so prolonged that Kennedy felt he could have asked them to march to the Berlin Wall and tear it down and they would have done it."[35] In Ireland Kennedy visited his ancestral home. In Italy he visited Rome, where the crowds were thin, perhaps weary after celebrating the new pope's coronation, but in Naples Kennedy drew the same kind of enthusiasm he had received in Germany and Ireland.

The major domestic issue facing Kennedy in 1963 was the civil rights issue. He had campaigned in 1960 promising improvements in the civil rights of blacks, but he had since hesitated taking action for fear of losing his political support in the South. In the summer the situation was bad:

> Bombs, riots, police dogs, burning, looting in scattered cities. The white South blamed the White House for stirring it all up. Blacks blamed the White House for not helping enough. The rest of the country was torn, with rumblings of conscience, hate, and fear.[34]

Kennedy spoke to the nation and declared that civil rights was a moral issue. On June 19, Kennedy sent Congress a comprehensive civil rights bill, which outlawed discrimination in public facilities of all kinds, withheld federal funds from schools that failed to desegregate, and outlawed discrimination in the application of voting laws. Although he never saw the bill passed, after his death Congress passed it and President Johnson signed it. On August 28 four hundred thousand African Americans marched in Washington, D.C., demonstrating their commitment to the civil rights movement; at this demonstration Martin Luther King Jr. delivered his famous "I have a dream" speech. Kennedy had opposed the planned march in Washington because he feared that a poor showing or the outbreak of violence might affect his legislation, but after it was successfully concluded, he praised it.

Two family events brought the president sadness in 1963. His father suffered a stroke and was confined to a wheelchair, a sad sight for Kennedy, who had been influenced by a strong father all his life. The other event was the death of his second son, Patrick Bouvier Kennedy, born prematurely and suffering from breathing problems. Seeing the frailty of life in the generation before him and the generation after him evoked a period of reflection and a preoccupation with death.

TEXAS AND DISASTER

In late November 1963 Kennedy had a scheduled trip to Texas, which he would have avoided had it not been politically important to go. There were stops planned in San Antonio, Houston, Dallas, and Austin. Crowds in San Antonio and Houston were enthusiastic and cheered especially for Jackie. The couple arrived in Dallas just before noon on Friday, November 21, for a motorcade to the Dallas Trade Mart, where Kennedy was to deliver a speech. As the presidential limousine passed the seven-story Texas School Book Depository, shots rang out: one hit Kennedy in the throat and he slumped forward, another shot off the right side of the president's head. Jackie cradled her husband in her lap telling him that she loved him even though she knew that someone had killed him. At the Parkland Hospital the president re-

President John F. Kennedy waves to his supporters from the presidential limousine moments before he was mortally wounded by an assassin's bullet.

ceived last rites, and he was declared dead at 1 P.M. Less than three hours after the shots were fired, Lyndon Johnson, aboard Air Force One on the flight to Washington, D.C., was sworn in as the thirty-sixth president of the United States. Within less than two hours after the shots, police had taken Lee Harvey Oswald into custody, believing that he had killed Kennedy and a Dallas patrolman who had stopped his car to question a man. On Saturday, Oswald was charged with murder. On Sunday, while the police were transferring Oswald to a county prison, Jack Ruby, a local nightclub owner who got past police guards because he knew them, shot Oswald dead, accusing Oswald of killing his president. Americans saw this murder live on television. Though some Americans still wonder if Oswald was part of a larger conspiracy, the official version found by the Warren Commission, set up to investigate the assassination, is that Oswald acted alone.

For three days the nation watched and grieved. The president's coffin lay in state in the Capitol Rotunda, and a quarter of a million people filed past to pay their respects, halting in silence as Jackie came to kneel and pray and again as the president's brother Ted came. The coffin was returned to the White House. On Monday, the day of the funeral, the cameras captured a vivid scene as Jackie, clad in black and wearing a black veil, held the hands of Caroline and John when the coffin left the White House. In one other vivid scene, John John saluted as his father's coffin left St. Matthew's Cathedral after the funeral mass on November 25, his third birthday. Two hundred foreign dignitaries and heads of state attended the funeral, walking behind the riderless black horse and the coffin carried on a caisson drawn by three pairs of matched gray horses, the right ones riderless. Kennedy was buried on a hill in Arlington National Cemetery, where an eternal flame burns in his honor.

When Kennedy was killed in 1963, he was immensely popular in America and around the world, and he has been an admired figure in the public imagination since his death. He was a hero and a role model to many people, an inspiration to young people to serve their country and be involved in its history. Admirers remember his image—a man bold, vibrant, confident, strong, daring, active—and they remember his good looks, his inspiring language, and his wit. The nation and the world also admired the Kennedys, what the president and the first lady meant as a couple. It was Jacqueline Kennedy's beauty and facility with languages that drew crowds and her contribution to the art and cultural life in the White House that elicited respect.

As a historical person, Kennedy symbolizes the advent of the sixties, the beginning of the Civil Rights Movement, and the Cold War struggle with Nikita Khrushchev and communism. Television made it possible for the nation to observe how this young president handled his mistakes, how he managed foreign affairs in order to hold Khrushchev and the threat of nuclear war in check, and how he reassured Berliners during the dark days of the Berlin Wall. In his televised speeches he promoted the Peace Corps as an opportunity to serve and presented civil rights as a moral issue confronting the nation's conscience.

This volume of Greenhaven Press's People Who Made History series portrays both the personal and the historical Kennedy. It focuses on his family and on his personal appeal as a campaigner. It focuses on his domestic agenda and his foreign policy. This anthology—the viewpoints along with the biography—invites the reader to explain the mystery of why this young American president so intensely captured the hearts and imagination of so many people even though his time in the limelight was but a few years.

John Kennedy Jr. salutes his father's coffin as the President's funeral procession passes.

Jacqueline Kennedy, in her own memorial to her husband, observed, "Someone who had loved President Kennedy, but who had never known him, wrote to me this winter: 'The hero comes when he is needed. When our belief gets pale and weak, there comes a man out of that need who is shining—and everyone living reflects a little of that light—and stores up some against the time when he is gone.'

"So now he is a legend," Mrs. Kennedy added, "when he would have preferred to be a man."[55]

Perhaps the letter writer is correct. Kennedy was the right man for the time. He saw a nation ready for a challenge, but a nation fearful of its Communist enemy. He was able to speak to young and old alike and give them a purpose, galvanize their ideals, and allay their fears. The nation was engaged with their president, and their leader brought out the best in the American spirit.

NOTES

1. Quoted in Ralph G. Martin, *A Hero for Our Time: An Intimate Story of the Kennedy Years.* New York: Macmillan, 1983, p. 23.

2. Quoted in Martin, p. 27.

3. Quoted in Martin, pp. 28–29.

4. Quoted in Martin, p. 43.

5. Quoted in Theodore Sorensen, *Kennedy.* New York: Harper & Row, 1965, p. 18.

6. Quoted in Martin, p. 48.

7. James MacGregor Burns, *John Kennedy: A Political Profile.* New York: Harcourt, Brace, 1959, pp. 57–58.

8. Martin, p. 52.

9. Quoted in Martin, p. 57.

10. Quoted in Martin, p. 60.

11. Allan Nevins and Henry Steele Commager with Jeffrey Morris, *A Pocket History of the United States.* 9th rev. ed. New York: Pocket Books, a division of Simon and Schuster, 1992, p. 564.

12. Quoted in Martin, p. 135.

13. Quoted in Martin, p. 154.

14. Quoted in Martin, p. 154.

15. Quoted in Martin, p. 183.

16. Quoted in Martin, p. 184.

17. David Farber, *The Age of Great Dreams: America in the 1960s.* New York: Hill and Wang, a division of Farrar, Straus and Giroux, 1994, p. 25.

18. Quoted in Martin, p. 186.

19. Farber, p. 30.
20. Martin, p. 197.
21. Quoted in Burns, p. 241.
22. Quoted in Martin, p. 204.
23. Quoted in Martin, p. 320.
24. Nevins and Commager, p. 545.
25. Quoted in Martin, p. 12.
26. Farber, p. 32.
27. Quoted in Martin, p. 331.
28. Martin p. 353.
29. Quoted in Martin, p. 354.
30. Quoted in Martin, p. 308.
31. Martin, p. 393.
32. Nevins and Commager, p. 561.
33. Martin, p. 490.
34. Martin, p. 513.
35. Quoted in Martin, p. 574.

WORKS CONSULTED

James MacGregor Burns, *John Kennedy: A Political Profile.* New York: Harcourt, Brace, 1959.

David Farber, *The Age of Great Dreams: America in the 1960s.* New York: Hill and Wang, a division of Farrar, Straus and Giroux, 1994.

Ralph G. Martin, *A Hero for Our Time: An Intimate Story of the Kennedy Years.* New York: Macmillan, 1983.

Allan Nevins and Henry Steele Commager with Jeffrey Morris, *A Pocket History of the United States.* 9th rev. ed. New York: Pocket Books, a division of Simon and Schuster, 1992.

Arthur Schlesinger Jr., "An Interview with Isaiah Berlin," *New York Review of Books* (October 22, 1998): 31–37.

Theodore Sorensen, *Kennedy.* NY: Harper & Row, 1965.

The Major Influences on John F. Kennedy's Development: The Fitzgerald and Kennedy Traditions

The Fitzgerald Influence: Charm, Energy, and Hard Work

Gail Cameron

Gail Cameron attributes the Kennedy family's work ethic and competitive spirit to the influence of Rose Kennedy, John F. Kennedy's mother. As the favorite daughter of John Fitzgerald, an aggressive Boston politician, Rose learned the art of politics—including the importance of congeniality, charm, hard work, and a determination to win. As a mother, she strove to develop these traits in her children. Gail Cameron, a *Life* magazine reporter who covered the Kennedys in 1960, was one of the first writers to extensively research the life of Rose Kennedy and the Fitzgeralds.

For Johnny Fitz [John F. Fitzgerald], who had grown up with nine brothers, the birth of a female Fitzgerald was not only a novelty but something akin to a miracle. In all his twenty-seven years, he had never known anything but a household of males. The fourth of ten sons born to Thomas and Rosanna Fitzgerald, he had only the cloudiest memory of his two younger sisters: the first, Ellen Rosanna, had died at the age of eight months, when he was only seven years old; the other, Mary Ellen, the last of his parents' twelve children, lived only four days. When his mother died three months later, the last vestige of female influence had abruptly disappeared from his family life. Of all his own children—three sons and three daughters—none would ever matter more to Johnny Fitz than the tiny, dark-haired infant girl who was born on that summer night [July 22, 1890] and whose eyes, even at birth, were as piercingly aquamarine blue as his own. And none would be more like him. She caught his infectious enthusiasm and kept it all her life; she had, from

Excerpted from *Rose: A Biography of Rose Fitzgerald Kennedy*, by Gail Cameron (New York: Putnam, 1971). Copyright 1971 by Gail Cameron.

earliest childhood, his will for hard work, his ambition, self-discipline, and instinctive ability to dazzle a crowd with consummate Irish charm. Rose, from the very beginning, was her father's daughter. . . .

John F. Fitzgerald, the President's namesake, was not yet "Honey" Fitz when his daughter Rose was born—he was still Johnny Fitz or Fitzie or Little Johnny Fitz—but he had come a long way, through difficulties and hardships that his daughter would come to understand but never experience.

THOMAS FITZGERALD—IRISH IMMIGRANT

Rose's grandfather, Thomas Fitzgerald, had left County Wexford in Ireland during the potato famine of 1845. The odors of death and putrefying vegetation were everywhere over that blighted land, and a half million people had already perished in their humble cottages or along the roadsides. Fleeing from panic, hunger, and despair, Thomas Fitzgerald joined the hordes of his countrymen who walked the rutted dirt roads to the seaport town of New Ross. There he boarded one of the "coffin ships" of the Cunard Line—ships that killed one out of every four passengers who crammed the steerage coops—and sailed westward in search of hope and a better life. . . .

When they arrived, the Irish lived in shantytowns, ghettos, "paddy-villes"—the first mass urban slums. The more they increased in number, the more they were scorned by the Yankees. "The scum of creation," they were called, "beaten men from beaten races, representing the worst failures in the struggle for existence.". . .

The Irish became blacksmiths, stevedores, coal heavers; they dug ditches for sewers and canals and leveled the hills of Boston; they were railroad workers and bartenders; they worked in sweatshops and lived in squalor. And they were called muckers and blacklegs and greenhorns and clodhoppers and micks. More than 2,000 Irish girls worked as domestics in Boston, and they were called biddies and kitchen canaries and bridgets. Johnny Fitz's ambition was as much *away from* this world, for himself and his family, as it was toward parity with the Yankees. . . .

Rose's father, John F. Fitzgerald, was born on February 11, 1863, in a red-brick tenement at 30 Ferry Street—a four-story, eight-family house near the Old North Church. His father ran a grocery and liquor store by this time, and his playgrounds, he liked to say, "were the streets and wharves, busy with ships from every part of the world.". . . .

YOUNG JOHNNY FITZ LEARNS
LEADERSHIP AND RESPONSIBILITY

With bare feet and patched pants, Johnny Fitz soon began to make his mark in the tight, bustling little Irish community, with its fish peddlers and tipcarts, its clattering horse-drawn wagons with ice and coal, fruit and vegetables—and its tough ward politics. He was neither the eldest nor the biggest of his brothers, but he was an instinctive leader— and his ambition was boundless. He joined and later led the most prominent social and athletic organizations in the North End and showed himself to be a natural politician at the frequent picnics, outings, minstrel shows, suppers, dances, and fairs. He played polo, football, and baseball; boys from all over Boston came to compete against him in footraces. He always vowed to "work harder than anyone else." And he did. Little Johnny Fitz, contemporaries said, was the swiftest sprinter, fastest swimmer, best dancer, most tuneful singer, and the most eloquent speaker in the North End. Even as an adult he would boast that he had never been beaten in a potato race. Later he would publicly adopt the slogan: "What I undertake, I do. What I want, I get."

He went to Boston Latin School, where he managed and played right field on the baseball team and captained the football squad for two years, and was in his first year at Harvard Medical School when his father died. . . ."We will never break up," he said. "I'll keep the family together." By his own account, he usually "washed dishes, made beds, scrubbed floors, sifted ashes, and brought up scuttles of coal and firewood, climbing three flights of creaky stairs. . . . I even washed the faces of the older boys every day, and oftentimes dressed them.

"My father left us a few thousand dollars," he later admitted. "It was not enough to educate me, and I thought my life belonged to my brothers, and that I could do better outside medical school, so I gave it up and took the examination for the Custom House." He passed and became a clerk under Leverett Saltonstall. . . .

JOHNNY FITZ TURNS TO POLITICS

Rose was born in an optimistic year. "If one couldn't make money in the past year," the Boston *Herald* announced in

1890, "his case was hopeless." Johnny's wasn't. He knew everyone and was ideally suited to the real estate and insurance business he ran, with flourishing success. The American dream was coming true, and Johnny Fitz, restless and ambitious, wanted his share along with those other "shanty Irish" who were rising, with ferocious determination, to higher social, economic, and political spheres. . . .

Politics were much more exciting than insurance, and within the North End Johnny Fitz was beginning to rise. His athletic ability had given him contacts with people from all over the city—and he used them. Short, stocky, handsome, and vivacious, with ruddy complexion and piercing blue eyes, he was a natural showman: full of drive, vigor, inexhaustible energy, and capable either of easy informality or true graciousness—whichever was needed. He learned and could teach Rose the "nuts and bolts" of ward and precinct politics, the endless lists and visits and street work. . . .

Fitz was already something of a minor legend in the North End when Rose was born, with his ability to talk at a dazzling machine-gun speed of 200 words a minute on any subject whatsoever, producing instant tears or sudden laughter in even the coolest campaign crowd with all the dexterity of a one-man soap opera. . . .

He was always immaculately dressed—dapper, debonair, and bubbling with good cheer. He was an indefatigable member of committees and organizations of all kinds—a trait his daughter would inherit. Organizations were spheres of influence, training grounds for larger spheres; they could even become pockets of political power. Fitz could throw out compliments with abandon, speak of his "dear mother born in County Mayo," practice the "Irish switch" (talking with one person—or two, or three—while pumping the hand of another), burst into song, and snipe at the "scions of the blue-blooded aristocracy." His "Fitzblarney" became a household word. But the Fitzblarney always stopped, in later years, when he recalled the hot summer night his Rosie was born. . . .

THE CLOSE RELATIONSHIP OF FATHER AND DAUGHTER

From the moment she was born she became the delight of his life, and he, in turn, the dominating and significant figure in her own. She even viewed herself at times not as Rose Elizabeth but as the mayor's daughter—and lived to meet this role. In many ways they were also incredibly alike—vivacious, gregarious, sharing a mutual flair for politics and for fashionable clothes, ambitious, athletic, severely self-disciplined. She even grew to share a good number of his idiosyncrasies—like taking catnaps in cars and later in planes and pinning notes to herself everywhere. Like him, she always wanted to be first—herself and her family. She would learn, in her own ways, to "work harder than anyone else.". . .

The [Fitzgerald] boys never became good students. They disappointed Johnny and "nearly broke their mother's heart." . . . [Johnny, or Honey, Fitz] poured all his magnificent hopes and enthusiasm into his daughter, took her on trips, talked to her constantly, and she, though she admired him immensely, learned from him but never lost something that was her own. . . .

Rose "took a real responsibility that none of the Fitzgerald kids did," says Marie Greene,[1] "like doing well in her studies. She always wanted to do well for her father; it meant everything to her." Rose herself says: "I found the role my father played in my life a decisive one. He talked to me incessantly, all the time I was growing up. He told me a lot about the history of the Irish people, about their culture; we discussed politics and government constantly." Rose did this with her own children; politics and current events were an inevitable part of the Kennedy household, usurping small talk and gabble, becoming the very fabric of the young Kennedys' lives.

Honey Fitz was also insatiably curious about everything, about how a trolley worked or a German municipal council; he always took pains to explain things to Rose, and gradually she developed his capacity for wide-reaching interest, for collecting unexpected bits of information on every possible subject from—for her—the Abyssinian Church to bikinis. She imparted this infectious curiosity to her own children. . . .

THE RACE TO BE BOSTON'S MAYOR

Rose loved politics from the beginning, really enjoyed it, found it fun and exciting and not a burden. She watched a master at work and learned every technique. But she was capable of translating what seems clearly a political ploy—concern for others—into a genuine character trait. . . . She learned how to make prospective voters feel important, by dressing carefully for them and addressing them on intimate

1. Rose's friend since their teen years

terms, but she never forgot that true concern comes from the heart, not the political head.

Her father's contacts had multiplied; his "Dearos," supporters who took their name from the number of times he spoke of his "dear old North End," were everywhere. . . . Fitz beat City Clerk Edward Donovan, the choice of Lomasney[2] and P.J. Kennedy, in the primaries and took on Republicans Henry Dewey and Louis Frothingham for the mayoralty [in 1905].

It was a marvelously theatrical campaign, and Rose saw it all, delighting in her father's extravagance—and his success. She heard the crowds and watched the way he moved them. She saw his impeccable preparations and his ceaseless energy, his unfailing interest in meeting each of the thousands of small demands that bring in the votes, one by one. His ringing motto—"Bigger, Better, Busier Boston"—was everywhere, but then so was he. His men pasted up posters of him on vacant walls faster than opponents could tear them down. He organized the first political motorcade and swept through the precincts in a large red car, followed by hordes of what were called Napoleon's Lancers. In every precinct, crowds of devoted Dearos met him and helped him and whooped up the crowd. He and his men worked harder and more imaginatively than anyone else.

On December 12, 1905, the final count was made; little Johnny Fitz had won by 8,000 votes. He proudly said that he would be the "mayor of the whole people.". . .

THE TRADITION CONTINUES: FROM DAUGHTER TO MOTHER

Early success as a family tradition had begun with Rose's father; she continued it, and her own children were remarkable for their early achievements. Whenever she had to defend Jack, Bobby, or Ted against charges of being too young, she would trot out an impressive family history of which she was a part. Not only youth but also youthfulness became part of the Kennedy-Fitzgerald legend; just as her mother was often mistaken for one of her own daughters, so would Rose be on countless occasions. . . .

Rose genuinely *liked* politics—not only the outward, center-stage frills of blaring brass bands and red, white, and blue tornadoes of confetti and signs, but all the musty back-

---

2. Martin Lomasney, political boss in Boston's Ward Eight

room strategy and behind-the-scenes maneuvering that brought things about. "She damn well knows all the nuts and bolts of politics," Pierre Salinger, John Kennedy's press secretary, remarked with some awe after watching her in two campaigns. "She knows how to get the votes out, how you make the phone calls, raise money, and all that; and as a speaker, she's an absolute spellbinder. I mean, people are just riveted by her and"—he added with some surprise—"she never talks about the issues; the issues are a total void with her, I think. She always talks about family." But for Rose, family and politics had always been synonymous, and when she reared her own children, she did so with politics in mind, just as she used carefully fashioned family stories as her primary stumping device. . . .

Rose's precepts of motherhood were simple, direct, and sometimes eloquent. "Whenever I held my newborn baby in my arms," she says, "I used to think that what I said and did to him could have an influence not only on him but on all whom he met, not only for a day or a month or a year, but for all eternity—a very, very challenging and exciting thought for a mother." She was a natural and determined teacher, who led the children by discovery, by story, by inspiration, by example, and by hard work; she had been a superior catechism instructor in the North End.

ROSE KENNEDY AS TEACHER

"Children," in her view, "should be stimulated by their parents to see, and touch, and know, and understand, and appreciate." She never preached or lectured to them about politics or art or religion but engaged them in conversation about these subjects, told them vivid stories, took them to Bunker Hill and Concord and Plymouth Rock. She did not let them merely listen, but drew them out. . . .

Even when the children were infants, Rose tried to take them to church every day, for a visit, so they would "form a habit of making God and religion a part of their daily lives, not something to be reserved for Sundays." She knew the value of repetition, the value of what is dramatic and concrete, so she always tried to key the discussions to what was immediate and present. . . .

She also encouraged them in the social graces and in athletics. When they were still quite young, all the children regularly attended dancing classes and took lessons in tennis and golf. Rose and Marie Greene would take the boys skating on a nearby flooded field, and all the children played lots of baseball and football, tennis and golf; they were taught to ski and to swim, and later all the Kennedys were to take a keen interest in sailing. . . .

Competition was always encouraged, not only by Joe[3] but also by Honey Fitz's daughter. "We would try to instill into them the idea that no matter what you did, you should try to be first," says Rose. A sharp rivalry developed between the oldest boys [Joe Jr. and John], who vied with each other throughout their teens and into their early twenties; they once rammed into each other on bicycles, because neither would yield. Rose insists: "The competition between the two boys was very good, as it is good for any children. . . ." She believed in having a full program planned for them, especially during holidays, and this usually included competitive activities: "They raced against one another and as a family team against others on foot, in swimming, and in boats during the summer.". . .

Rose instilled the idea that if you worked hard at something, you could do it—that everything involves hard work and that there is no easy way out. She gave the children the confidence to feel that they could do whatever they wanted to do or set out to do—by hard work. Even when they had a chauffeur, the boys had to fix their own bicycles, and they had to earn the money they received, which was always sparingly dispensed. They were brought up with the idea "that brains and talent and money should not be treated lightly," but that these "advantages" imposed obligations and responsibilities. She always preferred the word "advantages" to "money" or "wealth.". . .

Rose's summer philosophy included continuing efforts to improve the children in mind and body and also to keep them busy. "If you are not doing anything," said Rose, "you are just left in a corner." She made special lists of books for each of the children (and saw that reading lamps were placed all over the house to encourage reading); she saw to it that regular attention was paid to current events. Joe encouraged the children to swim and to play tennis and to sail, and there was usually a barefoot softball game every Fourth of July and a touch football game after Thanksgiving dinner. He de-

3. Joseph Kennedy—J.F.K.'s father

manded that his children "win, win, win"; as early as six or seven, the girls too were urged on, and Eunice remembers being told that "coming in second was just no good."

Rose was especially adept at finding fruitful chores and projects when the children got restless, or in poor weather. Busyness and activity held her father together and would always hold her together; she instilled these qualities in her family. Activity and prayer—these and her own solidity are what enabled her to keep her balance and to keep family balance and endurance in the often difficult coming years. There was something severely puritanical about her demands for activity, activity, but she also tried to keep vitality, even joy in the forefront.

Toughness Propels the Kennedys' Survival and Success

Richard J. Whalen

*Richard J. Whalen traces the paths of three genera-
tions of Kennedys—John Kennedy's great grandpar-
ents, his grandfather, and his father. These Kennedys
possessed a tough determination to survive, to seize
opportunities, and to improve their social standing
through politics, education, and money—traits that
can also be seen in John Kennedy. Richard J.
Whalen, a reporter and editor, was on the staff of
Time and Fortune magazines and the Wall Street
Journal newspaper. He worked for the State Department and served as an adviser to Ronald Reagan. He
is the author of several books, including A City Destroying Itself: An Angry View of New York and Taking Sides: A Personal View of America from Kennedy
to Nixon to Kennedy.*

Kennedy toughness can be traced back to Patrick [John
Kennedy's great grandfather], who survived the crossing [in
1848] and stepped ashore on Noddle's Island, in East Boston,
well enough to work. . . . With work available for the able-
bodied, many emigrants ended their journey where they dis-
embarked. Among those who stayed on the island and
squeezed into the cheap boardinghouses huddled near the
docks was Patrick Kennedy.

He found work as a cooper,[1] a thriving trade, for most of
the barrels held whiskey, and saloons multiplied with the
influx of Irish. Accused, not unjustly, of being a drunken lot,
the newcomers had cause to seek escape in cheap whiskey.
As they emerged from the steerage, blinking in the sunlight,

1. one who makes or repairs wooden barrels, casks, and tubs

Excerpted from *The Founding Father: The Story of Joseph P. Kennedy*, by Richard J.
Whalen (New York: NAL/World, 1964). Copyright ©1964 by Richard J. Whalen.
Reprinted by permission of the author.

they were met by boardinghouse runners and contract labor bosses, who spoke disarmingly of the dear, old country as they herded the greenhorns to their downfall. Cheated by conniving countrymen, sweated by native employers who paid a laborer a dollar for a fourteen-hour day, the Irish were stupefied with exhaustion and constantly bewildered. Unaccustomed to buying food, they found the prices at the store incredibly high, and here there was no place to cultivate the potato or keep a pig. As numbers pressed against inadequate space, rents jumped and crowding worsened. . . .

The clash of the native and the newcomer was bitter in such neighborhoods as the historic North End, a section of stately residences rapidly transformed into a slum. Conditions were better on the island where Patrick Kennedy had settled. . . .

These foreigners, taking a step fully as bold as their emigration, soon bound themselves to the new country. On small and uncertain wages, they married and raised large families. Among his friends, Patrick Kennedy met Bridget Murphy, a girl two years older than himself, whom he married. Three daughters were born to the Kennedys: Mary, Margaret, and Johanna; and on January 8, 1858, a son, christened Patrick Joseph. . . . The Kennedy children survived, but Patrick Kennedy, worn out at thirty-five, succumbed to cholera less than a year after his son was born. He died as poor as when he landed in East Boston.

WIDOW AND SON SURVIVE AND GET AHEAD

Left to support the family as best she could, Bridget Kennedy worked first in a small notions shop at the foot of Border Street, near the ferry landing; later she took a job as a hairdresser at Jordan Marsh in downtown Boston. Young Patrick, raised by his sisters, attended the neighborhood parochial school taught by the Sisters of Notre Dame. . . . As a boy, Patrick helped his mother at the store each afternoon and on Saturdays. In his early teens, with money scarce at home, he left grammar school and went to work as a stevedore[2] on East Boston's busy waterfront.

Fair-skinned, blue-eyed, and well-muscled, Patrick Joseph Kennedy, or "P.J." as his friends called him, had the strength for heavy work, but not the disposition. The hard-drinking, brawling crew around him lived carelessly from day to day,

2. one who loads and unloads ships

but he rebelled at slipping into his father's life of aimless drudgery. Even after putting money into his mother's hand each week, he managed to save part of his wages. His deep, instinctive urge to get ahead was practically his only resource.... Patrick Kennedy's opportunity to rise could come only within the immigrant community. As he worked and saved, he watched his chance.

Probably from his father's acquaintances in the whiskey trade, he learned of a saloon for sale in East Boston's Haymarket Square, and took it over on a shoestring. The quiet, self-possessed young man, working hard, made it a success. Year by year, he plowed back the profits, expanding into retail and wholesale whiskey distribution, eventually opening an office on High Street. He became a partner in two other saloons, one in the Maverick House, East Boston's finest hostelry since its opening in 1835, and the other opposite a shipyard, where the workers streamed in morning and evening for a drink and a bit of gossip....

Patrick Kennedy was unlike his neighbors in one respect: he preferred to listen. Though rarely seen lifting a glass containing anything stronger than lemonade, he stood behind the bar drinking in the endless conversation, absorbing names, occupations, and relationships, nodding at the liars and laughing with the jokers, becoming privy to the secrets, sorrows, and aspirations of the entire neighborhood. Soon or late, the talk of the Irish turned to politics....

PATRICK "P.J." KENNEDY ENTERS POLITICS

Politics, promising a frolic, a fight, and perhaps a steady job, drew spirited Irishmen like the skirl of bagpipes; they flocked into the Democratic party, a tough band full of blarney and bold as brass. And Patrick Kennedy, sensing opportunity, led the way.

With his wide circle of acquaintances, the saloonkeeper came naturally to political influence. He knew the office seekers and their supporters, the conspirators and their intended victims, because caucuses were held and plots hatched on his premises. His advice was sought and carried weight, particularly because it was not lightly given. Reserved, even austere, an elegantly curled moustache completing the picture of dignity, Kennedy commanded respect. Just as he ran an orderly pub, so he kept at arm's length the ward heelers in derby hats and loud vests. A man who sel-

KENNEDY VISITS HIS ANCESTRAL HOME IN IRELAND
*In 1947 John Kennedy visited the old family home in
New Ross, southeastern Ireland. He found his Irish
cousins living on a farm unaware of the American Kennedys.
The excerpt from James MacGregor Burns's book,* John
Kennedy: A Political Profile, *conveys the emotion Kennedy felt
when returning to his family roots and meeting his distant
Irish cousins.*

One August morning in 1947, a wealthy and engaging young
American congressman, son of the former Ambassador to the
Court of St. James's, drove off from Lismore Castle on an exploration back into time. He carried with him a letter from an
aunt in America giving directions to the old family home in
New Ross, fifty miles east of Lismore. At his side in his American station wagon sat an English lady from the company at
the castle. Through the soft green countryside along the
southeastern coast of Ireland and across the bottom tip of
Kilkenny County they motored on to the market town of New
Ross, settled on the banks of the Barrow River.

An Irishman standing on the road into town knew where
the Kennedys lived—"just up the way a hundred yards and
turn to the right." And there it was—an ordinary farm cottage
with thatch roof, whitewashed walls, and dirt floor. They
found a farmer and his wife and their half-dozen bright, tow-
headed children.

"I'm John Kennedy from Boston," the young congressman
said, sticking out his hand. "I believe this is the old Kennedy
homestead." The farmer and his wife greeted him cordially
while the children stared at the gleaming station wagon. The
New Ross Kennedys knew little, it seemed, about their American cousins. But they remembered a Patrick Kennedy from
Boston—John Kennedy's grandfather—who had visited them
some thirty-five years before.

"It sounded from their conversation as if all the Kennedys
had emigrated," Kennedy said later. "I spent about an hour
there surrounded by chickens and pigs, and left in a flow of
nostalgia and sentiment. This was not punctured by the English lady turning to me as we drove off and saying, 'That was
just like Tobacco Road!'[1] She had not understood at all the
magic of the afternoon. . . . "

James MacGregor Burns, *John Kennedy: A Political Profile.* New York: Harcourt,
Brace and World, 1961.

1. the setting for a novel about poor Americans

dom raised his voice, he was not cast in the iron-fisted mold of Martin Lomasney, an orphan bootblack and onetime city lamplighter dubbed "the Mahatma" for his uncanny ability to marshal the electorate of Boston's Ward Eight. . . .

Kennedy strengthened his grip on the precincts of East Boston by running a pocket-sized welfare state. The Irish, suspicious of the charity of outsiders, expected and honored help from their own kind. The Irish worker was at most two weeks away from starvation; the man who found him a job, or helped him keep one, had the gratitude—and votes—of his family and friends. A round or two of free drinks, the loan of a few dollars before payday, a bucket of coal for the family whose breadwinner was laid off—such small gestures brought Kennedy a large and loyal following. He was elected to office by landslide majorities, first to the Massachusetts House of Representatives in 1886, then to the state Senate six years later. But he disliked campaigning, could not make a speech, and had no appetite for office holding and public posturing. Why stammer through a speech when a word to his lieutenants could elect or defeat a candidate? With the clarity of the practical man, he saw that there was only one issue at stake in politics: who shall get what? His concern was with the substance of power. . . .

Patrick Kennedy was preeminently a realist: he cast his lot on the side of conquest. A member of the inner circle of power, popularly known as the Board of Strategy, he sat with like-minded men who doled out offices, jobs, and favors, wielding the Irish vote as a tool of their ambitions. . . .

PATRICK MARRIES AND HAS A SON

Patrick Kennedy had been courting pretty Mary Hickey, whose family stood a rung or two above the Kennedys; but Kennedy, a state representative at twenty-eight, had only begun to climb. They were married in 1887, and on September 6 of the following year, their first child was born. He was named Joseph Patrick. . . .

Patrick Kennedy moved astutely, investing the profits of saloon-keeping and whiskey-selling in such ventures as the Suffolk Coal Company and neighborhood banking. He helped organize the Columbia Trust Company in 1895 and the Sumner Savings Bank two years later. Over the years he invested in a small way in local real estate, mainly vacant land, and took an occasional speculative flier in the stock of mining companies. In steady, unspectacular fashion, Patrick Kennedy prospered. While Joe was a boy, the Kennedys left Meridian Street and moved up the hill to a four-story house at 165 Webster Street, overlooking the harbor.

Through his boyhood, Joe had before him the example of a determined man's ability to take the world as he found it and turn it to his own ends. A successful politician in an era of flagrant corruption, his father kept himself free of taint and was appointed to municipal office by Irish and Yankee mayors alike, serving as election, fire, and wire commissioners. In contrast to "Honey Fitz,"[3] Pat Kennedy stayed in the background, aloof from the brazen fraud and vote-stealing, yet well-informed of the work of his lieutenants. One of Joe's earliest memories was the visit of a pair of ward heelers who reported proudly: "Pat, we voted one hundred and twenty-eight times today." His father, then an election commissioner, was not displeased. . . .

JOSEPH DISPLAYS MONEYMAKING SKILLS AS A BOY

Most of Joe's friends came from poor families, and the pennies they could earn with odd jobs were needed at home. Patrick Kennedy watched with satisfaction as his son joined in the moneymaking scramble, not out of necessity, but out of a desire to excel in competition with his peers. Joe sold newspapers, worked in a haberdasher's, ran errands at the Columbia Trust, and even pocketed a few cents for lighting stoves and gaslights in the homes of Orthodox Jews on the Sabbath and holy days. . . .

A streak of shrewdness showed up early. Roast squab was a delicacy much admired in East Boston, and a chum, Ronan Grady, kept a coop. Pigeon-raising was slow work with a small flock; besides, the birds ate up most of the profits. Then young Grady took into partnership young Kennedy, who had a scheme to speed up matters. On a summer day, the boys would take birds from the coop, hide them under their shirts, and set off for Boston Common. With the birds struggling and tickling, the boys found transportation in the form of the slow-moving coal pungs, wagons drawn by two straining horses, which rumbled through the streets from the docks on Chelsea Creek toward the Boston ferry. Hopping on the rear of a long, flat coal pung, the free riders usu-

---

3. John F. Fitzgerald, John F. Kennedy's maternal grandfather

ally went undetected by the drowsing driver; in any event, they were well out of reach of his whip, a hazard on smaller, faster wagons. When they reached the Common, the boys released their birds among the wild pigeons and let nature take over. If all went well, at the coop that evening would be the two returning birds, plus two or more guests. Thus established on one of Boston's neglected resources, the boys' pigeon traffic thrived.

When he was fifteen, Joe gave further evidence of moneymaking skill. In the pickup games on the mud flats, his ownership of the best baseball and bat had long upheld his claim to the captaincy. Now he organized a neighborhood team called The Assumptions, after the church the boys attended, and led a money-raising drive to buy smart white uniforms with a blue English-script *A* on the shirt and matching stockings. . . .

Pat Kennedy, like every good parent, showed keen interest in his son's development; in addition, he managed the rarer feat of conveying his interest to his son. Joe sensed his father's support and involvement in everything he did. Life, he came to understand, was a joint venture between one generation and the next.

Just as he moved his family away from the mud flats to the fine house on Webster Street, so Patrick Kennedy decided early to set his son apart from the run of fellow Irishmen. After having attended Assumption School and then Xaverian School, both Catholic institutions, Joe deliberately was thrown into the company of the Protestants of the West Side and the regions of the Back Bay. He was enrolled at Boston Latin School, where the sons of New England's leading families had been educated since 1635. . . .

Early each morning, Joe ran to catch the North Ferry, which carried him across the ship canal for a penny, then dashed to the old Warren Avenue building, where the boy knew he was expected to compete hard for a place in the society that had been closed to his father.

Then as now one of the best preparatory schools in the country, Boston Latin rigorously upheld its tradition of scholarship. Joe entered the school in 1901, one of seventy-one members of the sixth class. He was a poor student, frequently reprimanded for his indifferent performance in the classroom by Headmaster Arthur Irving Fiske, a frail, scholarly classicist who was hailed in his day as the greatest

teacher of Greek in New England. But Joe's winning smile
and earnest promises usually enabled him to get around
Mr. Fiske. The single bright spot in his academic record was
in mathematics. . . .

An engaging personality was no substitute for passing
grades, however, and Kennedy was forced to remain behind
at Boston Latin for a year after his original class was graduated, making up his deficiencies. Still, it was no small accomplishment, as he later saw it, to stay in this fast intellectual company at all. . . .

From the first, the tall, slim, red-haired Kennedy made
friends easily and was one of the most popular boys in his
class. When he became colonel of the Latin School's cadet
regiment and led it to victory in city-wide drill competition,
he was the hero of the school's six-hundred-odd student
body. As a senior, he was elected president of the class. He
plunged into athletics, playing on the basketball team three
years and managing the football team. But baseball was his
consuming passion. . . .

The editors of the 1908 yearbook at Boston Latin tactfully
predicted that Joe Kennedy, a good fellow with a mediocre
academic record, would make his fortune "in a very round-
about way." The twists and turns would come later. Now his
first steps were as direct as the ambitions of Patrick and
Mary Kennedy could devise. Joe would surely go on to college. Once again, however, his path would be different. Few
Irishmen could afford to attend college in those days, and
most of those who did went to the Jesuits of Boston College
or Holy Cross, for the Church frowned on secular education.
While the Kennedys were devout Catholics, they wanted
something for their son that the Jesuits could not provide.
Let the Church frown and the neighbors gossip: Joe would
enroll at Harvard. . . .

For the grandson of an immigrant and the heir of a saloonkeeper, Harvard could be a hard experience. There
would be no crude discrimination of the bullying sort, but
a subtle, cruel exclusion, to remind one that he was an in-
truder in a place to which others were born. . . . Thus
Kennedy was doubly an outsider at Harvard, by choice and
by circumstance. But a tough-fibered young man with a
streak of cynicism might console himself with the thought
that Harvard and the Irish wards of Boston, in a sense,
were not so different after all. Each was controlled by a

self-perpetuating oligarchy.

Kennedy, by his own later account, did "all right" at Harvard, receiving passable grades as he concentrated in history and economics. His main interest, as at Boston Latin, was in making the grade socially. Unlike others in the Irish minority, who commuted to Cambridge each day by trolley and took little part in college life, Kennedy lived in the Harvard Yard and made it a point to meet the leading undergraduates. He did not depend on his personality to attract them but instead determinedly sought out and cultivated such popular classmates as Bob Fisher, the widely admired football All-American. . . .

Kennedy was, of course, ineligible for the "best" undergraduate clubs, such as Porcellian, A.D., and Fly, but then so were all but a relative handful of his classmates, those who had attended the "right" Episcopal prep schools. Club spotters, surveying the freshman crop, considered not only a young man's religion, but also his family's wealth, which must have been amassed in the right way, at the right time. . . .

During these years, Kennedy discovered an unsuspected love of good music when a classmate from New York initiated him into the old Boston ritual of the symphony concert on Friday afternoon. Later on, only a few intimate friends would know he liked to relax with his large collection of classical records. It was as though he feared that an admission of refined taste would endanger his reputation for toughness. . . .

[More than a decade and millions of dollars later] the Kennedys, Joe believed, had earned recognition as something more than moneyed Irish. As in the leading Yankee families, the Kennedy wealth was intended to serve as the foundation of a secure social position. . . .

But what good was money in Boston if it could not be translated into social prestige? His daughters, for instance, would not be invited to join the debutante clubs—"not that our girls would have joined anyway; they never gave two cents for that society stuff," [Joe] Kennedy once told a reporter. "But the point is they wouldn't have been asked in Boston."

In the spring of 1926, Kennedy packed his family and servants aboard a private railroad car and left Boston in grandly defiant style, bound for a new home in Riverdale, a suburb of New York City. Boston was "no place to bring up Catholic children," Kennedy later declared.

The Influence of Joseph Kennedy, the President's Father

James MacGregor Burns

James MacGregor Burns describes the impact that Joseph Kennedy had on his children, including John F. Kennedy. In his climb to economic and social success and his struggle against anti-Irish prejudice, Joseph Kennedy had learned that the world was harshly competitive. Therefore, according to Burns, he fostered competition and high expectations in his children. James MacGregor Burns taught political science at Williams College, Williamstown, Massachusetts, and lectured at the Institute of History of the Soviet Academy in Moscow. He is the author of *Roosevelt: The Lion and the Fox*, *Edward Kennedy and the Camelot Legacy*, and *The Power to Lead: Crisis of the American Presidency*.

Some East Bostonians raised their eyebrows when they heard that Pat's[1] eldest boy, Joseph Patrick Kennedy, had won the hand of Rose Fitzgerald, the mayor's[2] daughter, one of the most eligible Catholic girls in town. This was pretty good for the son of a ward boss and saloonkeeper. But those who knew Joe Kennedy were not surprised. He was a go-getter in everything he tried, they said, and he would be a good husband and a good provider.

They were right. Only nine years after his birth in 1888, Joe had sold peanuts and candy on Boston excursion boats, and a few years later had worked as office boy in a bank. He attended parochial school until seventh grade, then shifted to Boston Latin, the famed school where [founding father] Ben-

---

1. Patrick Kennedy, John F. Kennedy's grandfather   2. John F. Fitzgerald

Excerpted from *John Kennedy: A Political Profile*, by James MacGregor Burns. Copyright ©1959, 1960, 1961 and renewed 1987, 1988, 1989 by James MacGregor Burns. Reprinted by permission of Harcourt Brace & Company.

jamin Franklin and [noted historian] Henry Adams had been students. . . . His mother, ambitious for her son, wanted Joe to go to Harvard, and he entered with the class of 1912. . . .

JOE KENNEDY BUILDS A FORTUNE

Looking at the American scene through his calm, appraising eyes, Joe could see that sports and politics and literature were fun, but money really talked. During the summer vacations he and a partner earned several thousand dollars by running a sight-seeing bus to historic Lexington. He vowed to make a million by the time he was thirty-five, and he did, probably several times over. After he graduated from Harvard in 1912, he got a job as a bank examiner and learned the practical side of finance. When a small East Boston bank, owned in part by members of his family, was about to be taken over by another bank, Joe rounded up some capital and proxies and, with the help of his family, was elected bank president at the age of twenty-five, reportedly the youngest in the country.

By then he was courting Rose Fitzgerald, and the two were married in the private chapel of Cardinal O'Connell in Boston in October 1914. With her dark hair and rosy cheeks, the bride had her father's good looks and charm, but she also showed something of her mother's dignity and serenity. She had gone to parochial and public schools and studied music in Europe; she was popular and a good student. The couple settled down in a $6,500 house in a respectable, lower-middle-class neighborhood in Brookline. The groom, in debt at the time as a result of buying the bank stock, had to borrow money to make the down payment. But he was soon solvent. Children came rapidly: the first, Joe, Jr., within a year of the marriage, followed by another boy, John F., in 1917, then five girls and a son—Rosemary, Kathleen, Eunice, Patricia, Jean, and Robert F.—during the 1920's, and finally another son, Edward, in 1932.

With the coming of World War I in 1917, Kennedy resigned from the bank and became assistant general manager of Bethlehem Steel's huge shipyards in Quincy [Massachusetts]. After the war he moved swiftly toward his first million. Boston finance was still controlled by conservative Yankees not very sympathetic to aggressive Irishmen, but Kennedy, acting on the old political maxim "If you can't lick 'em, join 'em," deliberately studied the habits of Boston financiers, even to the point of taking a seat near them on the train. One of these, Galen Stone, was so impressed that he hired him as head of his investment banking house, Hayden, Stone and Company, and in this job Kennedy learned market operations and began to speculate on his own. He took some hard losses, recouped them, and then, with a group of Bostonians, bought control of a chain of thirty-one small movie theaters scattered throughout New England.

But many a Yankee banker still could not wholly accept Joe Kennedy. It was all right for Irishmen to run little East Boston banks and handle immigrants' remittances, they felt, but not to crash the central citadels of finance. So Kennedy, disgusted, began to operate more and more in New York and Hollywood. During the mid-1920's, he moved in on the booming, turbulent movie industry, won control of several motion-picture companies, reshuffled them, and sold out at a huge profit. . . .

By this time Kennedy was a business legend and a man of mystery. Long after he quit the movies in the late '20's, people were arguing about whether he had left behind him a string of strengthened companies or heaps of wreckage. When he deserted Hollywood and began to speculate in the bull market, his operations became even more obscure. "He moved in the intense, secretive circles of operators in the wildest stock market in history," *Fortune* later commented, "with routine plots and pools, inside information and wild guesses. . . ." But Kennedy came out of the bull market with many millions, made more in the crash, and even more by shrewd speculation in liquor importing, real estate, and numerous other enterprises joined together in a financial labyrinth that probably only the financier himself understood. . . .

MOVING UP THROUGH POLITICS

Having made his millions, he moved up through politics, as Pat and Honey Fitz[3] had done, but on a national scale. In 1932 he supported [Franklin D.] Roosevelt before the convention and gave $15,000 to the Democratic campaign fund, lent it $50,000 more, and probably contributed many more thousands indirectly. In 1934 the President made him first head of the new Securities and Exchange Commission—to the consternation of some—and, later, head of the Maritime

3. his father Patrick Kennedy and his father-in-law John F. Fitzgerald

Commission. Two years later, in 1936, Kennedy wrote a ringing endorsement of the Democratic nominee in a book called *I'm for Roosevelt,* and he gave the Democrats another big campaign donation. . . .

The President thought the book "splendid" and a help not only in the campaign but in the "sane education" of the country. Those who read the book carefully might have noticed that its support for the New Deal, while vigorous, was narrowly based. Kennedy liked the New Deal for its emphasis on welfare and security, for its bread-and-butter liberalism. He knew of "no higher duty or more noble function of the state," he said, "than caring for the needy among our citizens," and he quoted in his support the famous encyclical of Pope Leo XIII on the condition of the working classes. The noneconomic elements of liberalism—the relation of the New Deal to individual freedom—he laid aside scornfully as "question begging abstractions." What matters a vote to a hungry man? he demanded.

He was away from home often during the late summer of 1936 setting up businessmen's organizations for Roosevelt and looking for men in finance and business who would support the New Deal. But during the late '30's he became disenchanted with the direction of the New Deal. He said little publicly, and he remained on friendly personal terms with Roosevelt, but the radical fiscal policies he had begun to oppose in the first term disturbed him even more during the second.

Now in his late forties, Kennedy had become a national figure—a big, intense man, with sandy hair thinning a bit over a freckled forehead and horn-rimmed glasses that gave him a slightly owlish look. But he always remained something of an enigma to the public. For one thing, it was hard to place him. . . . The man himself was unpredictable, one moment overcoming you with his blarney, the next moment hard as steel, sometimes endlessly patient, then suddenly blowing up in a real Irish temper. And where did he live, anyway—Boston, New York, Hollywood, Washington, Palm Beach? He seemed to have homes everywhere.

Appearances were not too deceiving; Kennedy was indeed a lone wolf whom very few men knew. He never stayed in one job or enterprise very long; the moment he stepped in he seemed to be planning when he wanted to get out. He was never wholly accepted by either the business community or the liberals. The respectable rich looked on him as a political opportunist, the liberals as a Wall Street plunger. And of course there was the old problem of the Yankees. Kennedy left Boston primarily because he considered their attitude frigid and aloof. People were more tolerant in New York and Hollywood. But everywhere he went, he was labeled as an Irishman.

"I was born here," he exploded one day. "My children were born here. What the hell do I have to do to be an American?"

Joe Kennedy's great consolation in these strenuous years was his family. Indeed, he justified his feverish money-making largely as a way of ensuring his nine children's security in the years to come. Explaining to visitors why he could go on despite suspicion and criticism, he liked to quote a senator's reply to an angry voter who threatened to drive him out of office: "Home holds no terrors for me.". . .

Even among his family, however, Kennedy could not escape from the press of finance and politics; perhaps he did not try. At home he was pursued by telegrams and long-distance calls, and the house was full of aides, politicians, financiers. Visitors would find him happily stretched out on the big porch at Hyannisport, a stock-market ticker chattering away at his side.

Actually, Kennedy had no wish to seal his children off from the outside world. They might as well know at the start that it was harshly competitive. "Every single kid," a close friend of the family told a reporter, "was raised to think, First, what shall I do about this problem? Second, what will Dad say about my solution of it?" When he was home he encouraged talk at the dinner table about American government and politics, but money matters could not be raised. "I have never discussed money with my wife and family," Kennedy said years later, "and I never will."

COMPETITION AND UNITY

The father wanted his children to be competitive with one another, and they vied among themselves fiercely in parlor games and sports. Sometimes the girls would leave the tennis courts sobbing after being bested by their brothers. Touch football games were almost fratricidal. "They are the most competitive and at the same time the most cohesive family I've ever seen," said another long-time family friend some years after. "They fight each other, yet they feed on each other. They stimulate each other. Their minds strike sparks. Each of them has warm friends. But none they like and admire so much as they like and admire their own brothers and sisters."

He wanted his children, however competitive they might be with one another, to present a united front against the outside world. Consciously or not, he was copying the ways of his father and the Democratic bosses of old, who allowed fighting among the district leaders between elections but not on the day when they had to beat Republicans. The fierce loyalty of the Kennedys to each other exists to this day and was especially helpful to John Kennedy in his political campaigns.

During Kennedy's long absences, Joe, Jr. increasingly assumed his father's family responsibilities. He taught the others how to sail and swim with something of Joe, Sr.'s perfectionism. Indeed, he was much like his father—generous, considerate, and loving, and, at the same time, driving, domineering, and hot-tempered.

THE ROLE OF ROSE KENNEDY

But the main steadying element in this boisterous household was Rose Kennedy. Even as a young woman, she impressed her friends with her scrupulous sense of duty and her devotion to the church. What she lacked in intellectual brilliance she made up in her intense love for her family. Love and a sense of duty were needed in the Kennedy home. The children were so numerous that she had to keep records of their vaccinations, illnesses, food problems, and the like, on file cards, but she was still able to give each child some individual attention. . . .

In her husband's absence, she would even work up current-events topics and guide the discussion of them by the children at the table—her husband would have expected it. With him away so often and for so long, the daily routine, despite household help, was not simple, certainly not so easy as it later seemed to some of the family. Occasionally—and more often as the children went off to school—she got out from under her big family by taking vacations with her husband in Florida or Europe. She also devoted herself increasingly to the church. "She was terribly religious," Kennedy said. "She was a little removed, . . . which I think is the only way to survive when you have nine children. I thought she was a very model mother for a big family.". . .

EXPECTATION AND DISCIPLINE

As his father's riches piled up in the 1920's, Jack spent many winter vacations at the family's new resort home at Palm Beach and summers at another home at Hyannisport, on Cape Cod. He especially loved Hyannisport. . . .

But life was not always a victory. Wherever he was, at school or at home, Jack was conscious of his father's incessant concern that he do better, especially in his studies. His letters home were full of defensive, self-belittling remarks about his grades and his athletic skill. He offered excuses for his poor showing, at the same time denying that these were alibis.

"If it were not for Latin," he wrote his mother, "I would probably lead the lower school but I am flunking that by ten points." In a letter to his father his second spring at Choate, he listed the high points of a recent vacation and concluded: "I hope my marks go up because I guess that is the best way to say thanks for the trip." "Maybe Dad thinks I am alibing but I am not," he wrote on another occasion. "I have also been doing a little worrying about my studies because what he said about me starting of[f] great and then going down sunk in." Clearly Jack realized that what his father wanted above all was that he excel in his studies, as a prelude to competition in later life. . . .

If failure aroused parental frowns, achievement was recognized in a very material way. A sailboat, a pony, a trip to England were rewards for better grades. . . .

For Jack, competition was not some abstract thing that his father wanted. It was right in the family and its name was "Joe." In their father's long absences, Jack's big brother ruled the roost. Joe was bigger and heavier, more boisterous and outgoing than Jack. He demanded absolute obedience from the younger children in exchange for his brotherly help. . . . Bobby Kennedy remembered cowering with his sisters upstairs while his older brothers fought furiously on the first floor.

The boys' father knew about the rivalry but it did not bother him, except when it got out of hand. He wanted competition in the family as long as the children stuck together in dealing with the world outside. He knew, too, that Joe, Jr. made up for his bullying ways in generosity and kindness to his young brothers and sisters. Jack, too, for all his troubles at the hands of his older brother, felt that Joe's overbearing ways, when later smoothed out, were one reason for his own success in school and in the war.

The family competition was not just physical. The father encouraged political argument at the dinner table, especially among himself and the older boys. He asserted his own views strongly, but, though Jack said that his father was sometimes rather harsh, he did not force his views on Joe, Jr. or on Jack. The boys could not help being influenced, however, by their father's opinions, for he was forceful, knowledgeable, and articulate.

CHAPTER 2

The Kennedy Style of Politics

The Nixon-Kennedy Debate

Christopher Matthews

Christopher Matthews contrasts the performances of
John Kennedy and Richard Nixon in the first television debate between two presidential candidates to
explain why the 1960 event was a disaster for Nixon
and a success for Kennedy. Kennedy had the advantages of thorough preparation, an attractive appearance, and the confidence to intimidate his opponent.
According to Matthews, Nixon had made poor judgments before the debate and was caught off guard
during the confrontation. Christopher Matthews, a
nationally syndicated columnist, was a speechwriter
for Jimmy Carter and top aide to House Speaker
Thomas "Tip" O'Neill. He is a television commenta-
tor and author of *Hardball: How Politics is Played—
Told by One Who Knows the Game.*

Richard Nixon didn't understand the power of TV. "Television
is not as effective as it was in 1952," he told the *New York Herald Tribune's* Earl Mazo prior to the 1960 race. "The novelty
has worn off." With that odd mind-set in play, the first presidential debate between Nixon and rival Kennedy was set for
September 26 in Chicago, the city of Nixon's selection as the
vice-presidential candidate in 1952 and Jack Kennedy's melo-
dramatic run for the same office four years later. With the
country awaiting the televised confrontation between the two
men, their positions in the Gallup poll had frozen. An August
16 poll gave Nixon 47 percent, Kennedy 47 percent; an August
30 poll had it Nixon 47 percent, Kennedy 48 percent. A September 14 survey showed Nixon at 47 percent, Kennedy 46
percent. The electorate was waiting until it saw the two glad-
iators in the same arena, saw how they handled each other,
how each reacted to the sight and power of the other man.

Abridged with permission from Simon & Schuster, Inc., from *Kennedy and Nixon: The
Rivalry That Shaped Postwar America*, by Christopher Matthews. Copyright ©1996 by
Christopher Matthews.

Two weeks before the Great Debate, Nixon was asked a deflating question by CBS's Walter Cronkite. "I know that you must be aware . . . that there are some . . . who would say, 'I don't know what it is, but I just don't like the man; I can't put my finger on it; I just don't like him.' Would you have any idea what might inspire that kind of feeling on the part of anybody?" Nixon, who did not seem put off by the query, answered that it was hard for "the subject of such a reaction" to be objective. He then chalked it up to politics. "In my public life, I have been involved in many controversial issues. As a matter of fact, that is why I am here today." Finally, he raised the matter of cosmetics. "Then, of course, another thing might be the fact that when people take pictures of you or when you appear on television, you may not make the impression that they like. Oh, I get letters from women, for example, sometimes—and men—who support me, and they say, 'Why do you wear that heavy beard when you are on television?' Actually, I don't try, but I can shave within thirty seconds before I go on television and still have a beard, unless we put some powder on, as we have done today."

But if Nixon was also concerned about his notorious five o'clock shadow, a feature long satirized in editorial cartoons, Kennedy was already moving to exploit what he knew to be his own telegenic advantage. . . .

KENNEDY PREPARES

Kennedy and his team were aware that Nixon had a history of debating successes and that, if cornered, he could turn very nasty. In preparation, they commandeered the two top floors of Chicago's Ambassador East Hotel. . . . Kennedy had a fistful of cards in his hand, each with a probable question and its staff-prepared answer. Drilling him were the invaluable Ted Sorensen and his other legislative assistant, Mike Feldman. To offer further backup, Kennedy and his briefers had the help of a hefty research and speechwriting operation headed by Prof. Archibald Cox, on leave from Harvard Law School and now working for the campaign full-time. According to Harris,[1] after each card had been dealt with, Kennedy would throw it on the floor. As a backup document for the prep session, Feldman had produced a "Nixopedia" of the vice president's positions and statements over the years. . . .

1. Louis Harris, Kennedy's pollster

NIXON REFUSES TO PREPARE

Campaign manager Bob Finch was there for Richard Nixon's own hectic hours of September 26, 1960. Instead of resting or prepping, the candidate had spent the night before addressing rallies in five different Chicago wards, then getting up the morning of the debate for a speech to the Carpenters Union. "He was upset, because he had insisted on doing those last-minute car stops. He hadn't gotten his strength back from being in the hospital."

Nixon refused to engage in the kind of practice session being held at the Ambassador East, Finch revealed in frustration. "We kept pushing for him to have some give-and-take with either somebody from the staff . . . anything. He hadn't done anything except to tell me that he knew how to debate. He totally refused to prepare. . . ."

Now came the greatest miscalculation. Already handicapped by his hospital pallor and lack of warm-up, the Republican candidate chose the wrong strategy. Attorney General William Rogers, Nixon's counselor since the Hiss[2] case, coaxed him to be "the good guy," to be tolerant of Kennedy's shortcomings rather than reproachful. . . . Had Nixon known how polished and prepared Kennedy would be for the meeting, his predebate decision to go easy on his rival would have been different. . . .

In 1950 one in ten American families had a television set. By 1960 that number had increased to nine in ten. Anyone running for president should have realized what these figures meant: The audience, watching the first debate between Richard M. Nixon and John F. Kennedy, would be the largest yet assembled.

THE CANDIDATES IN THE STUDIO

The Republican candidate's arrival at Channel 2, the CBS affiliate in Chicago, was marked by bad luck. "He was in the right seat, I was in the left seat in the back," recalled Herb Klein,[3] who was with Nixon in the car. "When he got out of the car, he bumped his knee bad. It was the knee that had been infected." Others saw Nixon's face go "chalk white."

His discomfort didn't stop Nixon from making an ostenta-

2. Alger Hiss, a U.S. diplomat, was suspected of spying for the Soviet Union from 1926 to 1937. He was convicted of perjury in 1950. Recent evidence, the Venona descriptions of Soviet cable traffic, confirms his guilt of espionage right through 1945.   3. director of communications for Richard Nixon

tious display of good fellowship when he met with the phalanx of CBS executives, including CBS president Frank Stanton, who formed a reception committee for the two candidates. Despite the knee, Nixon seemed in lively spirits, taking time to banter with the men snapping pictures. "Have you ever had a picture printed yet?" he cruelly kidded one of the hardworking photographers.

Then it happened, the moment that would forever shake Nixon's confidence. "He and I were standing there talking when Jack Kennedy arrived," Hewitt[4] remembers. Tanned, tall, lean, well tailored in a dark suit, the younger candidate gleamed. Photographers, seizing their chance, abandoned Nixon and fluttered about their new prey like hornets. The senator bore no resemblance to the emaciated, wan, crippled, yellow figure he'd once been.[5] "He looked like a young Adonis," Hewitt would recall.

The psychological battle was on. Kennedy, asked to pose with his rival, appeared barely to notice him. His well-practiced Yankee chill froze the air between the two. "I assume you guys know each other," Hewitt said. At this, the two shook hands, "not warmly," Hewitt recalled, "not coldly," but as prizefighters "about to enter the ring."

"How're you doing?" Kennedy asked.

"You had a big crowd in Cleveland," Nixon rejoined.

They could have been strangers for all the interest Jack Kennedy showed in the colleague he'd known since 1947. Nixon, for his part, seemed intimidated. From the moment Kennedy strode in, hijacking the attention of the photographers, Nixon was not the same man. Visibly deflated by his rival's matinee-idol aura and seeming nervelessness, Nixon slouched in his chair, his head turned away, a man in retreat. . . .

Both candidates now retired to separate rooms. Ten minutes before the broadcast, however, Nixon was back in Studio B, nervously awaiting airtime. . . . [Lawrence O'Brian said,] "The countdown commenced over the loudspeaker. 'Five minutes to airtime.'" Nixon was staring at the studio door. Now there were only three minutes left. "Nixon was still watching the door, as tense a man as I had ever seen. By then, I was sure that no one had summoned Kennedy, and I

---

4. Don Hewitt, CBS producer directing the debate   5. Kennedy had had malaria and back injuries during World War II. As a senator he suffered complications after back surgery.

was about to dash after him, when the door swung open. Kennedy walked in and took his place, *barely glancing at Nixon.* Kennedy had played the clock perfectly. He had thrown his opponent off stride." He had set his rival up for the kill.

THE CANDIDATES' STRATEGIES

"The candidates need no introduction," moderator Howard K. Smith announced to 80 million Americans. Richard Nixon, for his part, looked like an ill-at-ease, unshaven, middle-aged fellow recovering from a serious illness. Jack Kennedy, by contrast, was elegant in a dark, well-tailored suit that set off his healthy tan. Kennedy sat poised, his legs crossed, his hands folded on his lap; Nixon had his legs awkwardly side by side, his hands dangling from the chair arms. Their faces presented an even starker contrast. "I couldn't believe it when the thing came on and he looked so haggard," Bob Finch recalls. Nixon's campaign manager also noticed something else. "I saw he didn't have any makeup on."

Too late. The debate was under way. By agreement, the focus of this first encounter was to be domestic policy. Believing that the audiences for the four debates would grow, the Nixon people had saved foreign policy until last. But in his opening statement, Kennedy made clear he could not only handle a foreign policy debate, he relished it. "Mr. Smith, Mr. Nixon," he began, slyly equating the status of a two-term vice president and a television newscaster. "In the election of 1860, Abraham Lincoln said the question is whether this nation could exist half slave or half free. In the election of 1960, and with the world around us, the question is whether the world will exist half slave or half free, whether it will move in the direction of freedom, in the direction of the road that we are taking, or whether it will move in the direction of slavery."

Then he dispensed with the rules to extol his global agenda. "We discuss tonight domestic issues, but I would not want . . . any implication to be given that this does not involve directly our struggle with Mr. Khrushchev for survival." He had cold-cocked his rival by introducing precisely the topic Nixon had agreed to postpone. His reference to the Soviet leader, who Kennedy noted was "in New York" (as if Nikita Khrushchev's current trip to the United Nations were a symbolic invasion of the country), was that of the classic Cold Warrior. The United States needed to be strong economically, Kennedy declared, not just to maintain the American standard of living but because economic strength buttressed our fight against the Communists. "If we do well here, if we meet our obligations, if we are moving ahead, I think freedom will be secure around the world. If we fail, then freedom fails. Are we doing as much as we can do?" he teased an anxious country. "I do not think we're doing enough." Was America to be led by the gutsy GI generation back from the Pacific or by slackers ready to let things slide?

To bolster his indictment of the White House, Kennedy recited a long list of national shortcomings: steel mills operating with unused capacity, West Virginia schoolkids taking their lunches home to hungry families, and the poor prospects facing the "Negro baby." Then he posed the challenge. "The question now is: Can freedom be maintained under the most severe attack it has ever known? I think it can be, and I think in the final analysis it depends upon what we do here. I think it's time America started moving again."

No matter that John F. Kennedy had delivered this self-same appeal scores of times before. His words now carried a martial cadence in the ears of his largest audience ever. In eight minutes a lean, smartly tailored young gentleman had made a proposal to the American man and woman sitting in the family parlor. In doing so, he had shown himself as infinitely more appealing than the fellow who had been vice president of the United States for eight years. There wasn't a word of his opening presentation that anyone could have argued with, not a sentiment that his fellow citizens couldn't share. No, the country was not meeting its potential. No, we were not the same nation of doers who had ended World War II. Yes, the country *could* do better. And, yes, we needed to "get the country moving again." Kennedy was playing a hawk on foreign policy, the activist at home, the same strategy he had used in the 1952 Senate race that sent Lodge[6] packing. By going to his rival's right on foreign policy and to his left on domestic policy, Jack Kennedy would leave Nixon scrambling for turf.

After observing this tour de force, Nixon began to betray the hunted look of a man dragged from a five-dollar-a-night hotel room and thrust before the unforgiving glare of a po-

6. Henry Cabot Lodge, Massachusetts senator, 1937–44, 1947–53, defeated by Jack Kennedy

lice lineup, a man being charged with a crime of which he knew himself to be guilty. Afraid to project the "assassin image," he was stymied. "Mr. Smith, Senator Kennedy, there is no question but that we cannot discuss our internal affairs in the United States without recognizing that they have a tremendous bearing on our international position. There is no question that this nation cannot stand still, because we are in a deadly competition, a competition not only with the men in the Kremlin but the men in Peking." Finally: "I subscribe completely to the spirit that Senator Kennedy has expressed tonight, the spirit that the United States should move ahead."

Incredibly, Nixon was agreeing with his challenger. Yes, domestic policies affect the country's foreign situation. Yes, we cannot afford to "stand still." Yes, Kennedy has the right "spirit" to lead. His only concern was that Kennedy's statistics made the situation appear bleaker than it was.

Regarding Kennedy's call for medical care for the aged: "Here again may I indicate that Senator Kennedy and I are not in disagreement as to the aim. We both want to help old people." Minutes later: "Let us understand throughout this campaign that his motives and mine are sincere." And, after a small reminder that he knew "what it means to be poor," he offered yet another genuflection to Kennedy's goodwill. "I know Senator Kennedy feels as deeply about these problems as I do, but our disagreement is not about the goals for America but only about the means to reach those goals."

Only? The race for the presidency is "only" about "means"? With staggering humility, Nixon was telling the largest American political audience ever assembled that his rival was not only a man of unquestioned sincerity but one of unassailable motive. It was merely a matter of method that separated the two applicants for the world's most exalted position. To avoid the "assassin image," Dick Nixon was presenting himself as Jack Kennedy's admiring, if somewhat more prudent, older brother.

He committed a second tactical error. Just as he had at McKeesport [Pennsylvania] thirteen years earlier, Nixon ignored the audience and fixed his attention exclusively on Kennedy. He seemed intent on getting Kennedy himself to agree that when it came to goals, there really wasn't much difference between them. Worse still, he seemed to crave Kennedy's *approval,* even to the point of rebuking his own

administration. "Good as a record is," he averred, "may I
emphasize it isn't enough. A record is never something to
stand on. It's something to build on.". . .

IMAGES, NOT WORDS, MADE THE DIFFERENCE

Yet at least one important listener thought the Nixon approach was working. Lyndon Johnson, following the pro-
ceedings on his car radio, gave most of the points to the Republican; so did the millions of others who followed the
sound but not the picture. . . .

But more than either contestant's words, it was their images, projected on millions of black-and-white Admiral and
General Electric televisions, that affected the American
judgment. Each time Kennedy spoke, Nixon's eyes darted toward him in an uncomfortable mix of fear and curiosity. . . .
When Nixon was on, Kennedy sat, sometimes professorially
taking notes, at other moments wearing a sardonic expression as he concentrated on his rival's answers. Sargent
Shriver would note that it was his brother-in-law's facial language, more than anything he said, that decided the results
of the Great Debate. By raising an eyebrow at Nixon, he had
shown he had the confidence to lead the country. . . .

After weeks of parity in the polls, one candidate now
moved into a clear lead. A Gallup survey taken in the days
following the Great Debate found Nixon with 46 percent,
Kennedy pulling ahead to 49 percent. Who had "won" the
debate? Forty-three percent said Kennedy; 29 percent called
it even. Just 23 percent gave it to Nixon.

Nixon partisans were furious. What could this man have
been thinking of, with all that unctuous nonsense of his
about Kennedy's motives being sincere, about the two men
having similar goals? . . . For the rest of his life Nixon would
refuse even to *look* at the tapes.

The New Frontier

Arthur Schlesinger Jr.

Arthur Schlesinger Jr. describes the early days of the
New Frontier, the name given to Kennedy's administration. Schlesinger identifies the people Kennedy
assembled for key positions and the qualifications
they brought to their jobs. While the initial spirit
was high, Schlesinger also cites criticism of the New
Frontier and catalogs the world realities facing the
president and his staff. Arthur Schlesinger Jr., historian and author of *The Rise of the City*, served as
adviser to President Kennedy.

The future everywhere, indeed, seemed bright with hope. By
the time I came back from Latin America in early March
[1961], the New Frontier was in full swing. The capital city,
somnolent in the Eisenhower years, had come suddenly
alive. The air had been stale and oppressive; now fresh
winds were blowing. There was the excitement which
comes from an injection of new men and new ideas, the release of energy which occurs when men with ideas have a
chance to put them into practice. Not since the New Deal
more than a quarter of a century before had there been such
an invasion of bright young men. Not since Franklin Roosevelt had there been a President who so plainly delighted in
innovation and leadership.

Before I went to South America, there had been a White
House reception for presidential appointees. We had all
wandered around the East Room in an intoxication of pleasure and incredulity. One's life seemed almost to pass in
review as one encountered Harvard classmates, wartime as-
sociates, faces seen after the war in ADA[1] conventions, workers in Stevenson[2] campaigns, academic colleagues, all
united in a surge of hope and possibility. The President him-

---

1. Americans for Democratic Action   2. Adlai Stevenson was the Democratic nominee
for president in 1952 and 1956.

self appeared to share the mood, though in his case it was a response to possibilities rather than to facts. He already had his gallery of anxieties—the sliding situation in Southeast Asia, the gold drain, the stagnation of the economy, the Cuban exiles in Guatemala. Yet anxiety did not disturb his easy composure, and he watched the exhilaration around him with pleasure, even if a skeptical smile played on his lips as he considered its more naïve manifestations.

Now, when I returned to Washington a month later, the New Frontier was hard at work. The pace was frenetic. Everyone came early and stayed late. I soon found myself arriving in the East Wing by eight or eight-thirty in the morning and remaining until seven-thirty or eight at night. Telephones rang incessantly. Meetings were continuous. The evenings too were lively and full. The glow of the White House was lighting up the whole city. Washington seemed engaged in a collective effort to make itself brighter, gayer, more intellectual, more resolute. It was a golden interlude.

THE NEW FRONTIER STAFF

Within the White House itself, things were beginning to settle into a pattern. Evelyn Lincoln and Ken O'Donnell guarded the two entrances into the presidential office. Pierre Salinger entertained the press with jocular daily briefings. Larry O'Brien, having won the critical fight to enlarge the House Rules Committee, was now deploying his people all over the Hill in support of the presidential program. Myer Feldman and Lee White were working on legislation and messages. Ralph Dungan was conducting the last stages of the talent hunt and supervising questions of government reorganization. Dick Goodwin was handling Latin America and a dozen other problems. Fred Dutton was Secretary of the Cabinet and dealt with many questions of politics and program.

It was already apparent that the key men around the President, so far as policy was concerned, were Theodore Sorensen and McGeorge Bundy. There had been predictions of conflict between the two. . . . But this did not seem to be taking place—and, indeed, the Kennedy White House remained to the end remarkably free of the rancor which has so often welled up in presidential households. One reason for this was that staff members had more than enough to do and therefore not much time for resentment or feuding. Another was that the President handled the situation with effortless skill, avoiding collective confrontations, such as staff meetings where everyone might find out what everyone else was up to. He tactfully kept the relations with his aides on a bilateral basis. . . . Contrary to the predictions, Sorensen accepted the new situation in the White House with imperturbable grace. The legislative program, domestic policy and speeches became his unchallenged domain; and speeches, of course, assured him an entry into foreign policy at the critical points. No one at the White House worked harder or more carefully; Kennedy relied on no one more; and Sorensen's suspicions of the newcomers, whatever they may have been, were under rigid control. Underneath the appearance of bluntness, taciturnity and, at times, sheer weariness, he was capable of great charm and a frolicsome satiric humor. His flow of comic verse always enlivened festive occasions at the White House.

For his part, McGeorge Bundy treated Sorensen and his relationship with Kennedy with invariable consideration. Bundy possessed dazzling clarity and speed of mind— Kennedy told friends that, next to David Ormsby Gore,[3] Bundy was the brightest man he had ever known. . . . He had tremendous zest and verve. He never appeared tired; he was always ready to assume responsibility; and his subordinates could detect strain only when rare flashes of impatience and sharpness of tone disturbed his usually invincible urbanity. One felt that he was forever sustained by those two qualities so indispensable for success in government—a deep commitment to the public service and a large instinct for power. . . .

QUALITIES COMMON AMONG NEW FRONTIERSMEN

The excitement in the White House infected the whole executive branch. A new breed had come to town, and the New Frontiersmen carried a thrust of action and purpose wherever they went. It is hard to generalize about so varied and exuberant a group; but it can be said that many shared a number of characteristics.

For one thing, like the New Dealers a quarter century earlier, they brought with them the ideas of national reconstruction and reform which had been germinating under the surface of a decade of inaction. They had stood by too long

---

3. an English friend of JFK; member of English Parliament; British ambassador to U.S. when Kennedy was president

while a complaisant government had ignored the needs and
potentialities of the nation—a nation whose economy was
slowing down and whose population was overrunning its
public facilities and services; a nation where the victims of
racism and poverty lived on in sullen misery and the ideals
held out by the leaders to the people were parochial and
mediocre. Now the New Frontiersmen swarmed in from
state governments, the universities, the foundations, the
newspapers, determined to complete the unfinished business of American society. Like Rexford G. Tugwell[4] in another age, they proposed to roll up their sleeves and make
America over.

For another, they aspired, like their President, to the
world of ideas as well as to the world of power. They had
mostly gone to college during the intellectual ferment of the
thirties. Not all by any means (despite the newspapers and
the jokes) had gone to Harvard, but a good many had,
though Sir Denis Brogan, after a tour of inspection, remarked that the New Frontier seemed to him to bear even
more the imprint of Oxford. Certainly there were Rhodes
Scholars on every side—Rostow and Kermit Gordon in the
Executive Office, [Dean] Rusk, Harlan Cleveland, George
McGhee, Richard Gardner, Philip Kaiser and Lane Timmons
in State, Byron White and Nicholas Katzenbach in Justice,
Elvis Stahr and Charles Hitch in Defense, as well as such
congressional leaders as William Fulbright and Carl Albert.
Many of the New Frontiersmen had been college professors.
([In *The Economics of the Political Parties*] Seymour Harris
has pointed out that of Kennedy's first 200 top appointments,
nearly half came from backgrounds in government, whether
politics or public service, 18 per cent from universities and
foundations and 6 per cent from the business world; the figures for Eisenhower were 42 per cent from business and 6
per cent from universities and foundations.) A surprisingly
large number had written books. Even the Postmaster General had published a novel. They had no fear of ideas nor,
though they liked to be sprightly in manner, of serious talk.
One day in March Robert Triffin, the economist, and I paid a
call on Jean Monnet.[5] We asked him what he thought of the
New Frontier. He said, "The thing I note most is that the con-

---

4. a staff member in F.D. Roosevelt's administration   5. French economist and politician

versation is recommencing. You cannot have serious government without collective discussion. I have missed that in Washington in recent years."

Another thing that defined the New Frontiersmen was the fact that many had fought in the war. Kennedy and McGov-

KENNEDY COINS THE PHRASE "THE NEW FRONTIER"

John Kennedy was nominated to be the Democratic candidate for president at the Democratic convention in Los Angeles in July 1960. In his acceptance speech, he outlined the challenges of the new frontier of the 1960s.

For I stand tonight facing west on what was once the last frontier. From the lands that stretch 3000 miles behind me, the pioneers of old gave up their safety, their comfort and sometimes their lives to build a new world here in the West. . . . Their motto was not "Every man for himself," but "All for the common cause.". . .

Today some would say that those struggles are all over, that all the horizons have been explored, that all the battles have been won, that there is no longer an American frontier. But . . . the problems are not all solved and the battles are not all won, and we stand today on the edge of a new frontier—the frontier of the 1960s, a frontier of unknown opportunities and paths, a frontier of unfulfilled hopes and threats. . . .

The new frontier of which I speak is not a set of promises— it is a set of challenges. It sums up not what I intend to *offer* the American people, but what I intend to ask of them. . . . It holds out the promise of more sacrifice instead of more security. . . . Beyond that frontier are uncharted areas of science and space, unsolved problems of peace and war, unconquered pockets of ignorance and prejudice, unanswered questions of poverty and surplus.

It would be easier to shrink back from that frontier, to look to the safe mediocrity of the past. . . . But I believe the times demand invention, innovation, imagination, decision. I am asking each of you to be new pioneers on that new frontier. . . .

For the harsh facts of the matter are that we stand on this frontier at a turning point in history. . . .

It has been a long road from that first snowy day in New Hampshire to this crowded convention city. Now begins another long journey. . . .

Arthur Schlesinger Jr., *A Thousand Days: John F. Kennedy in the White House.* Boston: Houghton Mifflin, 1965.

ern were not the only heroes in the new Washington. Lieutenant Orville Freeman had had half his jaw shot off by the Japanese in the swamps of Bougainville in 1943. Lieutenant Kenneth O'Donnell had flown thirty missions over Germany as a bombardier for the 8th Air Force; his plane had been shot up, and twice he had made emergency landings. Lieutenants McGeorge Bundy and Mortimer Caplin had been on the Normandy beaches on D-day plus 1, while a few miles away William Walton was parachuted in as a correspondent, accompanying Colonel James Gavin in the fighting for Ste. Mère-Eglise. Lieutenant Nicholas Katzenbach, a B-25 navigator, had been shot down in the Mediterranean and spent two years in Italian and German prison camps; he twice escaped and was twice recaptured. Lieutenant Commander Douglas Dillon had been under Kamikaze attack in Lingayen Gulf and had flown a dozen combat patrol missions. Captain Roger Hilsman had led a band of native guerrillas behind Japanese lines in Burma. Lieutenant Edward Day had served on a submarine chaser in the Solomons and a destroyer escort in the Atlantic. Lieutenant Byron White had fought in the Solomons. Ensign Pierre Salinger had been decorated for a dangerous rescue in the midst of a typhoon from his subchaser off Okinawa. Major Dean Rusk had been a staff officer in the China-Burma-India theater. Major Arthur Goldberg had organized labor espionage for the OSS[6] in Europe. Lieutenant Stewart Udall had served in the Air Force. Lieutenants Paul Fay and James Reed were veterans of the PT-boat war in the Pacific.

The war experience helped give the New Frontier generation its casual and laconic tone, its grim, puncturing humor and its mistrust of evangelism. It accounted in particular, I think, for the differences in style between the New Frontiersmen and the New Dealers. The New Dealers were incorrigible philosophizers—"chain talkers," someone had sourly called them thirty years before—and the New Deal had a distinctive and rather moralistic rhetoric. The men of the thirties used to invoke 'the people,' their ultimate wisdom and the importance of doing things for them in a way quite alien to the New Frontier. The mood of the new Washington was more to do things because they were rational and necessary than because they were just and right, though this

6. Office of Strategic Services

should not be exaggerated. In the thirties idealism was sometimes declared, even when it did not exist; in the sixties, it was sometimes deprecated, even when it was the dominant motive. The New Frontiersmen had another common characteristic: versatility. They would try anything. Most had some profession or skill to which they could always return; but ordinarily they used it as a springboard for general meddling. Kenneth Galbraith was an economist who, as ambassador to India, reviewed novels for *The New Yorker* and wrote a series of pseudonymous satiric skits for *Esquire*. Bill Walton was a newspaperman turned abstract painter. This was especially true in the White House itself. Where Eisenhower had wanted a staff with clearly defined functions, Kennedy resisted pressures toward specialization; he wanted a group of all-purpose men to whom he could toss anything. It seemed to me that in many ways Dick Goodwin, though younger than the average, was the archetypal New Frontiersman. His two years in the Army had been too late for the war, even too late for Korea. But he was the supreme generalist who could turn from Latin America to saving the Nile monuments at Abu Simbel, from civil rights to planning the White House dinner for the Nobel Prize winners, from composing a parody of Norman Mailer to drafting a piece of legislation, from lunching with a Supreme Court Justice to dining with Jean Seberg—and at the same time retain an unquenchable spirit of sardonic liberalism and an unceasing drive to get things done.

CRITICISM AND REALITY SET IN

Not everyone liked the new people. Washington never had. "A plague of young lawyers settled on Washington," one observer had said of the New Dealers. ". . . They floated airily into offices, took desks, asked for papers and found no end of things to be busy about. I never found out why they came, what they did or why they left." Even Learned Hand complained in 1934 that they were "so conceited, so insensitive, so arrogant." Old-timers felt the same resentments in March 1961. One could not deny a sense of New Frontier autointoxication; one felt it oneself. The pleasures of power, so long untasted, were now being happily devoured—the chauffeur-driven limousines, the special telephones, the top secret documents, the personal aides, the meetings in the Cabinet Room, the calls from the President. Merriman Smith, who had seen many administrations come and go, wrote about what he called the New People: "hot-eyed, curious but unconcerned with protocol, and yeasty with shocking ideas . . . they also have their moments of shortsightedness, bias, prejudice and needlessly argumentative verbosity." The verbosity, I have suggested, was marked only in comparison with the muteness of the Eisenhower days; but the rest was true enough, especially in these first heady weeks.

The currents of vitality radiated out of the White House, flowed through the government and created a sense of vast possibility. The very idea of the new President taking command as tranquilly and naturally as if his whole life had prepared him for it could not but stimulate a flood of buoyant optimism. The Presidency was suddenly the center of action: in the first three months, thirty-nine messages and letters to Congress calling for legislation, ten prominent foreign visitors (including Macmillan, Adenauer and Nkrumah[7]), nine press conferences, new leadership in the regulatory agencies and such dramatic beginnings as the Alliance for Progress and the Peace Corps. Above all, Kennedy held out such promise of hope. Intelligence at last was being applied to public affairs. Euphoria reigned; we thought for a moment that the world was plastic and the future unlimited.

Yet I don't suppose we really thought this. At bottom we knew how intractable the world was—the poverty and disorder of Latin America, the insoluble conflict in Laos, the bitter war in Vietnam, the murky turbulence of Africa, the problems of discrimination and unemployment in our own country, the continuing hostility of Russia and China. The President knew better than anyone how hard his life was to be. Though he incited the euphoria, he did so involuntarily, for he did not share it himself. I never heard him now use the phrase 'New Frontier'; I think he regarded it with some embarrassment as a temporary capitulation to rhetoric. Still even Kennedy, the ironist and skeptic, had an embarrassed confidence in his luck and in these weeks may have permitted himself moments of optimism. In any case, he knew the supreme importance of a first impression and was determined to create a picture of drive, purpose and hope.

---

7. Harold Macmillan, British Prime Minister; Konrad Adenauer, First Chancellor of West Germany; Kwame Nkrumah, President of Ghana in 1960, deposed in 1966

Kennedy: Master of the Art of Power

Gore Vidal

Shortly after Kennedy became president in 1961, Gore Vidal characterized the new administration by contrasting it with the previous years under Dwight D. Eisenhower. Vidal describes the new president's high level of energy, his attractive appearance, his intellectual curiosity, his extensive contacts with the world outside the White House, his effective relationships with staff—all threads Kennedy used to weave his fabric of power and to generate an atmosphere of hope. Gore Vidal, an American writer, published numerous works between 1946 and 1962, including: the novels *In a Yellow Wood, A Judgment of Paris,* and *Julian*; the play *Visit to a Small Planet*; and a collection of essays, *Rocking the Boat.*

Until last month, I had not been at the White House since 1957 when I was asked to compose a speech for President [Dwight] Eisenhower.

At that time the White House was as serene as a resort hotel out of season. The corridors were empty. In the various offices of the Executive Branch (adjacent to the White House) quiet grey men in waistcoats talked to one another in low-pitched voices.

The only colour, or choler, curiously enough, was provided by President Eisenhower himself. Apparently, his temper was easily set off; he scowled when he stalked the corridors; The Smile was seldom in evidence. Fortunately, Eisenhower was not at the White House often enough to disturb that tranquility which prevailed, no matter what storms at home, what tragedies abroad.

Last month I returned to the White House . . . to find the twentieth century, for good or ill, installed. The corridors

From "A New Power in the White House," by Gore Vidal, *The (London) Sunday Telegraph*, April 9, 1961. Copyright ©1961 by Gore Vidal. Reprinted by permission of Curtis Brown Ltd., on behalf of Gore Vidal.

are filled with eager youthful men, while those not young are revitalised.

As Secretary of Commerce Luther Hodges (at 62 the oldest member of the Cabinet) remarked: 'There I was a few months ago, thinking my life was over. I'd retired to a college town. Now . . . well, that fellow in there,' (he indicated the President's office) 'he calls me in the morning, calls me at noon, calls me at night: why don't we try this? Have you considered that? Then to top it all he just now asks me: where do you get your suits from? I tell you I'm a young man again.'

In the White House Press room reporters are permanently gathered. Photographers are on constant alert and television cameramen stand by, for news is made at all hours.

The affection of the Press for Kennedy is a phenomenon, unique in Presidential politics. There is of course the old saw that he was a newspaperman himself (briefly) and also that he is a bona fide intellectual (on the other hand, the working Press is apt to be anti-intellectual); but, finally, and perhaps more to the point, Kennedy is candid with the Press in a highly personal way. He talks to them easily. There is no pomp; there is little evasion; he involves them directly in what he is doing. His wit is pleasingly sardonic.

Most important, until Kennedy it was impossible for anyone under 50 (or for an intellectual of any age) to identify himself with the President. The intellectual establishment of the country opted for 'alienation,' the cant word of the '40s and '50s, and even those who approved of this or that President's deeds invariably regarded the men set over us by the electorate as barbarians (Truman's attack on modern painting, Roosevelt's breezy philistinism, Eisenhower's inability to express himself coherently on any subject.)

For 20 years the culture and the mind of the United States ignored politics. Many never voted; few engaged in active politics. Now everything has changed. From Kenneth Galbraith[1] to Robert Frost[2] the intellectual establishment is listened to and even, on occasion, engaged to execute policy.

KENNEDY'S APPEARANCE AND PERSONALITY

Close to, Kennedy looks older than his photographs. The outline is slender and youthful, but the face is heavily lined

---

1. Harvard professor of economics, accepted the post of ambassador to India in President Kennedy's administration   2. a popular New England poet; read a poem at the presidential inaugural ceremonies on January 20, 1961

for his age. On the upper lip are those tiny vertical lines characteristic of a more advanced age.

He is usually tanned from the sun, while his hair is what lady novelists call 'chestnut', beginning to go grey. His eyes are very odd. They are, I think, a murky, opaque blue, 'interested' as Gertrude Stein once said of [Ernest] Hemingway's eyes, 'not interesting'; they give an impression of flatness, while long blond eyelashes screen expression at will. His long fingers tend to drum nervously on tables, on cups and glasses. He is immaculately dressed; although, disconcertingly, occasional white chest hairs curl over his collar.

 ### THE MYTH OF CAMELOT

In And the Crooked Places Made Straight: The Struggle for Social Change in the 1960s, *David Chalmers explains how the Kennedy White House came to be called "Camelot."*

John F. Kennedy, handsome, young, and photogenic, with his crisp Boston accent, his eloquence and wit, his elegant wife, Jackie, and his rich, glamorous family, was a made-for-media natural. The Kennedy excitement was an energizing force in the consciousness of the 1960s. It was partly real and partly a myth, to which Jackie Kennedy gave the name "Camelot" after the then-reigning Broadway musical about the days of King Arthur and his Knights of the Round Table:

> Don't let it be forgot, that once there was a spot,
> for one brief shining moment that was known as Camelot.

The excitement touched not only Americans but also millions of people in other parts of the world.

David Chalmers, *And the Crooked Places Made Straight: The Struggle for Social Change in the 1960s.* Baltimore: The Johns Hopkins Press, 1996.

The smile is charming even when it is simulated for the public. Franklin Roosevelt set an unhappy tradition of happy warriors and ever since his day our politicians are obliged to beam and grin and simper no matter how grave the occasion. Recently, at a public dinner, I had a thoughtful conversation with Harry Truman. He was making a particularly solemn point when suddenly, though his tone did not change, his face jerked abruptly into a euphoric grin, all teeth showing. I thought he had gone mad, until I noticed photographers had appeared in the middle distance and it was the old politician's unconscious reflex to smile.

As for Kennedy's personality, he is very much what he seems. He is withdrawn, observant, icily objective in crisis, aware of the precise value of every card dealt him. Intellectually, he is dogged rather than brilliant. Over the years I've occasionally passed on to him books (including such arcane as Byzantine economy) which I thought would interest him. Not only does he read them but he will comment on what he's read when I see him next. . . .

After his defeat for the Vice-Presidential nomination in 1956, he was amused when I suggested that he might feel more cheerful if every day he were to recite to himself while shaving the names of Vice-Presidents of the United States, a curiously dim gallery of minor politicians. Also somewhat mischievously, I suggested he read *Coriolanus* to see if he might find Shakespeare's somewhat dark view of democracy consoling. Mrs. Kennedy and he read it aloud one foggy day at Hyannisport. Later he made the point with some charm that Shakespeare's knowledge of the democratic process was, to say the least, limited.

On another occasion, I gave him the manuscript of a play of mine whose setting was a nominating convention for the Presidency. He read the play with interest; his comments were shrewd. I recall one in particular, because I used it.

'Whenever,' he said, 'a politician means to give you the knife at a convention, the last thing he'll say to you as he leaves the room is, "Now look, Jack, if there's *anything* I can do for you, you just let me know!" That's the euphemism for "you're dead".'

KENNEDY'S FRIENDS AND ADVISERS

Kennedy's relationships tend to be compartmentalized. There are cronies who have nothing to do with politics whom he sees for relaxation. There are advisers whom he sees politically but not socially.

The only occasion where personal friendship and public policy appear to have overlapped was in his appointment of the perhaps-not-distinguished Earl Smith (our envoy to Cuba at the time of the débâcle) as Ambassador to Switzerland. The Swiss, who are acting for the United States in Havana, complained loudly. To save the President embarrassment, Earl Smith withdrew.

With chilling correctness, Kennedy is reported to have

called in the Swiss Ambassador to Washington and given him a lesson in international diplomacy (i.e. you do not criticise publicly an ambassadorial appointment without first apprising the Chief of State privately). The Ambassador left the White House shaken and bemused.

Kennedy is unique among recent Presidents in many ways. For one thing, he has ended (wistfully, one hopes for ever) the idea that the Presidency is a form of brevet rank to be given to a man whose career has been distinguished in some profession other than politics or, if political, the good years are past and the White House is merely a place to provide some old pol [politician] with a golden Indian Summer.

Yet the job today is, literally, killing, and despite his youth, Kennedy may very well not survive. A matter, one suspects, of no great concern to him. He is fatalistic about himself. His father recalls with a certain awe that when his son nearly died during the course of a spinal operation he maintained a complete serenity: if he was meant to die at that moment he would die and complaint was useless.

Like himself, the men Kennedy has chosen to advise him have not reached any great height until now. They must prove themselves *now*. Government service will be the high point of their lives, not an agreeable reward for success achieved elsewhere. Few men have the energy or capacity to conduct successfully two separate careers in a lifetime, an obvious fact ignored by most Presidents in their search, often prompted by vanity or a sense of public relations, for celebrated advisers.

KENNEDY POLITICS: LIBERAL, PRAGMATIC, AND HONORABLE

Nearly half the electorate was eager to find Kennedy and his regime 'Intellectual' (in the popularly pejorative sense), given to fiscal irresponsibility and creeping socialism. There is, by the way, despite the cries of demagogues, no operative Left in the United States. We are divided about evenly between conservatives and reactionaries. But now, having experienced his Administration, it is evident even to the most suspicious of the Radical Right that Kennedy is not an adventurous reformer of the body politic, if only because this is not the time for such a reformation, and he knows it.

Essentially, he is a pragmatist with a profound sense of history, working within a generally liberal context. Since the United States is in no immediate danger of economic collapse, and since there is no revolutionary party of Left or Right waiting to seize power, our politics are firmly of the Centre. The problems of the nation are lagging economic growth, which under an attentive Administration can be corrected, and foreign affairs, where the United States vis-à-vis Russia remains a perhaps-insoluble problem, but one Kennedy is addressing with coolness and a commendable lack of emotion. . . .

Perhaps the most distressing aspect of the last Administration was President Eisenhower's open disdain of politics and his conviction that 'politician' was a dirty word. This tragic view is shared even now by the majority of the American electorate, explaining the General's continuing appeal. Time and time again during those years one used to hear: 'O.K., so he is a lousy President, but thank God he isn't a politician!'

Kennedy, on the other hand, regards politics as an honourable, perhaps inevitable, profession in a democracy. Not only is he a master of politics, but he also takes a real pleasure in power. He is restless; he wants to know everything; he wanders into other people's offices at odd hours; he puts in a 10-hour office day; he reads continuously; even, it is reported, in the bathtub.

KENNEDY'S CONTACT WITH THE REAL WORLD

Most interesting of all, and the greatest break with tradition, have been his visits to the houses of friends in Washington, many of them journalists. Ever since the first protocol drawn up for George Washington, the President seldom goes visiting and never returns calls. Kennedy has changed that. He goes where he pleases; he talks candidly; he tries to meet people who otherwise might never get through the elaborate maze of the White House, in which, even during the most enlightened Administration, unpleasant knowledge can be kept from the President.

Inevitably, the President is delivered into the hands of an inner circle which, should he not be a man of considerable alertness and passion, tends to cut him off from reality. Eisenhower was a classic case. It was painfully evident at Press conferences that he often had no knowledge of important actions taken by the Government in his name; worse still, he was perhaps the only President not to read newspapers. The result was that when crises occurred, despite all his good intentions he was never sufficiently aware of the nature of any problem to have a useful opinion on its solution.

Only by constant study and getting about can a President be effective. As Harry Truman once remarked, despite the great power of the office, it was remarkably difficult to get anything done. 'You tell 'em what you want and what happens? Nothing! You have to tell 'em five times.'

The reason for this seeming disobedience is due, partly, to the hugeness of the Federal Government and, partly, to the fact that no matter what a President wants there are those who will oppose him within his own Administration. Most Presidential staffs inevitably take advantage of their President, realising that in the rush of any day's business he will make many decisions and requests which he cannot possibly follow up. Kennedy, however, has already shown an un usual ability to recall exactly what he requested on any subject and the impression he gives is of a man who means to be obeyed by his staff.

'He is deliberately drawing all the threads of executive power to himself,' remarked one close adviser. The cumbersome staff system of the Eisenhower Administration has been abandoned in favour of highly personal relationships between President and advisers. No one's function is ever clearly defined. The President moves men from project to project, testing them, extracting new points of view.

Not only is this a useful way of getting the most out of his staff, but it also ensures, rather slyly, Kennedy's own unique position at the centre of the web of power: he alone can view and manipulate the entire complex of domestic and interna tional policy. No one in his Administration may circumvent him because none can master more than a part of the whole.

This ultimate knowledge of the whole is power, and finally, the exercise of power is an art like any other. There is no doubt of John Kennedy's mastery of that art. He is a rare combination of intelligence, energy and opportunism. Most important, he is capable of growth. He intends to be great.

What he will accomplish depends largely upon his ability to rally the bored and cynical Western world, to fire the imagination of a generation taught never to think of 'we' but only of 'I'. There are fragile signs (the warm response to the 'Peace Corps'), and favourable omens (popular approbation reflected in polls) that a torpid society has at last been stirred by its youthful leader. If true, in the nick of time. Civilisations are seldom granted so vivid a second chance.

CHAPTER 3

Kennedy's Domestic Agenda

The President Versus the Steel Industry

Irving Bernstein

Irving Bernstein recounts President Kennedy's victorious efforts to prevent the steel industry from raising prices in 1962. He explains that the Kennedy administration worked hard for an agreement between management and labor that would prevent strikes, such as those that had occurred in five of the previous ten years. When U.S. Steel subsequently raised prices, Kennedy mobilized a successful government-wide attack against the company, heading off an industry-wide price hike. Irving Bernstein worked as a mediation officer for federal government agencies and the U.S. Department of Labor before teaching political science at the University of California in Los Angeles. He is the author of *The Lean Years: A History of the American Worker* and *The New Deal Collective Bargaining Policy.*

John Kennedy was baffled and frustrated in his relations with that immensely powerful American institution—business. He was the target of hostile attacks by industrial spokesmen and the business press as well as scatalogical abuse in golf club locker rooms.

Kennedy thought this unfair. His father, after all, had been an extremely successful businessman and he, like his brothers and sisters, was a beneficiary of the business system. . . .

CONFLICT BETWEEN THE ADMINISTRATION AND THE BUSINESS ADVISORY COUNCIL

The Kennedy versus business issue first came to a head in 1961 in a spat between [Secretary of Commerce] Luther Hodges, the courtly and elderly North Carolinian who liked to say that he was the administration's "only tie with the nineteenth century," and the Business Advisory Council. Hodges told the National Press Club that his department, while "primarily concerned" with business, would not be "its tool and automatic spokesman." This immediately locked him into conflict with the BAC.

The Council, formed in 1933, was, [journalist] Hobart Rowen wrote, "America's most powerful club." It consisted of a small number of the chief executives of the largest corporations. . . .

But now the Council was in trouble. Ralph J. Cordiner, chairman of General Electric, was the BAC chairman. GE, along with lesser electrical firms, had just pleaded *nolo contendere*[1] to price-fixing and bid-rigging in the most notorious such case in the history of the Sherman Act.[2] While Cordiner insisted that he knew nothing of these illegal activities and allowed his subordinates who went to jail to twist in the wind, he smelled, to mix the metaphor like a long expired fish. . . .

In late February 1961 Cordiner resigned [as chairman of the BAC] and was succeeded by Roger M. Blough, the chairman of U.S. Steel. Hodges then demanded that BAC extend its membership and agree that the government should name the members. The cozy fraternity voted him down. Blough recognized that Hodges could not be ignored and reached a settlement with the secretary which went part way. But the BAC spring meeting in May at the Homestead in Virginia under the new rules was a disaster. Hodges was the only high government official who showed up and the meetings, now open to the press, were dismal. BAC cut its ties to the government. . . . Hodges was left out to dry. Blough must have derived a good deal of satisfaction from having made the President back down; he may have concluded that Kennedy was spineless.

Blough soon had another and far more important confrontation with the President arising out of collective bargaining in the steel industry. . . .

HISTORY OF THE STEEL INDUSTRY'S PROBLEMS

In the 10 negotiations between 1946 and 1959 five resulted in strikes: 1946 (26 days), 1949 (45), 1952 (59), 1956 (36), and 1959 (116). No other important domestic industry or for-

1. a plea made by the defendant in a criminal action that is substantially but not technically an admission of guilt   2. Sherman Anti-trust Act, which opposed or intended to regulate business monopolies

eign steel industry came close in the propensity to strike. Steel stoppages were big because the industry was huge: half a million basic steel workers walked out. And since these companies owned support facilities organized by the Steelworkers, many more men in the iron mines, on the ore carriers, and in steel fabricating mills joined the strike. The captive coal mines and the coal-carrying railroads were affected immediately. "Thus," [author E. Robert] Livernash wrote, "the strikes are in some degree multi-industry in effect and nationwide in extent."

Steel was the classic oligopoly[3] with administered prices and U.S. Steel was the price leader. The industry's pricing had been the subject of the Kefauver[4] Committee investigation of the late fifties. It had exploited the wage agreements with the Steelworkers as occasions for simultaneous increases in prices, thereby creating the public impression that the union had pushed up the price of steel. In 1946 wages rose 18½ cents an hour and prices increased $5 a ton. In 1947 the numbers were 15 cents and $5; and in 1948, 13 cents and $10. And so on for 1949, 1950, 1953, 1954, and 1955. The 1956 agreement was for three years and the increases in the first year were almost 20 cents and $8.50. The 1959 agreement (because of the strike not signed till January 4, 1960) was again for three years. . . .

PRESIDENT DETERMINED TO AVOID A 1959 KIND OF DISASTER

Thus, the target date in steel became June 30, 1962, when the 1959 agreement expired. The Kennedy administration was determined that there must be no rerun of the 1959 disaster. [Secretary of Labor] Arthur Goldberg had battered his way through the negotiations of the fifties as the union's principal spokesman and wanted to break the pattern of rotten relations and strikes. . . .

Under the 1959 agreement steel wages and fringe benefits were scheduled to rise on October 1, 1961. Rumor had it that the industry would also increase prices. On August 2 Heller[5] wrote Kennedy that prices generally were steady, but "steel is the major threat to price stability over the next several months. Steel bulks so large in the manufacturing sector of the economy that it can upset the applecart all by itself." Sen-

3. a market condition in which sellers are so few that the actions of any one of them will affect price and have an impact on competitors   4. Estes Kefauver, Senator from Tennessee   5. Walter Heller, member of the Council of Economic Advisers, from Minnesota

ators Paul Douglas of Illinois and Albert Gore of Tennessee, primed by the administration, urged the President to prevent an increase. On September 7 he addressed identical letters that Kermit Gordon[6] had drafted to the chairmen of the twelve basic steel companies, urging them to absorb the prospective added labor costs. He pointed out that during the postwar era steel prices had risen much faster than wages and that the industry had enjoyed handsome profits. He warned that a rise in steel prices would spread through much of the economy, would significantly increase the cost of military procurement, would endanger the balance of payments, and would hamper economic recovery.

> If the industry were now to forego a price increase, it would enter collective bargaining negotiations next spring with a record of three and a half years of price stability. It would clearly then be the turn of the labor representatives to limit wage demands to a level consistent with continued price stability. The moral position of the steel industry next spring— and its claim to the support of public opinion—will be strengthened by the exercise of price restraint now.

On September 14 Kennedy wrote McDonald[7] asking him to act in the public interest. "This implies a labor settlement within the limits of advances in productivity and price stability.". . .

The bargaining opened on February 14 in Pittsburgh. The union's initial proposal, reflecting heavy unemployment in the mills along with government pressure, was quite modest—17 cents per hour, none in wages, all for job security. The talks recessed on March 2. Goldberg then met with Blough, who said that 17 cents was not acceptable because it was inflationary. Goldberg told McDonald that he would have to reduce the demand. The negotiations resumed on March 14 and led to agreement later that month and the signing of a new contract on April 6, 1962, almost three months before the expiration of the old one. It was, Rowen wrote, "an amazingly cheap settlement, so much so that McDonald refused to put an official value on the package." It came to 10 cents an hour, none in wages, everything to improve pensions and to mitigate unemployment. It was, obviously, within the wage guidepost.

The President, Goldberg, and Heller were jubilant.

6. member of the Council of Economic Advisers, from Williams College   7. David McDonald, of the Steelworkers Union

Kennedy congratulated the negotiators for their "high industrial statesmanship" and said the agreement was "obviously noninflationary and should provide a solid base for continued price stability." The business community and the press generally were enthusiastic, stressing that there would be no increase in steel prices. Kennedy, glowing, thought that steel was now safely behind him.

But on Tuesday afternoon, April 10, Blough called the executive committee of the U.S. Steel board into session in New York. The operating executives had proposed a 3½ percent price increase. The committee approved; the public relations department prepared a statement; and Blough phoned [presidential aide] Kenny O'Donnell to make an appointment with the President. He got one at 5:45 that afternoon and boarded a corporate plane for Washington. Kennedy was surprised to learn that Blough was coming and could not imagine what he had in mind.

"Perhaps the easiest way I can explain why I am here," Blough said, "is to give you this and let you read it." He handed Kennedy the mimeographed statement which at that moment was being released to the media. The first paragraph, which the President read carefully, was as follows:

> For the first time in nearly four years, United States Steel today announced an increase in the general level of steel prices. This "catch-up" adjustment, effective at 12:01 a.m. tomorrow, will raise the price of the company's steel products by an average of about 3.5 percent—or three-tenths of a cent per pound.

The remainder of the release, which Kennedy raced through, was a muddy justification for the action.

THE PRESIDENT FIGHTS U.S. STEEL PRICE HIKE

The President was furious. He protested, "I think you have made a terrible mistake." He then asked Evelyn Lincoln, his secretary, to summon Goldberg "immediately!" The Secretary broke the record for cabinet officers sprinting to the White House. Never at a loss for words, he launched into an argument against a price increase as he came through the door. "Wait a minute, Arthur," the President said. "Read the statement. They've raised the price. It's already done."

Goldberg was stunned and enraged. He asked Blough why he had come. He answered that it was a matter of courtesy. Goldberg said it was hardly courteous to present the

President with an accomplished fact. He then lectured Blough, calling the action a disservice to the nation, to U.S. Steel, and to the future of collective bargaining, as well as a deliberate double-cross of the President. Blough was somber as he left.

[Theodore] Sorensen, McGeorge Bundy,[8] and acting press secretary Andrew Hatcher, who had been waiting for a scheduled meeting, came into the Oval Office and were soon joined by Robert Kennedy, Heller, Gordon, and, somewhat later, [Maurice] Tobin. The President was seething. One aide said he had never seen him so angry. Another said there should have been a speedometer on his rocking chair. Kennedy then made the famous denunciation which leaked to the *New York Times:* "My father always told me that all businessmen were sons of bitches, but I never believed it until now." (He later said he meant steel executives, not "all businessmen.") Kennedy and Goldberg agreed: "This is war." The President felt that he had been betrayed, that the office of the presidency had been denigrated, and that the national interest had been flouted. This demanded a confrontation: the U.S. government versus U.S. Steel.

Given the pattern of administered pricing in the steel industry, no one at the White House had much hope that the other companies would refrain from raising prices. Nevertheless, Kennedy launched a massive government-wide 72-hour mobilization against U.S. Steel.

The President had a press conference scheduled for Wednesday, and Sorensen, Goldberg, and Heller prepared the statement. Experts from BLS[9] and the Council worked through most of the night gathering the numbers for a "White Paper." The Attorney General ordered the antitrust division to investigate the price increase. After Bethlehem raised prices, the Pentagon awarded a $5 million armor plate contract to Lukens, which had not. Senator Kefauver, "shocked" by U.S. Steel's action, said that his subcommittee would make an investigation. [Secretary of Defense Robert] McNamara stated that the hike would raise defense costs "in excess of $1 billion a year." A Bethlehem executive had told the press on April 9, "There shouldn't be a price rise." FBI agents summarily interrogated the reporters who had covered the story. Hodges said that he was "shocked and disap-

---

8. advisers to the President   9. Bureau of Labor Statistics

pointed" and charged that Blough's act was "anti-business." Solicitor General Archibald Cox, lecturing at the University of Arizona, was put to work drafting legislation.

Kennedy's statement on Wednesday was, a U.S. Steel executive granted, "a barnburner." In bitter fury he denounced the "irresponsible defiance of the public interest." In the inaugural address "I asked each American to consider what he would do for his country, and I asked the steel companies. In the last 24 hours, we have had their answer."

Anyone in the administration who knew an executive of a steel company was instructed to phone him and ask that his firm not follow U.S. Steel's lead. The phones hummed. But the early returns were discouraging. Bethlehem, Republic, Jones & Laughlin, Youngstown, and several smaller firms fell into line by Wednesday night. Five of the lesser companies, together 14 percent of the industry's capacity had not yet acted—Inland, Armco, Kaiser, Colorado Fuel & Iron, and McLouth.

Joseph Block of Inland held the key. The Chicago firm was probably the most efficient and profitable in the industry and would not have considered a price increase on its own. Block was friendly to the administration, close to Goldberg, and hardly an admirer of Blough. Vacationing in Japan, on Friday he issued this statement from Kyoto: "We did not feel that it was in the national interest to raise prices at this time. We felt this very strongly." Kaiser and Armco quickly followed Inland.

THE CHAIRMAN OF U.S. STEEL WAVERS AND BACKS DOWN

Kennedy had watched Blough on television the day before. If another major producer did not raise prices, he said, it would be "very difficult" for U.S. Steel. "I don't know how long we could maintain our position."

Kennedy sensed an opening and made his move, asking Clark Clifford, the noted Washington lawyer, to represent him. He met with Robert Tyson, vice president of the steel corporation, on one of its airplanes at Washington's National Airport that night. Clifford thought the conversation desultory, but Blough sent word the next morning that the meetings should continue.

Meantime, there were other and encouraging signs for the administration. In the struggle for public approval the President was winning. Few people, including businessmen, welcomed an increase in steel prices. Many of those who thought that the steel corporation had the right to fix its own prices condemned Blough for the way in which he did it. Blough did not help himself by stressing the technically correct point that U.S. Steel had never promised not to raise prices. The public recognized that the corporation had led everyone to believe that it would not. . . .

On Friday, Clifford and Goldberg flew to New York on a military plane where they met Blough, Tyson, and other U.S. Steel executives in a large suite at the Carlyle Hotel. Two phones rang almost simultaneously, one for Goldberg, the other for Blough. It was the same message: Bethlehem had caved in. Blough appeared "shaken." Goldberg poured it on— the White House would release the "White Paper," [Secretary of the Treasury, Douglas] Dillon would attack the "greed" of the steel companies, and so on. At 5:00 p.m. Blough surrendered. At 5:28 the tickers reported: "The United States Steel Corporation today announced that it had rescinded the 3½ percent price increase made on Wednesday, April 11." The companies that had followed Big Steel up now followed it down.

Kennedy did not gloat over his victory. Aside from damage control, there were good reasons not to do so. As [author] Grant McConnell pointed out, this was more a triumph for the presidency than for this particular President. Further, everyone knew that U.S. Steel would have gotten higher prices if it had gone about it quietly and selectively, as it did the next year. Kennedy met with Blough on April 17 and assured him that he held no grudges. That evening he informed [presidential aide Arthur] Schlesinger, "I told him that his men could keep their horses for the spring plowing." At the next press conference he said, "Nothing is to be gained from further public recriminations." The White Paper remained in its file. The antitrust division and Senator Kefauver folded their tents. But this was the President's public face. Privately he was deeply affected by the confrontation.

Kennedy's Failure to Work for Civil Rights

Henry Fairlie

Henry Fairlie argues that Kennedy procrastinated on his campaign commitment to support civil rights and never really delivered on his promises. When civil rights leaders warned him of coming protests, he ignored them until violence broke out and he had to take a stand. Henry Fairlie was a feature writer for the London *Observer*, a political editorial writer for the *London Times*, and a free lance writer. He is the author of *The Life of Politics*, *The Parties: Republicans and Democrats in this Century*, and *The Seven Deadly Sins Today*.

Just as [John Kennedy] did not mention civil rights in his inaugural address, so civil rights was the only significant area of domestic policy in which he did not appoint a task force. He might permit Frederick Hovde, the president of Purdue University, to tell him what he should do about education; or Joseph McMurray, the president of Queens Community College in New York, to prescribe what should be done about housing; . . . but he was not of a mind to allow them, or any like them, into the field of civil rights. In this area, the liberals and the intellectuals were not given the chance to set any awkward standards. They were invited where they could not cause any serious trouble. . . .

CIVIL RIGHTS LEADERS SPEAK OUT

On 3 February 1961, the Leadership Conference on Civil Rights, in the persons of Roy Wilkins, its chairman, and Arnold Aronson, its secretary, submitted to the new President a memorandum, in which they described the actions which they believed were necessary in that field. At a meeting at the White House three days later, they were told by

Theodore Sorensen that the President would neither introduce nor support any civil rights legislation, that he would rely instead on executive action, using the powers which were available to him. Late in March, the National Association for the Advancement of Colored People met in Washington in a stormy mood, and they were addressed by Harris Wofford, previously an active worker in the cause of civil rights, and by then one of John Kennedy's principal advisers. His speech was uncomfortable: "I do not mean that the new avenue of executive action will be easy. This course has plenty of contradictions, and it will not . . . resolve the built-in political contradictions." But it was these political contradictions, of course, which "consensus politics" was intended to bypass; and executive action, designed to avoid both public controversy and a struggle in Congress, was a part of the method.

During the campaign, when he was seeking the support of the liberals, John Kennedy had asked Joseph Clark, in the Senate, and Emanuel Celler, in the House of Representatives, to put the civil rights programme of the Democratic Party into legislative form; and, by the beginning of May 1961, they had introduced six bills, designed to implement the party's election pledges. The principal bill would have sought to hasten the desegregation of public schools by requiring every school board which was still operating a racially segregated school to adopt a desegregation plan within six months. Although they had already observed John Kennedy's determination to placate the Southern bloc in Congress, the sponsors hoped at least for his benevolent neutrality. Instead, on the day after they were introduced, [press secretary] Pierre Salinger publicly dissociated the President from them, saying that in his view legislation was at that time not necessary.

KING CRITICIZES KENNEDY'S INACTION

A year later, in *The Nation* of 3 March 1962, Martin Luther King said what he thought of this approach: "As the year unfolded, executive initiative became increasingly feeble, and the chilling prospect emerged of a general administration retreat." He argued that the "basic strategic goals" of the administration had been narrowed, and accused it of "aggressively driving towards the limited goal of token integration." He described its strategy and its tactics in this way:

The administration brought forth a plan to substitute executive order for legislative programs. The most challenging order, to end discrimination in federal housing, while no adequate substitute for the many legislative acts promised in the campaign platforms and speeches, nevertheless was alluring, and pressure abated for Congressional action. The year passed, and the President fumbled. By the close of the year, a new concept was adopted; the President now wished to "move ahead in a way which will maintain a consensus."

Yet, as Martin Luther King had pointed out earlier in his article, the conditions of "consensus" on this issue were no longer attainable. During 1961, "despite tormenting handicaps, Negroes moved from sporadic, limited actions to broadscale activities different in kind and degree from anything done in the past." The sit-ins and the Freedom Rides and the boycotts all carried the same message.

But even in the execution of his own moderate policy, John Kennedy still procrastinated. During his election campaign, for example, he had several times scoffed at Dwight Eisenhower for failing to order the desegregation of public housing. It could be done by executive action alone, he said; it required no more than "a stroke of the pen." But, in office himself, he delayed. Throughout 1961, he delayed, and throughout 1962, until an "Ink for Jack" campaign spread across the country, and bottles of ink began to arrive at the White House so that he might make the stroke of the pen that was needed. At last, immediately after the election of 1962, he signed a qualified executive order. It rejected the recommendations which had been made to him in 1961 by the majority of the Civil Rights Commission, and instead reflected the lowest common denominator of agreement which all its members, who included three Southerners, had been able to reach. It was no wonder, in these circumstances, that Martin Luther King, again appraising the year's progress, said in *The Nation* of 30 March 1963 that "If tokenism were our goal, the administration moves us adroitly toward it."

Martin Luther King was voicing the injury which the moderate leaders of the black population were beginning to feel. Wishing to co-operate with a President who was new and young, and who professed to support their cause, they were beginning to understand that they were being used: that they were being "moved adroitly" into a position in which they appeared to be willing to accept "tokenism." At a time when John Kennedy should have been anxious not to destroy the credit of the moderate leaders among their increasingly impatient followers, he recklessly did so. He neither gave them what they needed, nor allowed them to stand apart from him, able to criticise the slowness and the inadequacy of his actions. He required them in the "consensus" which he sought to maintain.

KENNEDY IGNORES WARNINGS OF PROTEST

Neither he nor his administration—including his brother who, as Attorney General, was in a strategic position—understood the magnitude of the movement which had begun. Loreen Miller, the publisher of the *California Eagle,* an old Negro newspaper, tried to make it clear in an article, specifically addressed to white liberals, which was published in *The Nation* of 20 October 1962. She recalled the recent statement of [novelist] James Baldwin that Negroes "twenty years younger than I don't believe in liberals at all," and said that the liberals who were shocked or surprised by it "haven't been doing their homework. Discontent with the liberal position in the area of race relations has been building up for the past several years." She concluded by bidding to liberals "a fond farewell with thanks for services rendered, until you are ready to re-enlist as foot soldiers and subordinates in a Negro-led, Negro-officered, army under the banner of Freedom Now." It is interesting to notice how early this statement was made.

The incomprehension was displayed again at the famous meeting which took place on 24 May 1963 between Robert Kennedy and two of his senior officers at the Department of Justice, on the one hand, and James Baldwin and several of his friends, on the other. When one of the blacks, Jerome Smith, remarked that, if the United States went to war with Cuba, he would not fight in it, Robert Kennedy was shocked, at which another of the blacks, Kenneth C. Clark, afterwards commented: "We were shocked that he was shocked, and that he seemed unable to understand what Smith was trying to say." Arthur Schlesinger reports that Robert Kennedy told him later: "They didn't know anything. They don't know what the laws are—they don't know what we've been doing or what we're trying to do. . . . It was all emotion, hysteria. They stood up and orated. They cursed. Some of them wept and walked out of the room." But one of the things which

Jerome Smith had been trying to tell him was that he felt "nauseous" to have to beg for protection when he was only fighting for his constitutional rights

As the protests became more violent throughout 1962 and the early months of 1963, their meaning began to penetrate the consciousness of the white liberal. In its issue of 8 May 1963, *Newsweek* carried a story in which it gave prominence to a remark of James Farmer [director of the Congress of Racial Equality]: "I like the word 'black.' I like to use it. It's an attempt to have some identity." It noticed the "increasingly restless and militant mood" of the Negro, saying that it was "freighted with dynamite." It ended by quoting [civil rights leader] Whitney Young: "We're liable to get some real violence: in Chicago, in Detroit, in New York." But the administration was still inclined to see only separate incidents, whether in Mississippi or in Alabama, and only separate villains, whether [Mississippi governor] Ross Barnett or Eugene T. "Bull" Connor [Birmingham's Commissioner of Public Safety]. As [journalist] I.F. Stone remarked on 24 June 1963, "the shot that killed Medgar Evers . . . was not simply the act of barbarity which the White House termed it. It was part of the system the South has used for a century to keep the Negro in his place." The problem was larger than that, since the problem had already moved to the North; but the administration was still refusing to face the question put by [journalist] Walter Lippmann at the time: "Is the rising discontent which is showing itself among the twenty million Negroes going to change in important ways the shape and pace of American politics?"

KENNEDY CHOOSES MORAL CONSENSUS OVER POLITICAL CONFRONTATION

John Kennedy may have seemed to face it on the television address which he gave on 11 June 1963. It did indeed represent a commitment on the part of the federal government to fight against discrimination, and he sought a "consensus" in support of it: "We face, therefore, a moral crisis as a country and as a people." But, even if such a "consensus" was possible, he was not in a strong position to call for it. He had himself moved on the issue only when the Negro had already moved out of the courts into the streets. At the beginning of the administration, Robert Kennedy had said of the demand for civil rights: "There has got to be—and there is going to be—leadership from the White House. That is going to make the difference." For two and a half years, this leadership had been absent, and the form in which it was now offered was predictable.

Once again, there was to be a spectacular display of personal leadership: an appeal for a national commitment which would obviate the necessity for a bitter political struggle. A moral "consensus" of a kind did indeed seem to have been created, in this atmosphere, during the march on Washington in the fall of 1963, which ended in the rally at which Martin Luther King proclaimed: "I have a dream." It is remembered by many white liberals today with a nostalgia which is as sweet as it is bitter. But the mood was false: at a crucial moment in a profound social and political upheaval, reliance was to be placed on professions of good will. The attitude of John Kennedy was characteristic. "When the Negro leaders announced the march," [civil rights activist] Bayard Rustin observed at the time, "the President asked them to call it off. When they thumbed—when they told him they wouldn't—he almost smothered us. We had to keep raising our demands . . . to keep him from getting ahead of us." In one mocking phrase, [journalist] Murray Kempton declared: "When the President finally mentioned the march in public, he issued something as close as possible to a social invitation."

Many of the accounts at the time as well as many of the memories in retrospect indicate how the march and the rally were indeed transformed into an almost festive occasion. It was characteristic that John Lewis of the Student Nonviolent Coordinating Committee was forced by the organisers of the rally to soften his words, in which he had proposed to challenge the white liberal leadership which the belated actions of John Kennedy had once again placed at the head of the civil rights movement. When the President welcomed the leaders of the march at the White House, he used the greeting, "I have a dream." In much the same way, when Lyndon Johnson addressed a joint meeting of the two houses of Congress nineteen months later, he used the slogan, "We shall overcome." This manner of political leadership is false. It not only has little to do with the real political struggle which lies ahead; it in fact makes that struggle more difficult to win. It distracts the energies which should be given to developing the kind of political strategy which, thirty years earlier, had carried the New Deal, deeply and irresistibly, into the heart of the political process of the country, and of the political attitudes of the people.

CONSENSUS POLITICS LEADS TO ELITE CONSENSUS

Significant political and social movements can be expected to engender conflict, since the claim of one group to a right which it has been denied must usually mean the surrender by another group of a privilege which it has enjoyed. It is false to try to manufacture a "consensus" in such a situation; and it was false in the 1960s to try to do so in the cause of civil rights. It could only be a distraction, certain in the end to provoke the frustration as much of the advocates of the cause, whose expectations had been aroused, as of its opponents, who felt with some justice that the political processes of the country had been bypassed. The attempt from 1954 onwards to deal with the problem of racial discrimination in the courts was similarly an attempt to achieve by a "consensus," that of the law, what the political processes of the country were failing to achieve.

If an attempt is made to ignore or to transcend the political processes of the country, these processes remain to be used, and the "populist movements" of opinion, as they have been designated, which have been evident in the electoral politics of the United States in recent years have at least one element in common: a desire on the part of a considerable number of people, who feel that they have been ignored, to use in their own interests the political processes of their country, which they also feel have been ignored. There clearly exists among them an impression that they have in recent years been governed by an elite, self-chosen and self-perpetuating; and one of the main criticisms put forward by some sociologists against the "consensus" view of society is that, if a "consensus" exists at all, it is an "elite consensus," formed by the persons and the organisations which are entrenched in the controlling positions in the existing society. There can be no question that the "consensus politics" which were practiced by John Kennedy and his administration were an attempt to impose an "elite consensus" on the American people; and it was done with such conviction that they eagerly responded. At home or abroad, it seemed, they had only to submit to a national commitment to which they had been called by their President, and good would prevail. It is never so easy.

Kennedy's Civil Rights Legislation Becomes Law

Allen J. Matusow

Allen J. Matusow explains how in 1963 the riots in Birmingham, Alabama, protest marches in cities across America, and Alabama Governor George Wallace's refusal to allow two black students to enroll in the University of Alabama moved President Kennedy to speak to the nation about its moral obligation to guarantee civil rights for all Americans. Kennedy promised to send legislation to Congress, but he was assassinated before it could be passed. Robert Kennedy subsequently worked with congressional leaders for its passage, and President Lyndon Johnson signed the bill into law in July 1964. Allen J. Matusow teaches history at Rice University in Houston, Texas, and has been visiting professor at Stanford University. He is the author of *Farm Policies and Politics in the Truman Years* and editor of *Twentieth Century America: Recent Interpretations.*

In 1960 civil rights had been just one among many tough political issues that candidate John Kennedy had to manipulate. By the beginning of 1963 it was a movement capable of delivering thousands of black demonstrators to the streets and summoning moral support from millions of white northerners. Eighty-nine members of the House submitted civil rights bills at the beginning of the new congressional session. Though manipulation of the issue was now beyond his capacity, Kennedy kept trying. His major civil rights proposal that winter was a bill to strengthen existing voting rights legislation. The staff of the Civil Rights Commission warned the White House that civil rights groups would greet it "with massive indifference or actual opposition." And they did.

The Kennedys in fact, could not even manage the Civil Rights Commission. The attorney general somehow dissuaded the commissioners from holding hearings in Mississippi; but John Kennedy failed to deter them from issuing a special report in April 1963, indicting Mississippi for wanton lawlessness and calling on the president to consider withholding federal funds from the state, pending compliance with the Constitution. Here was fresh evidence, if any was needed, that among those most engaged the time was ripe for a showdown with segregation.

SHOWDOWN IN BIRMINGHAM, ALABAMA

The showdown took place in Birmingham, Alabama. In response to an invitation from local black leaders, Martin Luther King initiated a carefully prepared campaign on April 3, 1963, to smash segregation in that grim, raw industrial city. King was aware of the stakes. "We believed that while a campaign in Birmingham would surely be the toughest fight of our civil rights careers, it could, if successful, break the back of segregation all over the nation," he wrote later. Demonstrations grew daily in size and intensity, until on April 10 a local judge issued an injunction banning further protests. King, who had never defied a court order, decided this time to take his Gandhian philosophy[1] to its logical conclusion and keep on marching. On Good Friday, April 12, he was arrested and jailed. One consequence was his famous "Letter from the Birmingham Jail"—an eloquent defense of demonstrations, civil disobedience, and nonviolent protest. If nonviolence had not emerged, King lectured whites, the streets of the South would "be flowing with blood," and millions of Negroes would have already turned for solace, and might yet, to "black nationalist ideologies."

After eight days King departed from his cell and resumed leadership of the demonstrations. When secret talks between white and black leaders broke down, he dramatically escalated tactics on May 2 by recruiting thousands of schoolchildren to join the protests and fill up the jails. The appearance of the children threw Bull Connor, Birmingham's Commissioner of Public Safety, into a rage. So far, Connor had handled the demonstrations with relative restraint. But

---

1. based on the philosophy of Mahatma Gandhi, Indian spiritualist who fought for Indian independence by practicing nonviolent disobedience

on May 3 he set upon the marchers with dogs, clubs, and fire hoses, making martyrs of his victims and assuring their triumph. The very caricature of a southern bully and perfect foil for King, Connor remarked after one civil rights leader, injured by water from a fire hose, was hospitalized, "I wish he'd been carried away in a hearse."

Connor's repressive tactics generated a massive outpouring of national sympathy for King's campaign. On the morning of May 4 Yankee newspapers featured a photograph of a police dog lunging at a demonstrator. Outrages were hardly a novelty in the South, and the North had seen many pictures of racist brutality over the years. But the conscience of northern liberalism was sensitized in 1963 as it had not been before. This fact transformed Birmingham into an extraordinary historical event. The pictures out of Birmingham helped create a mass constituency for civil rights for the first time since Reconstruction.

The administration remained unmoved. The president told a delegation from the Americans for Democratic Action on May 4 that, though the pictures in the paper made him "sick," he had no power to take action. The attorney general called for redress of "just grievances," but also suggested an end of demonstrations. Burke Marshall[2] flew to Birmingham to mediate the conflict and get it off the streets. On May 7, when 125 white businessmen of the Senior Citizens Committee met downtown to consider King's demands, their mood was so intransigent that Marshall despaired of a settlement. But, on breaking for lunch, the senior citizens went into the streets and confronted an extraordinary sight. King described it in his book, *Why We Can't Wait:*

> On that day several thousand Negroes had marched on the town, the jails were so full that the police could only arrest a handful. There were Negroes on the sidewalks, in the streets, standing, sitting in the aisles of downtown stores. There were square blocks of Negroes, a veritable sea of black faces. They were committing no violence; they were just present and singing. Downtown Birmingham echoed to the strains of the freedom songs.

That afternoon business leaders sent word to King that they were ready to negotiate. Three days later, truce terms were announced: the big department stores agreed to desegregate within 90 days and promote and hire Negroes; Negro leaders

2. head of the Civil Rights Division at the Justice Department

canceled demonstrations and called off the boycott of the stores. The crisis had apparently ended without the Kennedys having to choose.

RIOT IN BIRMINGHAM

But on Saturday night, May 11, two bombs exploded in Birmingham—one at the home of Dr. King's brother and the other at a motel used by black leaders. Word of the explosions quickly spread through the Birmingham ghetto, where the subtleties of King's nonviolent philosophy had never been much appreciated. More than 2,500 Birmingham blacks took to the streets that night and pioneered a form of social protest new to the 1960s: the urban riot. Rampaging for three hours, the rioters attacked police and firemen, wrecked cars, and burned stores. By the time order was restored, nine blocks of the ghetto were in ruins. On Sunday President Kennedy put the Alabama National Guard on the alert and sent federal troops to stations near Birmingham. But by then the spasm of black rage had passed.

The riot at Birmingham provoked a major reappraisal of policy inside the Kennedy administration. John Kennedy had long been worried by the violent possibilities of the black revolution. He knew of [author] Robert F. Williams's recent call for black self-defense in *Negroes with Guns,* of the growing influence of Malcolm X in the northern ghetto, and of the fading appeal of nonviolence among young blacks. That night in Birmingham Negroes shed white blood and put the torch to private property. In the space of a few violent hours civil rights for Negroes came to seem no longer the program of zealots, but a policy for moderate men. Two days after the riot Kennedy confided his fears at a private meeting with Alabama editors. If moderation and nonviolence failed, he said, Negroes might turn to violence and the black Muslims.

As the embers of the Birmingham ghetto were cooling, Kennedy decided at last to honor his 1960 campaign pledge of major civil rights legislation. Burke Marshall recalled that, except for the attorney general, "every single person who spoke about it in the White House—every single one of them—was against President Kennedy sending up that bill." The bill would not pass. It would destroy Kennedy in the South. It might stir up a white backlash in the North. Possessing a surer sense of the moment than any of those who counseled him, John F. Kennedy brushed aside all objections and bid for command of the civil rights movement. He did so even though he feared that his advisers might be right, that this bill was—as RFK phrased it—"maybe going to be his political swan song."

PROTESTS ACROSS AMERICA IN THE SPRING OF 1963

The Kennedys were right to fear for the civil peace that spring. Inspired by the example of Birmingham, demonstrators were marching in streets all over America. In southern cities like Jackson, Raleigh, and Tallahassee, marchers protested segregated accommodations. In Los Angeles, Philadelphia, and St. Louis, the issues were jobs and schools. One estimate put the number of Americans participating in racial demonstrations in May alone at 75,000. To better comprehend this social earthquake, Robert Kennedy met privately in New York on May 24, 1963, with a group of blacks assembled for him by novelist James Baldwin. Among those present were social psychologist Kenneth Clark, singer Harry Belafonte, actress Lena Horne, and playwright Lorraine Hansberry. Beginning with a civil rights worker saying that being in the same room with the attorney general made him feel like vomiting, the meeting degenerated into an emotional, sometimes tearful, three-hour denunciation of administration policy. Kennedy endured most of it sitting in angry silence. In despair he said afterward, "We seem to be shut out everywhere."

There seemed no escape from crisis in the spring of 1963. George Wallace had won election as governor of Alabama the previous year, vowing to defend segregation by standing "in the schoolhouse door." When two black students arrived on the University of Alabama campus on June 11 with a federal court order requiring their admittance, there he stood, blocking the entrance. Assistant Attorney General Nicholas Katzenbach stepped forward with a presidential proclamation commanding Wallace to desist "in unlawful obstructions." The governor read a proclamation of his own and refused to move. Wallace, however, was no Ross Barnett.[3] Having had his hour on national TV, he yielded to superior force later in the day after the president nationalized the Alabama National Guard. Kennedy had planned to address the

3. governor of Mississippi, whose resistance to the enrollment of James Meredith, a black man, ended in violence and a confrontation between government marshalls and local whites

nation that night in case of trouble at the university. Now that there was no trouble, he decided to speak anyway.

KENNEDY SPEAKS TO THE NATION

The speech Kennedy gave was the speech the civil rights movement had been awaiting for nearly three years—the most moving speech of his presidency. Ted Sorensen finished writing it only a few minutes before delivery, and Kennedy extemporized the conclusion on the air.

> We are confronted primarily with a moral issue. It is as old as the scriptures and is as clear as the American Constitution. ... If an American, because his skin is dark, cannot eat lunch in a restaurant open to the public, if he cannot send his children to the best public school available, if he cannot vote for the public officials who represent him, if, in short, he cannot enjoy the full and free life which all of us want, then who among us would be content to have the color of his skin changed and stand in his place? Who among us would then be content with the counsels of patience and delay? ...
>
> Are we to say to the world, and much more importantly, to each other that this is a land of the free except for Negroes; that we have no second-class citizens except Negroes; that we have no class or caste system, no ghettoes, no master race except with respect to Negroes?

Kennedy informed the nation of the legislation he intended to send to Congress, called upon individuals to fight race prejudice in their homes and communities, and asked for help in making equality of opportunity a reality for Negro Americans. The President, noted the *New York Times,* delivered his speech with unaccustomed "fervor." Later that same night, a white sniper shot and killed Medgar Evers, leader of the Mississippi NAACP,[4] in Jackson.

On June 19, 1963, Kennedy sent Congress a civil rights bill embodying most of the movement's urgent demands. The best efforts of the Justice Department having failed to enfranchise blacks in the Deep South, Kennedy's bill further strengthened the voting rights laws. Massive resistance had practically nullified the Supreme Court's 1954 *Brown*[5] decision; his bill empowered the attorney general to initiate school desegregation suits. Roy Wilkins and Martin Luther King were demanding termination of federal support for dis-

---

4. National Association for the Advancement of Colored People   5. In *Brown v. Board of Education of Topeka* the Supreme Court ruled that legally enforced school segregation was unconstitutional.

criminatory state programs; Kennedy's bill granted the president discretionary authority to cut off funds. Blacks in Birmingham had marched by the thousands to petition for equal treatment in public places; the president's bill outlawed discrimination in such places of public accommodation as hotels, motels, movie theaters, sports arenas, retail stores, gas stations, restaurants, and lunch counters.

But the civil rights lobby, determined to exploit this unique moment, pressed not merely for most of its objectives, but for all of them. That meant a civil rights bill even more far-reaching than Kennedy's. Specifically, civil rights spokesmen demanded a ban on job discrimination, enforced by a fair employment commission; statutory authority for the attorney general to initiate suits protecting the constitutional rights of private citizens against deprivation by state and local officials; and stronger voting provisions than Kennedy was proposing.

Kennedy's bill contained less than the movement wanted because his top priority was enactment. Senate Majority Leader Mike Mansfield had told him the votes in Congress to pass any bill were not there. The only way Kennedy might find them was by converting Republicans not ordinarily sympathetic to him or civil rights. Accordingly, before submitting the bill, the president draped the flag around it, consulted with Republican leaders, and urged the parties to join together, as in wartime, to deal with a national crisis. Only by fending off demands for a stronger bill could he hope to secure necessary bipartisan support.

THE MARCH ON WASHINGTON

Kennedy also tried to fend off the March on Washington, which was planned that summer by civil rights leaders as a giant demonstration in support of civil rights legislation. Kennedy warned black leaders at a meeting late in June that key congressmen might interpret the March as intimidation and turn against the bill. "Frankly," Martin Luther King replied, "I have never engaged in any direct action movement which did not seem ill-timed." Once the March became inevitable, the administration virtually took over its management to assure success. Kennedy remained nervous, nevertheless. As the March approached, he privately expressed fears of violence, a small turnout, a backlash in Congress. He declined to speak to the crowd, though he did agree to meet with its leaders at the conclusion. On the day of the March, in case the worst happened, he had four thousand soldiers stationed nearby to defend the capital.

The March on Washington, August 28, 1963, was the great day of the civil rights movement. Nearly 200,000 Americans, most of them black, gathered at the Lincoln Memorial in the largest assembly for redress of grievances ever seen in Washington. The good-humored crowd, dressed in their Sunday best, "had come," said the *New York Times,* "in the spirit of a church outing." Many on the fringes could not hear entertainers Bob Dylan, Joan Baez, and Dick Gregory. And no one heard the militant speech that SNCC's[6] John Lewis had prepared but that nervous moderates in the March persuaded him to rewrite. Concluding a slashing attack on Kennedy's bill, Lewis had intended to say, "We will march through the South, through the heart of Dixie, the way Sherman did. We shall pursue our own 'scorched earth' policy and burn Jim Crow to the ground—nonviolently. We shall fragment the South into a thousand pieces and put them back together in the image of democracy."

Those who heard Martin Luther King's speech learned, if they did not already know, why this black man had become the unrivaled leader of his people. Eloquently distilling the liberal faith on which the movement had been built, King said, "When the architects of our great republic wrote the magnificent words of the Constitution and the Declaration of Independence, they were signing a promissory note to which every American was to fall heir. This note was a promise that all men, yes, black men as well as white men, would be guaranteed the inalienable rights of life, liberty, and the pursuit of happiness." King's critics in the movement might accuse him of failure as an organizer, hit-and-run tactics in the South, monopoly of civil rights funds, and willingness to compromise at critical moments. But on this occasion, as on so many others, declaiming in the cadence of the southern pulpit his dream that the sons of slaveholders and the sons of slaves might "sit down together at the table of brotherhood," he elevated the March from a mere political tactic into a spiritual event.

In September 1963 Congress began serious work on the bill that so many were so earnestly pressing upon it. Admin-

6. Student Nonviolent Coordinating Committee

istration strategy paid off in the form of working relations with Representative William McCulloch, Republican of Ohio, the key minority member of the Judiciary Committee. Mc-Culloch, it seemed, would support Kennedy's bill and carry enough Republicans with him to assure House passage. These calculations were nearly wrecked when Emanuel Celler, the aging chairman of the committee, yielded to pressure from civil rights lobbyists and joined with other liberals to force a bill through the civil rights subcommittee containing the full menu of militant demands. McCulloch threatened to mutiny, and the committee's southern Democrats moved in for the kill. The southerners decided to join with liberals in the full committee to report out the strongest possible bill and then vote with Republicans on the House floor to defeat it. The episode confirmed the belief of the Kennedys that their father's judgment on businessmen applied just as well to liberals. Said RFK, "They're sons of bitches."

It took the president's personal intervention to undo the subcommittee's liberal mischief and restore the bipartisan alliance on which passage of a civil rights bill realistically depended. As a result of meetings he held with Democratic liberals and House Republican leaders, the administration's original bill was revised to contain a section outlawing discrimination in employment. Conservatively drafted, the new employment section strengthened the bill sufficiently to appease most liberals but not enough to alienate McCulloch. In the meantime, McCulloch extracted a promise from the administration not to sacrifice any part of the bill to obtain passage in the Senate without his permission. Rejecting the militant bill previously approved by its subcommittee, the full Judiciary Committee voted 23 to 11, on October 23, 1963, to report out the administration's amended measure.

By November 1963 John Kennedy had cause to be satisfied with his recent civil rights performance. His pending bill had made him a hero to most liberals and won him respect from all but the militant fringe of the civil rights movement. His parliamentary strategy had assured early passage in the House and given him an even chance in the Senate. In addition, the white backlash was drawing less blood than he had feared. Pollster Louis Harris reported that fall that Kennedy had lost 6.5 million voters who had supported him in 1960— 4.5 million because of his civil rights stand. But he had also attracted 11 million Nixon voters, giving him a substantial lead over all his likely Republican challengers in 1964. The civil rights issue might well cost Kennedy the South, and, as he learned in October on a tour of deserted Italian neighborhoods in Philadelphia, was doing him no good in white ethnic neighborhoods in the North. But 63 percent of the American people backed his civil rights bill and 60 percent continued to approve his conduct of the presidency. Prepared to concede nothing to the Republicans, Kennedy took his fateful trip to Texas to lay the groundwork for his forthcoming presidential campaign in that southern state.

After the president's assassination in Dallas, millions of Americans felt bereft of a truly great leader in large measure because Kennedy had cast his lot with civil rights. Comparisons with Abraham Lincoln, another president martyred before completing the work of liberation, were immediate. Especially among blacks, grief was tinged with anxiety. The first Emancipator had been succeeded by a southern president named Johnson, who shattered the dream of a racially reconstructed South. At an overflow memorial service for Kennedy in Harlem, a minister spoke the fear of his race when he said, "Let us pray that what happened 100 years ago will not repeat itself."

But, as civil rights leaders who knew him understood, Lyndon Johnson would finish Kennedy's work, not destroy it. As a Texas senator, he had broken with the South in 1957 to pilot through Congress the first civil rights bill since Reconstruction. As chairman of the President's Committee on Equal Employment Opportunity, he had revealed an honest, if ineffective, commitment to a colorblind labor market. In the spring of 1963 he had counseled Kennedy against sending a civil rights bill to Congress because he expected its defeat, but in meetings of prominent citizens at the White House that summer he had been the most eloquent and emotional advocate for its passage. Indeed, he had privately urged Kennedy to tour every southern state to tell white people in person that segregation was morally wrong, utterly unjustifiable, and in violation of the tenets of Christianity. A complex man notorious for ideological insincerity, Johnson's simple motive on this issue was to make the Constitution a living document in his native region.

Civil rights leaders required of Johnson only that he reaffirm Kennedy's commitment to trade away none of the civil rights bill in the Senate. Meeting with them one by one in the days following the assassination, Johnson pledged to stand by the bill as written. Indeed, he had even less freedom to compromise than Kennedy, for only by proving himself on the civil rights issue could he allay the skepticism about him so long nourished in liberal circles. Georgia's Richard B. Russell, the leader of the southern contingent in the Senate and an old friend of Johnson's, grasped this point early. There was less chance of compromise now, he said, "than there would have been had President Kennedy not met his tragic fate."

The civil rights bill passed the House in February 1964 and proceeded to the Senate. Southerners promptly mounted a determined filibuster to prevent the bill from ever coming to a vote. The Senate had never before produced the two-thirds majority to vote cloture on a civil rights debate, and success was by no means assured now. If all 100 Senators were present, the bill's managers could count on only 42 Democratic votes for cloture. That meant that 25 of the 33 Senate Republicans would have to supply the winning margin. Again and again in early 1964, Johnson would ask Robert Kennedy, to whom he had delegated complete authority for managing the bill, "Where are we going to get the votes?" Only one Republican commanded enough prestige to produce the requisite number, but that man, Minority Leader Everett McKinley Dirksen, seemed something less than a champion of the rights of man.

Dirksen, whom Richard Russell called "the most accomplished thespian who has ever trod" the Senate floor, reveled in the spotlight now focused on him. Carefully cloaking his ultimate intentions, he had few kind words to say about the bill, especially its public-accommodations and fair-employment sections. On May 5, 1964, after months of doleful comment, Dirksen finally sat down with Robert Kennedy for the first of a series of meetings to spell out the amendments he would require as the price of his support. They turned out to be mainly technical. The ritual of doubt, agonizing appraisal, and eventual conversion that Dirksen had so publicly enacted had merely been contrived to make it easier for other Republicans to join him in voting to close debate and enact the bill. Quoting a line he said was the last in [French novelist] Victor Hugo's diary but actually came from Hugo's *Histoire d'un crime*, the unlikely hero of this parliamentary drama declaimed, "No army can withstand the strength of an idea whose time has come."

PRESIDENT JOHNSON SIGNS THE CIVIL RIGHTS BILL

The Civil Rights Act that Johnson signed in July 1964 was the great liberal achievement of the decade, though at the time not every liberal thought so. Critics belittled the act because it did not attack de facto segregation or because it left untouched vast areas of subtle discrimination or because it was irrelevant to the scandal of black poverty. None of these were its purpose. The act's main intent, limited but indispensable, was the accomplishment of legal equality in a region where it did not exist. Because the act passed and was eventually enforced, the southern segregation system soon vanished into history. The southern black men and women who lived through this attempt to reconcile American principle and black reality knew best what it had cost and what had been gained. Hartman Turnbow, a black farmer in the Mississippi delta, was one of those who had gone to a SNCC freedom school and risked his life to register. Looking back a decade later, he rendered his judgment:[7]

> Anybody hada jus told me 'fore it happened that conditions would make this much change between the white and the black in Holmes County here where I live, why I'da just said, "You're lyin'. It won't happen." I just wouldn't have believed it. I didn't dream of it. I didn't see no way. But it got to workin' just like the citizenship class teacher told us—that if we would redish to vote and just stick with it. He says it's gon' be some difficults. He told us that when we started. We was looking for it. He said we gon' have difficults, gon' have troubles, folks gon' lose their homes, folks gon' lose their lives, peoples gon' lose all their money, and just like he said, all of that happened. He didn't miss it. He hit it ka-dap on the head, and it's workin' now. It won't never go back where it was.

7. in an interview with Howell Raines, author of *My Soul Is Rested*

CHAPTER 4

Kennedy and Foreign Policy

The Bay of Pigs Disaster

Thomas G. Paterson

Thomas G. Paterson argues that Kennedy inherited the problem of Cuba and Fidel Castro from the Eisenhower administration, but rather than solve it, he made it worse. Paterson explains how Kennedy approved a CIA plan to invade Cuba and make it look like an attack by Cuban exiles and how the plan unraveled from the start, resulting in lost planes and men. The failure was an embarrassment for the new Kennedy administration and caused critics to doubt Kennedy's judgment and resolve. Thomas G. Paterson has taught history at the University of Connecticut in Storrs. He is the author of several books, including *Soviet-American Confrontation, On Every Front: The Making of the Cold War*, and *Meeting the Communist Threat: Truman to Reagan.*

The [Dwight D.] Eisenhower Administration bequeathed to its successor an unproductive tit-for-tat process of confrontation with Cuba and a legacy of failure. In 1959–1960, with Ambassador Philip Bonsal thinking that Castro suffered "mental unbalance at times" and Eisenhower concluding that the Cuban leader "begins to look like a madman," Havana and Washington traded punch for punch. In November 1959 the President decided to encourage anti-Castro groups within Cuba to "check" or "replace" the revolutionary regime, and thus end an anti-Americanism that was "having serious adverse effects on the United States position in Latin America and corresponding advantages for international Communism." In March of the next year Eisenhower ordered the CIA [Central Intelligence Agency] to train Cuban exiles for an invasion of their homeland—this shortly after Cuba signed a trade treaty with the Soviet Union. The CIA,

From "Fixation with Cuba: The Bay of Pigs, Missile Crisis, and Covert War Against Fidel Castro," by Thomas G. Paterson, in *Kennedy's Quest for Victory: American Foreign Policy, 1961–1963*, edited by Thomas G. Paterson. Copyright ©1989 by Oxford University Press, Inc. Used by permission of Oxford University Press, Inc.

as well, hatched assassination plots against Castro and staged hit-and-run attacks along the Cuban coast. As Cuba undertook land reform that struck at American interests and nationalized American-owned industries, the United States suspended Cuba's sugar quota and forbade American exports to the island, drastically cutting a once-flourishing commerce. On January 3, 1961, fearing an invasion and certain that the American embassy was a "nest of spies" aligned with counter-revolutionaries who were burning cane fields and sabotaging buildings, Castro heatedly demanded that the embassy staff be reduced to the small size of the Cuban delegation in Washington. The United States promptly broke diplomatic relations with Cuba.

Eisenhower failed to topple Castro, but American pressure accelerated the radicalization of the revolution and helped open the door to the Soviets. Moscow bought sugar, supplied technicians, armed the militia, and offered generous trade terms. Although the revolution's radicalization was probably inevitable, it was not inexorable that Cuba would end up in the Soviet camp. Hostile United States policies ensured that outcome. Revolutionary Cuba needed outside assistance to survive. "Russia came to Castro's rescue," Bonsal has concluded, "only after the United States had taken steps designed to overthrow him."

KENNEDY INHERITED AND WORSENED THE CUBA PROBLEM

Kennedy's foreign policy troubles have sometimes been explained as inheritances from Eisenhower that shackled the new President with problems not of his own making. To be sure, Kennedy inherited the Cuban problem from Eisenhower. But he did not simply continue his predecessor's anti-Castro policies. Kennedy greatly exaggerated the Cuban threat, attributing to Castro a capability to export revolution that the Cuban leader never had and lavishing on him an attention he did not deserve. Castro was "an affront to our pride" and a "mischief maker," [columnist] Walter Lippmann wisely wrote, but he was not a "mortal threat" to the United States. And because of his obsession with Cuba, Kennedy significantly increased the pressures against the upstart island. He thus helped generate major crises, including the October 1962 missile crisis. Kennedy inherited the Cuban problem—and he made it worse.

The new President actually made his first important policy choice on Cuba before he entered the White House. On the day Cuban-American relations were severed, Secretary of State Christian Herter telephoned Secretary-designate Dean Rusk and asked for Kennedy's reaction. Rusk talked with Kennedy and reported that the President-elect "would not associate himself with the Administration stand, i.e., he would not take a position for or against it at the present time. . . ." By saying nothing, Kennedy accepted a decision that reduced his own options for dealing with Cuba. The United States lost an embassy which had served as a first-hand listening post; now Washington would have to rely upon a fast diminishing number of CIA informants and deep-cover agents or upon often exaggerated information from exiles. Most important, with economic coercion having failed to bring down Castro and diplomacy now impeded, the rupture in relations elevated covert action—especially an invasion by Cuban exiles—as one of the few means left to resolve the contest with Cuba.

The questions of whether and under what conditions to approve an exile expedition dominated the President's discussion of Cuba in his first few months in office. Although Kennedy always reserved the authority to cancel the operation right up to the moment of departure, his choices, made after much deliberation, pointed in one direction: Go. National security adviser McGeorge Bundy later said that the President "really was looking for ways to make it work . . . and allowed himself to be persuaded it would work and the risks were acceptable." Not simply a prisoner of events or of the Eisenhower legacy, Kennedy associated so closely with the covert operation that it became identified as *his.* He listened to but rejected the counsel of doubting advisers, and he never revealed moral or legal qualms about violently overthrowing a sovereign government. He never requested a contingency plan to disband the exile brigade. In questioning aides, the President worried most about which methods would deliver success and whether the guiding hand of the United States could be concealed. Kennedy sought deniability of an American role, but never the demise of the project. . . .

THE BAY OF PIGS PLAN AND ITS FAILURE

Officials moved fast. The CIA devised a plan for dawn landings in the area of Bahía de Cochinos (Bay of Pigs). The existence of an air strip at the town of Playa Girón, the surrounding Zapata swamps with few access roads, and the region's sparse population made this an appealing entry site. In a Miami motel, a CIA operative bluntly forced exiles to form the Cuban Revolutionary Council under José Miró Cardona, a former foe of Batista[1] and a onetime member of Castro's government. [Presidential adviser Arthur] Schlesinger quickly produced a White Paper. Issued on April 3, this propagandistic justification for anti-Castroism condemned the Cuban radical for betraying his revolutionary promises, delivering his island to the "Sino-Soviet bloc," and attempting to subvert Latin American governments. After several high-level meetings and [CIA Director Allen] Dulles's assurance that the prospects for Operation Zapata were even greater than they had been for the successful CIA plot in 1954 against Guatemala, Kennedy set April 17 as D-Day.

The Bay of Pigs plan began to unravel from the start. As the brigade's old, slow freighters, obtained from the United Fruit Company, plowed their way to Cuba, B-26 airplanes took to the skies from Nicaragua. On April 15, D-Day minus 2, the brigade pilots destroyed several parked planes of Castro's meager air force. That same day, as part of a pre-invasion ploy, a lone, artificially damaged B-26 flew directly to Miami, where its pilot claimed that he had defected from the Cuban military and had just bombed his country's airfields. But the cover story soon cracked. Snooping journalists noticed that the nose cone of the B-26 was metal; Cuban planes had plastic noses. They observed too that the aircraft's guns had not been fired. The American hand was being exposed. The President, still insistent upon hiding American complicity, decided to cancel a second D-Day air strike against the remnants of the Cuban air force. CIA officials protested, because they believed the invasion force could not succeed unless Castro's few planes were knocked out. After conferring with Secretary Rusk, Kennedy stuck with his decision.

Shortly after midnight on April 17, more than 1400 commandos motored in small boats to the beaches at Bahía de Cochinos. The invaders immediately tangled with Castro's militia. Some commandos never made it, because their boats broke apart on razor-sharp coral reefs. In the air, Castro's marauding airplanes shot down two brigade B-26s and, in the

1. Fulgencio Batista y Zaldivar, Cuban dictator who was president, 1940–1944 and 1952–1959; his corrupt authoritarian regime was overthrown by revolutionaries led by Fidel Castro on January 1, 1959.

water, sank ships carrying essential communications equipment and ammunition. Fighting ferociously, the brigade nonetheless failed to establish a beachhead. Would Washington try to salvage the mission? Kennedy turned down CIA appeals to dispatch planes from the nearby USS *Essex*, but he did permit some jets to provide air cover for a new B-26 attack from Nicaragua. Manned this time by American CIA pilots, the B-26s arrived an hour after the jets had come and gone. Cuban aircraft downed the B-26s, killing four Americans. With Castro's boasting that the *mercenarios* had been foiled, the final toll was grim: 114 of the exile brigade dead and 1,189 captured. A pall settled over the White House.

"How could I have been so stupid, to let them go ahead?" Kennedy asked an assistant. Stupid or not, Kennedy knew the answers to his own question. First, he dearly sought to oust Castro and score a victory in the Cold War. Second, his personality and style encouraged action. Always driven to win, Kennedy believed "that his disapproval of the plan would be a show of weakness inconsistent with his general stance." One foreign policy observer [Louis Halle] explained "how the President got such bad advice from such good advisers":

> The decision on which they were asked to advise was presented as a choice between action and inaction. . . . None of the President's advisers wants it said of him by his colleagues . . . that he . . . loses his nerve when the going gets hot. The Harvard intellectuals are especially vulnerable, the more so from being new on the scene. They are conscious of the fact that the tough-minded military suspect them of being soft-headed. They have to show that they are he-men too, that they can act as well as lecture.

Third, fear of nasty political repercussions influenced the President. Told to disband, brigade members might have refused to give up their arms or even have mutineed. In any case, Republicans would have scorned a weak-kneed Administration. Kennedy approved the operation, finally, because he felt a sense of urgency. . . .

Failures in intelligence, operations, decision-making, and judgment doomed the Bay of Pigs undertaking. Arrogant CIA architects knew too little and assumed too much about Cuba, particularly about the landing site. Although [Deputy Director for Plans Richard] Bissell and Dulles have staunchly denied that they ever told the President that the invasion would ignite an island-wide rebellion against the Castro regime and thus ensure the ascendancy of Miró's provisional government,

Kennedy decision-makers nonetheless believed that the invasion would stimulate a popular revolt against an unpopular government. But the CIA did not coordinate the invasion with the anti-Castro underground in Cuba, because the agency feared leaks and the likely infiltration of opposition groups by Castro's security forces. No rebellion erupted. Kennedy and his advisers also assumed that, should the brigade prove incapable of taking territory, it could melt into the mountains and become a guerrilla army. But, because the invasion site had been shifted, the mountains now lay some 80 miles away, with impassable swamps between. Neither Kennedy nor CIA advisers had explored this problem. The guerrilla option, which, like the belief in a rebellion, probably led Kennedy to suppress doubts about the operation, was actually impossible.

CIA planners failed in other ways. If they overestimated Cuban discontent with Castro, they underestimated the effectiveness of his military. They anticipated that he would crack; in fact, he expertly led his forces at the Bay of Pigs, where he had vacationed. CIA analysts had failed to detect the coral reefs. CIA-issued equipment malfunctioned; crucial communications gear was concentrated in one ship that sank; paratroopers did not drop far enough inland to cut off causeways. Another operational failure remained a tightly held secret. The CIA had been attempting since 1960 to kill Fidel Castro, even employing Mafia thugs for the task. The CIA activated assassination plots in March and April. It seems likely that assassination was part of the general Bay of Pigs plan. Bissell has admitted that he was hopeful "that Castro would be dead before the landing."

The most controversial operational question remains the cancelled second D-Day air strike. Post-crisis critics have complained that the President lost his nerve and made a decision that condemned the expedition to disaster. Castro and Bissell have agreed that Cuban air supremacy was important to Cuba's triumph. But was it decisive? A pre-emptive strike on D-Day against the Cuban air force would not have delivered victory to the invaders. After the first air attack, Castro had dispersed his planes; the brigade's B-26s would have encountered considerable difficulty in locating and destroying them. And, even if a D-Day assault had disabled all of Castro's planes, then what? *La brigada's* [the exile brigade] 1400 men would have had to face Castro's army of 25,000 and the nation's 200,000 militia. The commandos most likely would not have survived the overwhelming power of the Cuban military.

A flawed decision-making system also contributed to failure. Bissell and Dulles were too emotionally committed to the project to see the shortcomings in their handiwork. CIA planners were less than candid with the President, for fear that he would terminate the project. Operation Zapata was even kept a secret from many other CIA professionals responsible for intelligence analysis. Had they been asked to assess the chances for national rebellion, for example, they probably would have reported negatively, pointing out Castro's continued popular appeal. CIA officials also contributed to the President's thinking that American participation could be hidden and plausibly denied. But how could Kennedy ever have thought that secrecy was possible? Wishful thinking provides the best answer. "Trying to mount an operation of this magnitude from the United States," a CIA official wrote later, "is about as covert as walking nude across Times Square without attracting attention." Nonetheless, until his decision to cancel the second strike, Kennedy clung to the fiction of deniability.

The Joint Chiefs of Staff and Secretary of State also failed as advisers. Although the generals and admirals had serious reservations, they always evaluated the operation favorably. Sworn to secrecy, they did not seek close staff analysis of the CIA plan. Not "cut in" until the later stages of planning, they hesitated to "pound the desk," because the operation was "not our show." Nor did Dean Rusk provide rigorous scrutiny or press his case against the invasion. A "good soldier" who went along with the apparent consensus, he seemed to believe that he should preside over debate rather than influence it. Rusk later regretted his restraint:

> As a colonel of infantry [in the Second World War], I knew that this brigade didn't have the chance of a "snowball in hell." But I wasn't a colonel of infantry; I was sitting there in a very special cubicle. I failed President Kennedy by not insisting that he ask a question that he did not ask. He should have turned to our Joints Chiefs of Staff and said to them: "Now gentlemen, I may want to do this with U.S. forces, so you tell me what you would need. . . ." By the time the Joint Chiefs had come in with their sustained and prolonged bombing, their several divisions, a massive fleet, and their big air force, it would have become obvious to the President that that little brigade didn't have a chance at all.

One wonders, of course, why Kennedy himself did not think to ask the question. Rusk also kept departmental intelligence and Cuban specialists in the dark.

Kennedy encountered a good deal of dissenting opinion and he rejected it. Schlesinger, for example, wrote several memoranda to the President, arguing that time was actually not on Castro's side and that the Cuban leader, at least for the moment, remained popular. The skeptics included [Kennedy appointees] Richard Goodwin, John Kenneth Galbraith, Charles E. Bohlen, Chester Bowles, and Adlai Stevenson. In making his decision, Kennedy also bypassed Congress, further ensuring that he received limited advice. Only Senator J. William Fulbright, Foreign Relations Committee chairman, was let into the inner circle, and, at that, only once. Picking up rumors of a forthcoming invasion of Cuba, Fulbright sent the President a memorandum that strongly disapproved invasion—it was "of a piece with the hypocrisy and cynicism for which the United States is constantly denouncing the Soviet Union . . . ," he wrote. Kennedy thereupon invited the Arkansas senator to attend an April 4 meeting. Fulbright spoke forthrightly to the assembled top-level advisers, chiding them for exaggerating the Cuban threat. As he had told the President earlier, the Castro regime "is a thorn in the flesh; but it is not a dagger in the heart." No one in the room agreed with Fulbright.

"Mr. President, it could have been worse," remarked a Stevenson assistant. How? "It might have succeeded." Had all gone well with the chain reaction of beachhead, rebellion, and Castro's death or departure, the victory would only have "exchanged a Castro pest-house for a post-Castro asylum." Tainted as an American stooge, the head of the new government would have struggled to win public favor. Well-armed Castroites, including Fidel's brother Raúl and Che Guevara, would probably have initiated a protracted guerrilla war against the American-created regime. The Soviets might have helped these rebel forces, and volunteers from around the world might have swelled the resistance—like the Spanish Civil War of the 1930s, Schlesinger had warned. The United States would have had to save its puppet government through military aid, advisers, and maybe even troops. To have sustained a successful Bay of Pigs invasion, then, the Kennedy Administration probably would have had to undertake a prolonged and expensive occupation of the island.

The Peace Corps

Charles Lam Markmann and Mark Sherwin

Charles Lam Markmann and Mark Sherwin explain President Kennedy's proposal for a Peace Corps, an organization of volunteers that would provide education and aid social and economic development in poor countries around the world. The proposal received immediate national and international support, and people began volunteering within two days. The authors identify the staff, which included business managers, journalists, lawyers, a football coach, and a doctor. Congress provided the funding, and well-known Americans lent their support as advisors. Charles Lam Markmann has been associate foreign editor of the *New York Times* and consultant to publishers and television producers. He has co-authored, along with Francis Trevelyan Miller, *History of World War II*. Mark Sherwin, who has written about American anticommunists, politics, and government, is the author of *One Week in March* and *The Extremists*.

On March 1, [1961] President Kennedy issued an executive order establishing a Peace Corps, which he described as a "pool of trained men and women sent overseas by the United States Government or through private institutions and organizations to help foreign governments meet their urgent needs for skilled manpower." He also sent a message to Congress asking legislation to make the Corps permanent. "Life in the Peace Corps," the President said, "will not be easy. Members will work without pay, but they will be given living allowances. They will live on the same level as the inhabitants of the countries to which they are sent." In his message to Congress he said: "There is little doubt that the number of those who wish to serve will be far greater than our capacity to absorb them." He said by the end of the year he hoped to have 500 to 1,000 trained corpsmen working abroad.

Excerpted from *John F. Kennedy: A Sense of Purpose*, by Charles Lam Markmann and Mark Sherwin (New York: St. Martin's Press, 1961). Copyright ©1961 by Charles Lam Markmann and Mark Sherwin.

IMMEDIATE NATIONAL AND INTERNATIONAL SUPPORT

The news ignited greater public enthusiasm than any other program sponsored by the new Administration. Two days after the message, 8,000 letters had been received. Rarely had a Presidential directive evoked such universal approval. George Meany, president of the American Federation of Labor and Congress of Industrial Organizations, offered immediate cooperation and assigned Henry Pollock, a staff specialist in foreign affairs, as liaison officer to study the use of trained workers in countries where skilled labor was scarce. Building-trades unions said the likeliest source of their volunteers would be two age groups. The first would be apprentices, finishing their work-and-education phases. Most of these were in their early twenties and had high school educations. The second would be older workers whose children had married and who were already serving as teachers in apprenticeship programs. Applications were requested by many young skilled construction workers who had wide experience in living under the rugged conditions of dam-building in Colorado or constructing the Distant Early Warning system across Arctic Canada.

Students and educators also gave swift support to the program. Arthur S. Adams, president of the American Council on Education, declared after a survey that 300 colleges and universities would cooperate in training members for the Peace Corps. Replies to a questionnaire that went to 468 institutions of higher learning showed that 441 approved and only 27 disapproved the Corps in principle. The National Student Conference endorsed the Peace Corps but opposed loyalty oaths for volunteers. The Administration declared it had no loyalty data requirement.

The reaction from the diplomatic corps was favorable and sound. Nigeria received the news "warmly"; Brazil called it a "very imaginative move that would add dynamism to programs already under way . . . public opinion in our country would be very sympathetic." Dr. Carlos Samz de Santamaria, the ambassador from Colombia, said it was "romantically and pragmatically good from all angles. I am wonderfully well impressed." Britain gave the Peace Corps a hearty reception. *The Yorkshire Post* explained that the program "would appeal only to the most dedicated of young people or those with a large allowance from a millionaire parent. America being what it is, both these types are likely to be represented in the Corps." A government spokesman in Bonn said: "The idea would certainly find a potent echo among the Western allies." Italian officials said they favored the idea so much that their country might wish to start similar projects.

This "spiritual mobilization" of American youth was first broached to Kennedy by Senator [Hubert] Humphrey [of Minnesota] and Representative Henry Reuss of Wisconsin, who felt that the present generation needed a romantic and dramatic challenge to match earlier generations that helped Roosevelt revamp the economy and destroy the Fascist threat to liberty. Kennedy first introduced the plan in a campaign speech at San Francisco's Cow Palace on November 2, 1960, saying that, while "we cannot discontinue training our young men as soldiers of war, we also want them to be ambassadors of peace." No single utterance in his campaign drew more mail or a greater response. There were, of course, dissenters after the President sent his message to Congress. Representative Otto E. Passman, Louisiana Democrat and chairman of the House Foreign Aid Appropriations Subcommittee, objected on the ground of cost, and the Daughters of the American Revolution objected tremulously that this might lead to a universal civilian draft and job assignment.

ADMINISTRATION OF THE PEACE CORPS

The President named his brother-in-law, R. Sargent Shriver, 45, former president of the Chicago Board of Education, who had headed the planning of the Peace Corps since January, as director. There was no salary with the job. In an interview with Senator Kenneth B. Keating, New York Republican, Shriver declared that "anybody who joins us with the idea that this will be a glorified joy ride is doomed to disappointment. No Americans in modern times will have been asked to do harder work. It's going to be work carried on in the underdeveloped part of the world, under difficult living conditions, different diet, different culture, different language, sometimes in remote places."

The White House created a nucleus staff to assist Shriver in carrying out his program. Some would remain permanently with the organization, others would serve as temporary consultants. They were:

Bradley Patterson, 39, career Civil Service official, former Assistant Secretary of the Cabinet during the Eisenhower

Administration. John D. Young, 41, an executive with McKinsey & Co., management consultants. Lester Gordon, 38, deputy assistant managing director for planning and economics of the Development Loan Fund. Forest Evashevski, 43, of Iowa City, Iowa, University of Iowa athletic director and former football coach. Lawrence E. Dennis, 40, of University Park, Pa., former Iowa journalist and vice-president in charge of academic affairs for Pennsylvania State College. Dr. Arthur S. Adams of Harvard, president of the American Council of Education, who accepted supervisory responsibility for the Peace Corps training program. Thomas H.E. Quimby, 42, East Lansing, Mich., business executive; he set up a recruitment program. Louis E. Martin, 48, of Chicago, editor of *The Chicago Defender,* a Negro daily, working on the development of programs with the United Nations and other international agencies. Dr. Howard A. Rusk of New York, professor and chairman of the Department of Physical Medicine and Rehabilitation, New York University Medical Center. Albert G. Sims, 43, of Riverside, Conn., vice president in charge of operations for the Institute of International Education, in charge of the development of university programs. Gordon Boyce, 43, of Putney, Vt., president and international secretary-general of the Experiment in International Living. Morris B. Abram, 42, Atlanta lawyer and Rhodes scholar, who was to set up a legal office. Edwin R. Bayley of Madison, Wis., 42, former reporter for *The Milwaukee Journal.* Warren W. Wiggins of Washington, 38, assistant deputy director for programs of the International Cooperation Administration.

To add some luster (as if it were needed) to the group, the President appointed a National Advisory Council, a 33-member bi-partisan group, headed by Vice President Johnson and including Supreme Court Justice Douglas, a renowned traveler, explorer and outdoors man; Mrs. Roosevelt, John D. Rockefeller 4th, Dr. Mary Bunting, president of Radcliffe; David E. Lilienthal, former chairman of the Atomic Energy Commission; the Reverend James Robinson, director of New York's Morningside Community Center, and Thomas J. Watson Jr., president of the International Business Machines Corporation. The other members included representatives of the arts, sciences, business and various hues of political opinion, demonstrating a national unity rarely achieved in any piece of legislation.

FINANCING THE PROGRAM

The first financing of the program came through already appropriated funds of the Mutual Security Agency. Subsequently special funds would have to be set aside by Congress to cover the estimated cost of $10,000 to $12,000 a year for each overseas worker, including training, transportation, medical care and administrative overhead. With about 2,000 workers overseas, the cost would run to about $24 million, considered a modest sum in the more than $80 billion Federal budget.

In presenting the fiscal portrait of the Corps, the Administration stated its official purpose: The Peace Corps volunteers of both sexes would operate as teachers and technicians in the fields of education, agriculture, public health, English-language instruction, urban renewal and public administration. The first emphasis would be on teaching. The volunteers would work only on projects that by Peace Corps standards showed the need as well as the possibility of improvement. They would work only at the invitation of the host country and largely under its authority. The plans called for the volunteers to fill the void between technical advisers already in the field and the unskilled local labor. One official explained that the volunteers were not expected to perform tasks that could be done by native manpower.

The Peace Corps was organized as a semi-autonomous agency under the State Department, but the workers would also function in approved programs undertaken by private universities, voluntary private agencies, the ICA[1] and United Nations groups. Ambassador Stevenson[2] suggested to UN Secretary General Hammarskjold that the idea of an international Peace Corps be considered. He said it was Kennedy's hope that other countries would join in a similar effort so that the American program would be only one step in a major international drive in the sharing of knowledge and techniques with underdeveloped areas. Stevenson noted that the British Voluntary Overseas Services group already had 89 workers in 25 countries teaching, training and working with youth clubs. Only a few, he said, were university graduates; most were secondary-school graduates with plans for college after they had completed their overseas duty of a year or so. Voluntary Services Overseas was founded by youth and religious orga-

1. International Cooperative Alliance   2. Adlai Stevenson, U.S. ambassador to the United Nations

nizations, and is supported largely by grants and pays for the transportation of its workers. Host countries are required to supply food and lodging and $2.80 a week in pocket money.

SCREENING, TRAINING, AND SUPERVISION

In his recruiting drive, Shriver made it clear that men and women with trade skills, in construction or home economics, were just as welcome as those with college degrees. While the minimum age was set at 18, it was expected that the majority of those accepted would come from the 22-to-35 age group. Candidates would be thoroughly screened for intelligence, skills and emotional stability, the plan being to fit volunteers into projects already designated. The screening procedures would include a security check by the F.B.I., written tests and carefully annotated interviews. The training program would begin in a number of universities and continue in Peace Corps staff centers and overseas stations. Each candidate would have three to six months of intensive instruction in language, foreign culture and his chosen occupation. The training period was also expected to evolve into a further screening process where the recruits would be observed under conditions as close to actual assignments as possible.

In order to ease the anxieties of parents of some of the younger workers, especially the women, the Peace Corps gave the assurance that experienced supervision would be the foundation of the overseas units. Depending upon the place of assignment, a Peace Corps volunteer would spend two to three years abroad. He would get only a basic allowance sufficient to equal local living standards. For example, a teacher would get only enough money to live as the local teachers do. Technical helpers would work under the guidance of ICA technical advisers and would be expected, for example, to follow through a demonstration of malaria control by remaining in the area, mapping the mosquito-infested marshes and doing the field testing required. It was stressed that the Peace Corps was not designed as a propaganda agency or a means of spreading the American influence on the local political scene. This, of course, did not preclude the setting of the best possible example of the American way of life, which could be considerably more influential than a publicity release or a speech. It was stated as a fixed policy that the Peace Corps could not be used for religious missionary purposes or by the Central Intelligence Agency. The legal status of the volunteers would be governed by treaties now covering ICA personnel abroad. Some countries give the agency diplomatic immunity, others do not. At the end of his tour of duty, a volunteer would get travel expenses home and an accumulated "bonus" of $50 to $75 for each month of overseas service. In addition, a Peace Corps career board would seek to develop job opportunities for its veterans.

PEACE CORPS UPDATE

In "Peace Corps at a Glance," Chuck Meyers gives basic facts about the Peace Corps at the end of 1995.

Current Director: Mark Gearan
Budget: $219.7 million (fiscal 1995)
Volunteers since 1961: 140,000
Current volunteers: over 7,000
Program countries: 96—in Africa, Asia, South and Central America, the Caribbean, Eastern Europe, the former Soviet Union and various island nations.

Chuck Meyers, "Peace Corps at a Glance." Knight-Ridder/Tribune News Service, December 21, 1995.

Volunteers of draft age were not promised automatic exemption. General Lewis B. Hershey, Director of Selective Service, said that, barring some national crisis, the corpsmen would be able to get indefinite deferments (de facto exemption) if they worked on some occupation "in the national interest." It was presumed that the Peace Corps could be construed as in the national interest.

The President was so gratified by the reception the Peace Corps proposal received that he announced later that he was studying the establishment of a Peace Corps Foundation to channel aid to private United States groups working overseas. These would include projects that did not meet official United States criteria; proposals by several Roman Catholic and Mormon organizations to couple missionary efforts with work projects, and those countries that would prefer non-governmental help from the United States. Congress was empowered to create such foundations, and even state governments could grant them charters. Funds would come from private sources, but the United States might also provide some money. The Peace Corps received a number of private donations, which had to be returned.

Another facet of Kennedy's program came to light in a television conversation he had with Mrs. Roosevelt. He announced that the Administration was seriously considering methods of using the Peace Corps concept in slum and depressed areas at home. He referred to the "reservoir of talent" that had been uncovered in the applications for jobs sent to the Corps. He mentioned retraining and education in blighted sections of the country as needing the same kind of attention as was planned for foreign nations. "I think that we have hundreds of thousands of people in this country who genuinely want to be of service," he said.

THE FIRST VOLUNTEERS TO TANGANYIKA

The organization of the Peace Corps moved ahead so rapidly that by April 21 the President was able to announce definite plans to send the first group of 28 volunteers to Tanganyika in east central Africa. The group, consisting of surveyors, geologists and civil engineers, was scheduled to arrive in Dar-es-Salaam in September to help local technicians and construction workers to plan and build roads. "There is nothing more important in Tanganyika," the President said, "than the development of roads to open up the country." Tanganyika was a British-administered United Nations trust territory with a population of 9 million, scheduled to gain its full independence on December 28. The country's Ministry of Communications and the Ministry of Commerce and Industry had promised to provide the American volunteers with native armed game scouts, transportation, tents, mosquito netting and other non-technical supplies. During the dry season the volunteers would camp out three weeks at a time and labor on farm-to-market road surveys, on engineering of main bridges and roads and on geological research and mapping. Sir Ernest Vesey, finance minister, described as vital the three-year development program undertaken by the Peace Corps. He dramatized his statement by saying that his country could train only two surveyors in the next five years. The need was for simple dirt roads that would change the country's farmers from living under a barter economy to a cash economy. After the dry season, when rains made outdoor work impossible, the American volunteers would teach the Tanganyikans engineering and surveying techniques. Two- and three-man teams would fan out from Mount Kilimanjaro to Lake Tanganyika in a romantic and practical trek that should make for excellent reminiscence in the future.

The United States began negotiations with United Nations groups, such as the World Health Organization, and with foreign governments for the most effective use of the Peace Corps. Ten nations almost at once expressed an interest in the program. Among the first possible host countries were Brazil, the Philippines, Nigeria, Pakistan, Colombia, Chile and India. There would be more as the Peace Corps demonstrated its abilities. It promised to be a long and arduous assignment of trial and error, failure and success. This was emphasized by Shriver in his report to the President when he warned that "no matter how well conceived and efficiently run, there probably will be some failures and some disappointments. These could be costly and have serious effects both at home and abroad. Nevertheless the Peace Corps over the long run may create a substantial popular base for responsible American policies to reward the world. Thus the Peace Corps could add a new dimension to America's world policy—one for which people here and abroad have long been waiting."

There were many who regarded the Peace Corps as Kennedy's dynamic reply to the Birchers,[3] the right-wing students, the security-conscious conformists and their bewildered fathers and mothers.

3. members of the John Birch Society, an anti-communist organization founded in 1958

The Alliance for Progress

Bruce Miroff

The Alliance for Progress was Kennedy's program to improve living conditions and prevent revolution and communism in Latin America. The Alliance was formalized at a conference in Punta del Este, Uruguay, in August 1961. In the following essay, Bruce Miroff argues that the Alliance's goals of economic development and social reform never materialized because Latin Americans were skeptical of the program and because Kennedy allowed American corporations to use the Alliance for their own economic gain. Bruce Miroff, a political historian, is the author of *Icons of Democracy: American Leaders as Heroes, Aristocrats, Dissenters, and Democrats.*

John F. Kennedy's record in the Third World was, on the surface, a puzzling blend of the generous and the ignoble. Among Kennedy and his fellow New Frontiersmen, a sophisticated yet compassionate understanding of Third World problems seemed to exist. Marking that understanding were fresh departures in American foreign policy: the idealistic Peace Corps, a solicitous concern for the new nations of Africa, and, most notably, the Alliance for Progress campaign for economic development and social justice in Latin America. Yet, parallel to these undertakings was a history of repressive military intervention in the affairs of the Third World. Here, too, there were landmarks: the invasion of Cuba and the increasingly bitter struggle against the Viet Cong guerrillas in South Vietnam.

Doubtless there was genuine ambivalence in Kennedy's approach to the Third World, ambivalence fostered by a liberal's simultaneous desire for, and fear of, change. But ambivalence should not, in this case, be equated with incon-

Excerpted from *Pragmatic Illusions: The Presidential Politics of John F. Kennedy*, by Bruce Miroff (New York: David McKay, 1976). Copyright ©1976 by Bruce Miroff. Reprinted by permission of the author. (Endnotes in the original have been omitted in this reprint.)

sistency. For one consistent theme ran through almost all of Kennedy's ventures in the Third World—counterrevolution. Whatever other sympathies he professed, John Kennedy was a determined counterrevolutionary. His overriding aim was to banish the specter of radical revolution from the underdeveloped nations by channeling the forces of change into a "democratic revolution." The "democratic revolution" promised evolutionary change within a democratic framework, free from the disruption and violence of a radical social upheaval. It turned out to mean only the status quo in an elaborate new guise. . . .

The history of the Alliance for Progress can be recited relatively quickly; it takes only a few pages to describe its major events and achievements. What requires fuller consideration is the story of what didn't happen—the Alliance's glaring failure to fulfill its own goals or, indeed, to make even a dent in the stagnant economic and social order of the Latin American countries. That failure reveals much about the nature of present-day Latin America; it reveals far more about the political understanding of John Kennedy and his circle of advisers.

The Alliance for Progress was hailed, when it was announced in March 1961, as the start of a new era in United States–Latin American relations. But reassessment of America's hemispheric policy had already begun in the Eisenhower Administration. After Vice-President [Richard] Nixon's ill-starred trip to South America in 1958, and the triumph of the Cuban revolution in 1959, Washington policy makers had observed with alarm the rising tide of discontent in an area long taken for granted. By 1960, they were agreed on the need to pour more energy and money into Latin America. At the Bogotá Conference the Eisenhower Administration thus pledged $500 million as an American "social progress fund" for Latin American development.

Despite Eisenhower's initiative, Kennedy as a presidential candidate considered the Republicans vulnerable on the subject of Latin America. He made it one of his key campaign issues, adopting the slogan "Alliance for Progress" (coined by Richard Goodwin[1]) to describe his own prospective program. After his election, plans for this Alliance rapidly took form; by March 13, 1961, Kennedy was ready to

1. Deputy Secretary of State for Inter-American Affairs

unveil them to a White House assemblage of the Latin American diplomatic corps.

He painted his program in glowing terms. "I have called on all people of the hemisphere to join in a new Alliance for Progress—Alianza para Progreso—a vast cooperative effort, unparalleled in magnitude and nobility of purpose, to satisfy the basic needs of the American people for homes, work and land, health and schools. . . ." The new partnership of North and South would encompass both economic development and social restructuring—national planning and technical aid, agrarian reform and tax reform, public housing, education, and health care. And it would operate within the framework of democratic institutions, proving definitively the compatibility of representative government with material progress. Kennedy did not hesitate to call his Alliance a new hemispheric "revolution": "Let us once again transform the American continent into a vast crucible of revolutionary ideas and efforts. . . ."

The Alliance for Progress was born in hope, but also in fear. Little was said about it at the time, yet it was apparent to everyone concerned that the Alliance was America's response to the Cuban revolution, its contrivance for heading off the eruption of Castro-style revolutions throughout the hemisphere. The rapid promulgation of this new Latin American policy betrayed the nightmare of Fidelismo at its base. "It was," Ronald Steel observed [in *Pax Americana*], "neither charity nor a guilty conscience but Fidel Castro who provided the inspiration for the Alliance for Progress. . . . The Alliance for Progress might never have seen the light of day, let alone grown into childhood, had Fidel not injected the fear of communism into official Washington."

Barely more than a month after the announcement of this program for forestalling copies of the Cuban revolution, Kennedy struck at the original. On April 17, a brigade of 1400 Cuban exiles under the direction of the CIA were set ashore at Cuba's Bay of Pigs. Their hope was to spark a general uprising against the Castro regime; if this did not occur in a few days the invaders could melt away into the mountains and commence guerrilla warfare. The CIA was highly optimistic about the scheme; Kennedy, while expressing some doubts, went along in the faith that the Cuban populace would rise up against what he himself had characterized as a government "seized by aliens." But in a matter of days the Cuban militia crushed the invasion force and took most of its members prisoner. . . .

In the immediate aftermath of the Bay of Pigs . . . Kennedy was too irate to hide the threat [of force which accompanied the Alliance].

Let the record show that our restraint is not inexhaustible. Should it ever appear that the inter-American doctrine of non-interference merely conceals or excuses a policy of nonaction—if the nations of this Hemisphere should fail to meet their commitments against outside Communist penetration—then I want it clearly understood that this Government will not hesitate in meeting its primary obligations which are to the security of our Nation!

The Kennedy Administration was soon eager to forget its blundering Cuban invasion. But for Latin Americans the invasion was not so easily forgotten; it remained a powerful object lesson in the U.S. response to social revolution in the hemisphere.

While Kennedy's popularity in Latin America sagged temporarily after the Bay of Pigs, hopes for the Alliance for Progress remained high. The Alliance was formally organized at a conference of the Inter-American Economic and Social Council held in Punta del Este, Uruguay, in August 1961. In his written message to this conference Kennedy returned to the generous purposes of his March speech. Profound changes in the social and economic structure of Latin America were again foretold: "For there is no place in democratic life for institutions which benefit the few while denying the needs of the many, even though the elimination of such institutions may require far-reaching and difficult changes such as land reform and tax reform and a vastly increased emphasis on education and health and housing." And a vast infusion of American care, as well as American money, was pledged: "Only an effort of towering dimensions—an effort similar to that which was needed to rebuild the economies of Western Europe—can ensure fulfillment of our Alliance for Progress."

Although some of the Latin American delegates to the conference were skeptical in private, publicly all (except Cuba's Che Guevara) endorsed the plans of Kennedy and his chief representative, Treasury Secretary Douglas Dillon. When the conference ended on August 17, those plans had been incorporated into an official Charter of Punta del Este. The ambitions of the Alliance can be seen in the social goals

which the Charter set forth: comprehensive agrarian reform, tax reform, accelerated urban and rural housing development, accelerated programs of health and sanitation,
elimination of illiteracy. The economic goals were equally
ambitious: a national development plan for each country,
fair wages, stable prices, Latin American economic integration, and a per capita growth rate of 2.5 percent a year. There
was also a clear political goal: to protect and strengthen the
institutions of representative democracy in the hemisphere.
Toward all these ends the United States pledged $20 billion
over the next ten years, slightly more than half in public assistance, the rest in private funds.

The history of the Alliance during the remainder of
Kennedy's Presidency presents a dreary picture of inaction or
failure. A year or two after Punta del Este the bright hopes of
its founding had all but dissolved. Growth rates for the Latin
American economies as a whole lagged far below the 2.5 percent figure. Land and tax reforms were, in most cases, hope-
lessly bottled up in conservative legislatures. As for the Alliance's commitment to democracy, the years 1962–63
witnessed repeated setbacks for democratic institutions in
Latin America in the face of a resurgent militarism. In 1962
the governments of both Argentina and Peru were toppled by
military coups; in 1963 four more governments—Guatemala,
Ecuador, the Dominican Republic, and Honduras—fell under
military control. These developments could not, of course, all
be attributed to the Alliance. Still, it had rapidly become apparent that the Alliance could not live up to its name—and
would not disturb Latin America's stagnation.

Confronted persistently with criticisms of the Alliance,
Kennedy found it hard to disguise his gloom. All that he could
do was to cite the difficulties that the Alliance faced—the
complexity of Latin America's problems, its shortage of
trained personnel to develop and administer reform programs, the opposition of vested interests to such programs—
and to counsel patience. Sometimes even he found it difficult
to follow that counsel. On the second anniversary of the
Punta del Este conference, for example, he responded to a
press conference query on Latin America with obvious frustration: "The problems are almost insuperable. . . ." Yet the
grandiloquent rhetoric was never abandoned completely;
four days before his death Kennedy declared: "The task we
have set ourselves and the Alliance for Progress, the develop-

ment of an entire continent, is a far greater task than any we have ever undertaken in our history."

At the time of Kennedy's death, supporters of the Alliance still could claim that its reforms would take hold in a few more years. By the end of the decade, those supporters had to admit that the critics had been right all along—by almost any standard imaginable the Alliance was a failure. None of the goals fixed at Punta del Este had been achieved. As Susanne Bodenheimer[2] notes, figures compiled by the United Nations Economic Commission for Latin America actually show that "Latin America's problems of urban poverty, unemployment (particularly in rural areas), slow industrialization, inequalities of income and living standards, dependence upon foreign capital, foreign indebtedness, and slow expansion of foreign markets have become more critical during the [decade of the 1960's] . . . the annual average growth rate during the 1960's was lower than that of the previous decade and fell far short of targets established in 1961." Progress in land and tax reform was pathetically slow. Housing, sanitation, health care were no better for the great majority of Latin America's poor in 1970 than they had been in 1960. The fate of the Alliance could be summed up by its campaign against adult illiteracy; after ten years, statistics showed no appreciable increases in adult literacy in Latin America.

REASONS FOR THE ALLIANCE'S FAILURE

Why was the Alliance for Progress such a failure? Before this question can be answered, a prior question must be asked: what was the real intention of those who created the Alliance? What purposes, and whose interests, was the Alliance designed to serve? On this question opinion has, for the most part, been divided into two camps. Liberal supporters have regarded the Alliance as a sincere effort to bring material progress and social justice to Latin America. Radical critics, on the other hand, have viewed it as simply a new tool for preventing revolution and protecting America's economic stake in Latin America. A noble experiment which foundered on the rock of Latin American realities, or an ideological fraud which in good measure succeeded in fore-

2. author of *The Ideology of Developmentalism: The American Paradigm-Surrogate for Latin-American Studies*

stalling social change for yet another decade—these have been the terms in which most discussions of the Alliance have been couched.

While there is greater substance, in my opinion, in the argument of the critics, both sides have a hold on part of the truth about the Alliance for Progress. The Alliance goal of social change was genuine—as was its calculation of American self-interest. I shall treat the Alliance in each of these aspects—first as a failed "democratic revolution," then as a successful strategy for preserving the American economic empire in Latin America.

If we turn to writers who supported the Alliance, we find an interesting explanation proposed for the failure of Kennedy's "democratic revolution." Beyond the festering problems, bureaucratic inertia, and conservative resistance that hamstrung the Alliance, these writers stressed its incapacity to create a political "mystique" in Latin America. Despite the grand purposes and elevated language at its founding, the Alliance had come to seem just another aid program. As Tad Szulc, a *New York Times* journalist, put it,

> . . . the concept of the Alliance somehow failed to electrify Latin America, contrary to what optimists in Washington had hoped and notwithstanding the early Latin American enthusiasm for the new Administration. Despite the noble and inspiring words of President Kennedy, the Alliance quickly proved to be virtually empty of the desperately needed political and psychological content. It was unable to project a mystique that would captivate the attention and the imagination of Latin Americans—as the Castro revolution had done in Cuba and in the rest of the Hemisphere.

That the Alliance for Progress failed to develop a mystique that inspired and involved the people of Latin America was true enough. But that failure could not, as these writers imagined, be attributed to an inattention to ideology or a paucity of public-relations efforts on the part of Washington. Though its backers did not realize it, the weakness of its political appeal was inherent in the basic theory of the Alliance itself.

If we examine the major premises of that theory closely, we can begin to see why it was bound to fail in Latin America. I shall consider four of these premises: (1) elitism and the fear of mass action (revolution from the top); (2) social change as manipulation by outside agencies (revolution from the outside); (3) maintenance of existing economic arrangements while "expanding the pie" for all (nondisruptive revolution); and (4) violence as the prerogative of the established order (nonviolent revolution). Each premise was essential to Kennedy's global liberalism. Each had its counterpart, too, in his domestic liberalism. The Alliance was to be an elaborate projection of the Kennedy Administration's pragmatic liberal faith—and a telling commentary on the illusions sustaining that faith. . . .

THE ALLIANCE FURTHERED IMPERIALISM

The Alliance for Progress, despite its noble pretensions, furthered American imperialism[3] in Latin America. While most of its reforms failed to take hold, its efforts to maintain and increase American investments in the hemisphere were substantially successful. To some backers of the Alliance this outcome was no doubt satisfactory; their commitments had always been to the American corporate order in Latin America. In Kennedy's case, however, the Alliance was a profound disappointment. Kennedy was not a self-conscious or cynical imperialist. His motives were more complex; indeed, they were a prime source of the sort of contradictions that beset the Alliance from the outset.

Kennedy's relationship to the business community with regard to Latin America illustrated some of these contradictions. During the early days of the Alliance he spoke of putting the national interest of the United States (in Latin American development) above the interests of American corporations; further, he criticized the traditional idea that private investment was the panacea for Latin America's problems. In the Charter of Punta del Este encouragement of private enterprise was only one of the numerous goals—and it was overshadowed by the more dramatic reforms. But American business was not happy about being relegated to this secondary place in U.S. policy toward Latin America. Hence, Schlesinger[4] reports, the Alliance came under "growing pressure from United States companies doing Latin American business to talk less about social reform and more about private investment."

As investment in Latin America lagged, Kennedy eventually succumbed to the pressure. References to the virtue of foreign investments now became more frequent in his

3. the policy of extending a nation's authority by territorial acquisition or by the establishment of economic or political predominance over other nations 4. Arthur Schlesinger, presidential adviser and author of *A Thousand Days*

speeches. By the time of his 1963 message to Congress on foreign aid, this had become a dominant theme: "The primary initiative in this year's program relates to our increased efforts to encourage the investment of private capital in the underdeveloped countries." Such capital was, he told the Inter-American Press Association on November 18, 1963, a key to the Alliance's eventual success: "If encouraged, private investment, responsive to the needs, the laws, and the interests of the nation, can cooperate with public activity to provide the vital margin of success as it did in the development of all the nations of the West. . . ."

. . . It was not business pressure, however, or business connections that ultimately made John Kennedy the servant of American imperialism in Latin America. A more crucial factor was his own ideological conviction. Kennedy saw himself, not as a tool of American corporations, but as a proponent of Latin American modernization. In the theory of modernization he had adopted, American investment was an aid to Latin American development; the profits flowing back to the United States were matched by the Latin Americans' profit in obtaining a modern industrial base. The protection and extension of the American economic stake in the hemisphere benefited all concerned. Kennedy thus was ill equipped to notice the contradictions: capital flowing out of Latin America faster than it flowed in, American corporations "developing" Latin America by exploiting its resources and subordinating its economic needs to their own, "nationalistic" and "progressive" bourgeoisie who collaborated with American corporate allies in maintaining a stagnant status quo. For all his analysis of Latin America's problems, Kennedy never grasped what was the single greatest roadblock to its progress—American imperialism.

Kennedy's goals in Latin America—material progress linked with reform, military suppression of revolutionary activity, protection of American property holdings—were, in his mind, fully consistent and congruent. But the first did not materialize; the record for the second was mixed; only the last was effectively accomplished. Reform and growth could not coexist in Latin America with repression and imperialist exploitation. Whatever generous and liberating impulses Kennedy's mode of global liberalism possessed were, therefore, inevitably subordinated in Latin America to its more selfish and repressive aims.

CHAPTER 5

Confronting Khrushchev and Waging the Cold War

The Kennedy-Khrushchev Meeting in Vienna

Kenneth P. O'Donnell and David F. Powers with Joe McCarthy

Kenneth P. O'Donnell recalls the first meeting between President Kennedy and Nikita Khrushchev in Vienna, Austria, in June 1961, five months after Kennedy had taken office. O'Donnell describes three phases of talks: light conversation, testing of one another's resolve, and serious disagreements and threats over the issue of Berlin. According to O'Donnell, Kennedy remained firm and calm during the discussions; afterward, in private, Kennedy reflected on Khrushchev's threats and the ramifications of a war over Berlin. Kenneth P. O'Donnell was Kennedy's political strategist from 1952 to 1963. David F. Powers, Kennedy's closest friend, was a campaign and presidential aide and a staff member on the John F. Kennedy Memorial Library. Joe McCarthy was the president's friend and confidant.

Despite his determination to avoid a nuclear war, President Kennedy was equally determined not to back away from a threat of such a war if there was no other means of stopping the Soviets from dominating the Western world. He came into office realizing that Khrushchev was certain that the United States would never take the risk of atomic war to defend its position of world leadership, and he decided that one of his first hard duties as President was to convince Khrushchev and the other Communists that their confident assumption was wrong. "I have to show him that we can be just as tough as he is," Kennedy said when he first discussed the possibility of a meeting with Khrushchev. "I can't do that sending messages to him through other people. I'll have to

From *Johnny, We Hardly Knew Ye*, by Kenneth P. O'Donnell and David F. Powers (with Joe McCarthy). Copyright ©1970, 1972 by Kenneth P. O'Donnell, David F. Powers, and Joe McCarthy. Reprinted by permission of Little, Brown and Company.

sit down with him, and let him see who he's dealing with."
Negotiations for a Kennedy-Khrushchev meeting in Europe began in March, less than two months after the 1961 inauguration, but the date and the place, the first weekend in June at Vienna, were not finally set until May. . . .

We had arrived that morning in Vienna in a downpour of rain, but a huge crowd of Austrians had turned out to give Jackie and the President a wild welcome when our motorcade made its way through the streets from the airport to the Alte Hofburg, the Austrian White House, where the Kennedys were received by President Adolf Scharf. . . .

KENNEDY AND KHRUSHCHEV TEST EACH OTHER'S RESOLVE

The first talk at the American Embassy started with some bantering between the President and the Premier. Khrushchev reminded the group that he had met Kennedy before, in 1959, at a meeting of the Senate Foreign Relations Committee in Washington. "I remember you said that I looked young to be a Senator," Kennedy remarked, "but I've aged a lot since then.". . .

But when the conversation moved into serious channels, Khrushchev began to get rough and blustery. "He is no slouch in an argument," Kennedy told us later. "When I complained about his support of Communist minorities fighting popular majorities, he came back at me with our support of Franco and Chiang Kai-shek." But those of us who were with Kennedy during the Vienna talks—and that includes the principal American advisers, such as Rusk,[1] Llewellyn Thompson, Charles Bohlen and Foy Kohler, who sat in on the conversations—have no recollection of the President being cowed or overpowered by Khrushchev's fist-waving as some of the recent Kennedy-downgraders now claim. In every exchange of hard shots, Kennedy gave as good, and often better, than he received. Khrushchev himself said later that he came away from Vienna with a respect for Kennedy's reasoning and firmness. "Unlike Eisenhower," Khrushchev said in his memoirs, "Kennedy had a precisely formulated opinion on every subject."

Khrushchev was often backed into a corner where he had no choice but to change the subject. Kennedy's intensive study of previous American-Russian discussions and his

1. Dean Rusk, Secretary of State

own debating skill made him well prepared to handle Khrushchev's thrusts. At one point Khrushchev complained because he had not been invited to sign the Japanese peace treaty. "You went over that at length with President Eisenhower in 1959," Kennedy said. "Why bring it up again? It's an old issue." Khrushchev drew back in surprise and switched to another question. When Khrushchev was demanding a withdrawal of Allied troops from Germany, he pointed out that Roosevelt had promised at Yalta to make such a withdrawal within two to four years after the end of World War II. "President Roosevelt said we would withdraw our troops if Germany was reunited under one government," Kennedy said. No further argument.

At another point in a heated debate, Kennedy said, "Do you ever admit a mistake?"

"Certainly," Khrushchev said. "In a speech before the Twentieth Party Congress, I admitted all of Stalin's mistakes."

"Those were Stalin's mistakes," Kennedy said. "Not your mistakes.". . .

It was at lunch that day that Kennedy made his remark about the Lenin peace medal that Khrushchev was wearing: "I hope you get to keep it." After the luncheon, Kennedy and Khrushchev went outside for a walk in the garden, alone except for their two interpreters. . . . Khrushchev was carrying on a heated argument, circling around Kennedy and snapping at him like a terrier and shaking his finger, while Kennedy strolled casually on the lawn, stopping now and then to say a few words, not at all upset or angry. . . .

SERIOUS DISCUSSIONS CONCERNING BERLIN

Khrushchev had been complaining in the garden about the Berlin situation and the American support of a reunified Germany. He had no sympathy for Germany, he said, because his son was killed in the war by the Germans. "I reminded him that my brother had died in the war, too," Kennedy told us, "and I also reminded him that we didn't come here to Vienna to talk about a war of twenty years ago. I told him that we can't turn our backs on the West Germans and pull out of Berlin, and that's that. But he keeps on yelling about signing a separate treaty with East Germany, just as [French president Charles] De Gaulle said he would threaten to do."

When the formal talks resumed that Saturday afternoon, Khrushchev gave in quickly and easily on the Laos problem, agreeing to a cease-fire in the war there between the Communists and the government troops. "I thought he would use Laos to give himself more leverage against us in Berlin, as he could have done," Kennedy said later. But Khrushchev refused to budge on the Berlin issue and on Kennedy's request for a nuclear test ban. Urging the test ban, Kennedy used the Chinese proverb, "A journey of a thousand miles begins with one step."

"You seem to know the Chinese very well," Khrushchev said.

"We may both get to know them better," Kennedy said.

Khrushchev groaned, and said, "I know them well enough now."

 KHRUSHCHEV INTIMIDATES KENNEDY

In an excerpt from his book, A Question of Character: A Life of John F. Kennedy, *Thomas C. Reeves portrays the Vienna meeting as a Kennedy failure and a Khrushchev victory.*

Khrushchev publicly called his talks with Kennedy "a very good beginning." The Soviet Foreign Ministry spokesman said that the premier was "very satisfied." A *New York Times* reporter observed that Khrushchev "left the impression with Austria that he was quite confident he had achieved what he had come here to obtain."

The Soviet leader's elation may well have been over his belief that his earlier estimation of Kennedy was correct: he was a lightweight. (In his memoirs Khrushchev recalled thinking at the time that the young president "was a reasonable man" who "knew he wouldn't be justified in starting a war over Berlin.") Scholar-diplomat George Kennan said later that he was sure Kennedy had given the premier that impression. After reading the transcript of the Vienna conclave himself, he was "very disappointed" and thought Kennedy "strangely tongue-tied." Kennan ascribed this failing to the President's youth, inexperience, and lack of a well-thought-out policy on communism.

Thomas C. Reeves, *A Question of Character: A Life of John F. Kennedy.* New York: The Free Press, a division of Macmillan, 1991.

That night at the Austrian President's state dinner at the Schonbrunn Palace, Khrushchev sat next to Jackie Kennedy and joked with her all evening. On Sunday morning the Kennedys went to a nine o'clock mass at Saint Stephan's Cathedral, where they listened to the Vienna Boys' Choir, and an hour later the President went to the Soviet Embassy for the last of his scheduled meetings with Khrushchev. Their talk was so unsatisfactory that Kennedy asked for one more session alone with Khrushchev after lunch. "I can't leave here without giving it one more try," he said.

That afternoon in their last private talk together Khrushchev flatly threatened Kennedy with war if the United States insisted on defending its rights in West Berlin after Russia signed a separate treaty with East Germany, which, he said, would take place in December of that year, six months away. All of Berlin would then become East German territory, and if the Western Allies did not withdraw their troops from the city before that deadline, "force would be met with force." The only concession that Khrushchev tentatively offered was one that he knew Kennedy could not accept: the Russians and East Germans might agree to let a small token force of American and Western European troops remain in West Berlin, not as occupation forces but as a part of a United Nations police force along with an equal number of Soviet military units. But, Khrushchev shouted, his decision to sign the treaty allowing East Germany to seize West Berlin in December was "firm" and "irrevocable" and "you can tell that to Macmillan, De Gaulle and Adenauer,[2] and if that means war, the Soviet Union will accept the challenge."

Kennedy looked at Khrushchev calmly and said to him, "It's going to be a cold winter."

A few minutes later when Kennedy and Rusk were leaving the Soviet Embassy and the President and the Premier posed before the photographers with a final handshake, Khrushchev was his old merry self again, laughing and joking, but Kennedy was not smiling. I would describe the President's mood when he returned to the American Embassy that afternoon as cool and controlled, not at all rattled or discouraged by Khrushchev's attempt to bully him. . . .

[Kennedy said,] "I'd like to get across to the people at home the seriousness of the situation, and the *New York Times* would be the place to do it. I'll give Scotty[3] a grim picture. But actually, as De Gaulle says, Khrushchev is bluffing and he'll never sign that treaty. Anybody who talks the way he did today, and really means it, would be crazy, and

2. Harold Macmillan, Prime Minister of Great Britain; Charles de Gaulle, President of France; Konrad Adenauer, Chancellor of West Germany 3. James "Scotty" Reston

I'm sure he's not crazy.". . .

Reston's story in the *New York Times* described Kennedy as "shaken" and "angry." He was certainly angry with Khrushchev's attitude and with the situation that Khrushchev was creating, but if he felt any panic, he kept it well concealed. That night on the plane, while we were flying from Vienna to London, he called me[4] into his cabin and talked with me alone for more than an hour about what he had been through with Khrushchev over the past two days, and about the danger of a possible war with Russia that he would be facing in the months to come. . . .

KENNEDY REFLECTS ON THE BERLIN CRISIS

Uppermost in his mind that night, and during the months of tension in our dealings with Khrushchev that followed over the next year, was the disproportion between cause and effect in allowing a dispute over questionable West German rights to Berlin to start a nuclear world war. "All wars start from stupidity," Kennedy said. "God knows I'm not an isolationist, but it seems particularly stupid to risk killing a million Americans over an argument about access rights on an Autobahn in the Soviet zone of Germany, or because the Germans want Germany reunified. If I'm going to threaten Russia with a nuclear war, it will have to be for much bigger and more important reasons than that. Before I back Khrushchev against the wall and put him to a final test, the freedom of all of Western Europe will have to be at stake.". . .

Kennedy honored our commitment in West Berlin as a pledge that never could be broken, because he felt that pulling out of the city would turn West Germany against the United States and Britain, and lead to a breakup of the NATO alliance. At the same time he was realistic enough to see the hope of a reunited East and West Germany as an impossible dream, and he could understand Russia's dissatisfaction with the continued presence of Western occupation forces and a pocket of Western free enterprise economy in Berlin, deep in the heart of Communist German territory. The real reason why Khrushchev wanted to seize and seal off West Berlin, Kennedy said that night—and Khrushchev himself later frankly admitted in his memoirs—was an economic one. The Soviet leader wanted to shut down West Berlin's

4. Kenneth O'Donnell, political strategist for Kennedy

thriving capitalistic business system, which was luring thousands of job-hungry East Germans from the socialist side of the city and seriously draining East Germany's manpower. "You can't blame Khrushchev for being sore about that," Kennedy said. . . .

Again Kennedy expressed strong doubt that Khrushchev, for all his shouting, would ever actually sign a separate treaty with East Germany. But we would have to be careful in the months to come, he added, not to make a sudden military move or a quick buildup of force that might alarm Khrushchev into making a rash countermove. I particularly remember Kennedy's closing remark when the plane was descending for its landing in London. "If we're going to have to start a nuclear war," he said, "we'll have to fix things so it will be started by the President of the United States, and nobody else. Not by a trigger-happy sergeant on a truck convoy at a checkpoint in East Germany."

KHRUSHCHEV SOFTENS HIS RHETORIC

Even though Kennedy's meeting with Khrushchev in Vienna ended in flat disagreement on the two big issues, Berlin and nuclear testing, both of them gained an understanding and a respect for each other during the talks that served the United States and Russia well in the later crisis periods. As annoyed as he was at times with Khrushchev over the next two years, Kennedy often found him more reasonable than some of our allies. It was obvious in their later correspondence that Khrushchev had a strong personal admiration for Kennedy. His first letter to the President after their rough farewell session in Vienna sounded as if he was anxious to assure Kennedy that his threats at the conference table should not be taken too seriously:

Dear Mr. President,

In Vienna, you told me that you are fond of collecting models of vessels. It is with pleasure that I am sending you a model of an American whaler of which I told you during one of our conversations. This model made of walrus tusk and whalebone was carved from memory by a talented, self-taught Chuktchi craftsman. Such sail-steam vessels were in use in the end of the 19th century in the Chuktchi Sea for whale-fishing and they would visit Russian harbors. I will be glad if the model of this vessel becomes part of your collection.

It is also a pleasure for Nina Petrovna and myself to fulfill Mrs. Kennedy's wish and to send to you and your family little

"Pushinka," a direct offspring of the well known cosmos-traveler "Strelka," which made a trip in a cosmic ship on August 19, 1960, and successfully returned to earth.

I would like to express my hope that the model of the vessel and "Pushinka" will be of pleasure to you and will serve as a good remembrance of our meetings and conversations in Vienna.

I avail myself of this opportunity to extend on behalf of Nina Petrovna and myself our best wishes to you, your wife and all your family.

Yours respectfully,
N. KHRUSHCHEV

Dave[5] and I happened to be with the President and Jackie in their apartment in the White House on the day when the Soviet Ambassador and two of his staff men appeared with the ship model and Pushinka, a nervous and white fluffy puppy, and a daughter of the dog that traveled into outer space on the second Soviet Sputnik flight. The President stared at the dog and then stared at Jackie, who put her hand to her mouth and whispered, "I was only trying to make some conversation." It seems that at the state dinner in Vienna she had asked Khrushchev about the space-flying dog, and when he said that the dog recently had pups, she said, "Why don't you send me one?" In due time, Pushinka made herself at home in the White House and became a pampered member of the family.

The summer the growing crisis in Berlin and the urgent question of how to cope with Khrushchev took up almost all of the President's working hours. . . .

THE BERLIN WALL

Then, on August 13, the East Germans built the Berlin Wall. It was said and written at the time that the building of the wall shocked and depressed Kennedy. Actually, he saw the wall as the turning point that would lead to the end of the Berlin crisis. He said to me, "Why would Khrushchev put up a wall if he really intended to seize West Berlin? There wouldn't be any need of a wall if he occupied the whole city. This is his way out of his predicament. It's not a very nice solution, but a wall is a hell of a lot better than a war."

To reassure the excited West Berliners, Kennedy sent Lyn-

5. Dave Powers, presidential aide

don Johnson to their city to wave the American flag and to make a fiery speech pledging our armed support to their freedom and independence. The Vice-President was not happy about making the trip, especially when he learned that the President had ordered a battle group of fifteen hundred American troops to move into West Berlin from Helmstedt in West Germany while he was there. "There'll be a lot of shooting, and I'll be in the middle of it," Lyndon said. "Why me?" It took some coaxing before he agreed, with a deep sigh, to undertake the mission.

But the convoy of American infantry soldiers moved along the Autobahn in East Germany into Berlin with no interference from the Soviet occupation troops. Johnson was waiting to greet them when they arrived, and his appearance in the city was a big success. He came back to Washington thrilled by the whole experience. When the Berlin Wall was built, Kennedy was attacked by some critics because he did not knock it down. I asked him later if anybody in the government had suggested such a move. "Not one person in the Defense Department or the State Department ever mentioned such an idea," he said. "What right did we have to touch that wall? It was in East German territory."

As Kennedy had predicted, the building of the wall brought the situation in Berlin down to a slow simmer, stemming the flow of refugees from East Germany, the immediate cause of Khrushchev's dissatisfaction. . . .

On October 21, Khrushchev told the Congress of the Soviet Communist party that he was not going to insist on signing a separate treaty with East Germany before the end of the year. Temporarily, at least, the Berlin crisis was over.

The Berlin Crisis

Theodore C. Sorensen

Theodore C. Sorensen explains Kennedy's handling of the Berlin crisis, which was initiated at a meeting between Kennedy and Soviet president Nikita Khrushchev in Vienna in June 1961. At that meeting, Khrushchev threatened to sign a separate treaty with East Germany and eliminate the western presence in Berlin. Kennedy decided that western rights in West Berlin had to be preserved regardless of risk or cost to the United States. Sorensen identifies Kennedy's strategy: to build troop strength in Europe, to talk to the American people about the importance of remaining in Berlin, and to solicit support from American leaders and western allies. Though Khrushchev erected the Berlin Wall, the crisis gradually receded and a permanent western presence in Berlin was established. Theodore C. Sorensen was legislative assistant to Senator Kennedy from 1953 to 1961 and special council to and speech writer for President Kennedy from 1961 to 1963. Sorensen is the author of Decision-Making in the White House.

The President's first and most basic decision [after meeting with Khrushchev in Vienna] was that the preservation of Western rights in West Berlin was an objective for which the United States was required to incur any cost, including the risk of nuclear war. It was reported by some that he was obsessed by the fear that he might be ordering his country's semiextinction. He was, in fact, calmly convinced that an unflinching stand for West Berlin's freedom would, in the long run, lessen the prospects for a nuclear war, while yielding on West Berlin would only weaken the future credibility of our defenses. Asked at a July [1961] news conference about a report that the Soviet Ambassador, departing Washington for a new post, had sneered that "when the chips are down, the

United States won't fight for Berlin," Kennedy replied matter-of-factly: "We intend to honor our commitments."...

KENNEDY PLANS TROOP BUILD-UP

Kennedy regarded the existing strategy as a weak and dangerous position. The imbalance of ground forces which the two sides could readily deploy in the area was an excessive temptation to Khrushchev to cut off access to West Berlin so gradually that we would never respond with a nuclear attack. "If Mr. Khrushchev believes that all we have is the atomic bomb," he said, "he is going to feel that we are . . . somewhat unlikely to use it."

The President sought therefore to fill that gap with a rapid build-up of combat troops in Central Europe—with a contingent large enough to convince Khrushchev that our vital interests were so deeply involved that we would use any means to prevent the defeat or capture of those forces. This required a force large enough to prevent any cheap and easy seizure of the city by East German guards alone, which would weaken our bargaining power—and large enough to permit a true "pause," a month instead of an hour before choosing nuclear war or retreat, time to bring up reserves, to demonstrate our determination, to make a deliberate decision and to communicate at the highest levels before the "ultimate" weapons were used. Only in this way, Kennedy was convinced, could Khrushchev be dissuaded from slowly shutting off West Berlin. . . .

On the afternoon of Wednesday, July 19, [1961] meeting at 3 P.M. with a small group of us in his living quarters on the second floor of the Mansion, the President put the finishing touches on his plan. After six weeks of intensive meetings, he stated each decision in firm, precise tones. The additional military budget requests would total $3.2 billion rather than $4.3 billion. The Congress would be asked to provide stand-by authority to call up the Reserves, rather than an immediate mobilization. Draft calls would be more than tripled, West Berlin would be readied, Allied agreement on economic sanctions would be sought, a temporary tax increase would be requested (this decision . . . was later reversed) and no declaration of national emergency would be proclaimed. . . .

The President also decided, contrary to Acheson's paper and the initially prevailing view among his advisers, that the West should "lean forward" on negotiations. . . . He had no intentions of lulling the West into believing that a meeting at the negotiating table reduced all danger. But he did have hopes of persuading Khrushchev to postpone his treaty as long as alternatives were being actively explored.

Before Khrushchev could be presented with any agreed-upon new ideas, however, the West had to produce some new ideas and agree upon them—and neither had happened by mid-July. Indeed, the difficulty of finding any new ideas which could be sold to all concerned would remain throughout Kennedy's term. The French were against all negotiations; the British were against risking war without negotiations; and the Germans, as their autumn elections drew nearer, were against both of these positions and seemingly everything else. The necessarily generalized passages dealing with diplomatic approaches were thus the weakest parts of the President's July 25 TV address. Nevertheless, by underlining our willingness to talk "with any and all nations that are willing to talk, and listen, with reason"—our willingness "to remove any actual irritants in West Berlin [though] the freedom of that city is not negotiable"—and our willingness to submit the legality of our rights to "international adjudication" and our presence in West Berlin to a free vote among its people, he at least struck in a few moments more positive notes than he had been able to obtain in seven weeks from the American and Allied diplomats. . . . Its basic message was firm and urgent without resort to threats or fear. I had completed the first draft over the weekend. . . .

Finally, with all changes and clearances completed and coordinated along the lines of the President's instructions, I took his reading copy for the 10 P.M. talk over to the Mansion around eight o'clock. I found the President sitting up in bed, a hot pad behind his back, scribbling out a personal note with which to close.

When I ran for the Presidency of the United States, I knew that this country faced serious challenges, but I could not realize, nor could any man realize who does not bear the burdens of this office, how heavy and constant would be those burdens. . . . In these days and weeks I ask for your help, and your advice. I ask for your suggestions, when you think we could do better. All of us, I know, love our country, and we shall all do our best to serve it. In meeting my responsibilities in these coming months as President, I need your good will, and your support and, above all, your prayers.

It was a somber close for a somber speech—a speech more somber, in fact, than the American people were accustomed to accept, more somber than any previous Presidential speech in the age of mutual nuclear capabilities. "West Berlin has now become," he said,

the great testing place of Western courage and will, a focal point where our solemn commitments . . . and Soviet ambitions now meet in basic confrontation.

We cannot and will not permit the Communists to drive us out of Berlin, either gradually or by force. For the fulfillment of our pledge to that city is essential to the morale and security of Western Germany, to the unity of Western Europe, and to the faith of the entire free world. . . . It is as secure . . . as the rest of us, for we cannot separate its safety from our own. . . . We will at all times be ready to talk, if talk will help. But we must also be ready to resist with force, if force is used upon us. Either alone would fail. Together, they can serve the cause of freedom and peace. . . .

To sum it all up: we seek peace, but we shall not surrender. That is the central meaning of this crisis, and the meaning of your government's policy. With your help, and the help of other free men, this crisis can be surmounted. Freedom can prevail and peace can endure.

THE BERLIN WALL GOES UP

. . . In mid-August a crisis within the crisis came dangerously close to the flash point. The Communists had for some years, over Western protest, gradually increased the legal—and in some cases physical—barriers between West and East Berlin, including temporary closings of most crossing points, special traffic and entry permits and a prohibition against West Berliners working in East Berlin. Sensing that they were gradually becoming imprisoned, East Germans and East Berliners poured increasingly across the dividing line between East and West Berlin, the principal hole in the Iron Curtain. By the summer of 1961 some 3.5 million had left their homes and jobs for the refugee centers and airports of West Berlin, draining the already depressed East German economy of its lifeblood and dramatizing to all the world their choice of freedom over Communism. In August, as the fear of war or more repression increased, the daily flow of refugees rose from the hundreds to the thousands. Khrushchev's response on August 13—due possibly in part to Kennedy's speech and to [Charles] De Gaulle's veto of four-power negotiations, but certainly due primarily to the hemorrhage of East German manpower—was the Wall.

The Berlin Wall—sealing off the border between the two cities with a high, grim barrier of concrete and barbed wire, separating families and friends, keeping East Germans in, free Germans out and Western access to East Berlin on a more limited basis—shocked the free world. Kennedy promptly turned to his aides and allies for advice; but there was little useful they could say in such a situation.

All agreed that the East German regime had long had the power to halt border crossings, was bound to do it sooner or later and had at least done so before the West could be accused of provoking it. All agreed also that the Wall—built on East German territory, the latest and worst in a thirteen-year-long series of such actions in the Soviet-administered zone—was illegal, immoral and inhumane, but not a cause for war. It ended West Berlin's role as a showcase and escape route for the East, but it did not interfere with the three basic objectives the West had long stressed: our presence in West Berlin, our access to West Berlin and the freedom of West Berliners to choose their own system. Not one responsible official—in this country, in West Berlin, West Germany or Western Europe—suggested that Allied forces should march into East German territory and tear the Wall down. . . .

KENNEDY'S RESPONSE TO THE WALL

The President was nevertheless convinced that some response was required—not to threaten the Communists for their blatant admission of failure but to restore morale among the shocked and sickened West Berliners. Our contingency plans had been prepared for interference with our access to West Berlin, not emigration from the East. Our intelligence estimates, although recognizing that the Communists would have to control their loss of manpower, had offered no advance warning of this specific move. Kennedy thus had to improvise on his own; and meanwhile crucial time—too much time—went by.

Finally, to test Communist intentions and demonstrate our own, he dispatched an additional contingent of fifteen hundred American troops down the *Autobahn,* riding in armored trucks through the East German checkpoints to West Berlin. Obviously fifteen hundred more troops could not hold the city against a direct Soviet attack, he said, but "the West Berliners

KENNEDY TOUCHES THE HEARTS OF BERLINERS
In A Hero for Our Time: An Intimate Story of the
Kennedy Years, *Ralph G. Martin describes the powerful surge of emotion Kennedy set off in the crowd of Berliners gathered on the platform of City Hall when he expressed
his identification with them in their own language.*

Bobby had talked to his brother informally about saying
something in German while he was in Berlin, and the President explored the idea with McGeorge Bundy.

"*Ich bin ein Berliner*[1] was not my idea; it was his," Bundy
insisted. "I just told him how to say it in German. He had
no feeling for the German language. He had no feeling for
any foreign language. That's because he had no sense of
music, no *ear.* So there we were in the goddamn airplane,
coming down on Berlin, while he repeated the phrase over
and over again—I don't know how many times. But they
knew what he said, and it worked. God, how it worked!"

As far as Kennedy could see there were thousands of
faces so closely packed they seemed almost a single mass
with a single voice chanting his name over and over again.
These were a people in danger and he was their hero who
would save them, protect them. Such was their emotion
that some of the Kennedy staff on the platform were in
tears.

The crowd's emotion caught Kennedy when he shouted,
"Today in the world of freedom, the proudest boast is *Ich
bin ein Berliner.*"

The response was unimaginable, almost an animal roar,
as if every person there was venting the frustration of a
lifetime in a single exciting, exhilarating moment. He had
touched the exact nerve with the exact phrase.

He intensified the hysteria when he added "There are
many people in the world who really don't understand, or
say they don't, what is the great issue between the free
world and the Communist world.

"Let them come to Berlin! . . ."

The roar was so intense and so prolonged that Kennedy
felt he could have asked them to march to the Berlin Wall
and tear it down and they would have done it.

Ralph C. Martin, *A Hero for Our Time: An Intimate Story of the Kennedy Years.*
New York: Macmillan, 1983.

1. I am a Berliner.

would benefit from a reminder of [our] commitment... at this time," and the Soviets would recognize the troops as "our hostage to that intent." It was his most anxious moment during the prolonged Berlin crisis, his first order of American military units into a potential confrontation with Soviet forces. Postponing his usual weekend change of scenery to the Hyannis Port White House, he kept his military aide in constant touch with the convoy's commander. When the first group of sixty trucks turned unimpeded into West Berlin, he felt that a turning point in the crisis had been reached.

Simultaneously he dispatched Vice President Johnson to address the people of West Berlin, to rally their hope and their will, and to restate this nation's commitment in the language (personally approved by the President) of our most solemn pledge: "our lives, our fortunes, our sacred honor."

Accompanying Johnson—and returning to West Berlin shortly thereafter for a prolonged stay as Kennedy's personal emissary—was retired General Lucius Clay, a hero to West Berliners. Clay had been in command in 1948 when a Soviet land blockade of West Berlin had required a massive Western airlift. A constant spur to Allied effort and a beloved symbol to West Berliners, Clay's presence was highly valued by the President despite his tendency to be something of an alarmist in his private cables, sometimes hinting he might resign unless his requests were granted. . . .

The basic objective of the military, the Johnson and the Clay missions was to rekindle hope in West Berlin. Its spirit had been damaged by the Wall, its role altered, its future as the ultimate capital of a reunited Germany darkened. Khrushchev predicted that it would soon be a dying, withering city. Many Westerners as well saw little prospects of inducing new industry and labor to locate there or even inducing its present residents to remain. Some urged its complete incorporation into West Germany; but Kennedy felt that that would close out all hope of ever reuniting the city, and merely provoke the Soviets into further acts with no real gain for the West. Instead, starting with these three missions, a major effort was made under Walt Rostow to maintain and increase the viability of West Berlin—to enhance its economic, educational and cultural roles—to attract young families, new investments and world understanding. That effort succeeded, and in the years that followed West Berlin not only survived but flourished.

The Wall, however, remained—and it was an ugly source of tension. At one stage Western and Soviet tanks and troops faced each other across the barricade until the Soviets drew back. American tests of our rights to enter East Berlin—and to ignore Red warnings about keeping Westerners one hundred meters away from the Wall in West Berlin—were all successful. But no one knew when either side, convinced that the other would back down, might precipitate a situation from which neither could back down. The Soviet resumption of nuclear testing in September added to the atmosphere of belligerence. . . .

TENSION RECEDES

The President speculated as to when the great confrontation would come, when a Soviet-German peace treaty would be signed and when a move would be made to cut off access. But the confrontation never came. The December, 1961, deadline passed without any treaty. Slowly, imperceptibly, the tides of crisis receded. From time to time they would rise suddenly again, with an incident at the Wall or on the access routes. The most serious was a deliberate Soviet test in the early months of 1962 on the air corridors from West Germany to West Berlin. . . . In time the interference ended, and the tides of crisis once more receded.

They receded in part, we must assume, because Khrushchev recognized more clearly that turning access over to the East Germans was a highly dangerous venture—and in part because the ending of East German emigration eased the pressure on him for immediate action. But they also receded because Kennedy finally succeeded in getting his side ready to talk as well as fight, in changing the East-West confrontation to one of words instead of weapons. "Winston Churchill," observed the President, "said it is better to jaw, jaw than war, war, and we shall continue to jaw, jaw and see if we can produce a useful result. . . . That [is] the purpose . . . in calling up 160,000 men [and] adding billions of dollars to our defense budget . . . not to fight a nuclear war."

THE PRESIDENT'S PLAN FOR TALKS

To jaw, jaw, however, Kennedy had to overcome stout resistance within his own administration and within the Western Alliance; and it must be said that he never fully succeeded with either. . . .

The President decided, therefore, that the United States would jaw, jaw on its own as a self-appointed agent for the Alliance. Theoretically we were to engage, not in "negotiations," but in "exploratory talks to see whether serious negotiations could be undertaken.". . .

The talks were carried on—in New York, Moscow, Geneva and Washington, in meetings between [Dean] Rusk and [Andrei] Gromyko, [Llewellyn] Thompson and Gromyko, Rusk and [Anatoly] Dobrynin, and Kennedy and Gromyko. Proposals were discussed in the Kennedy-Khrushchev letters and in Kennedy's meetings with Adzhubei.[1] But no real progress was made. . . .

The talks nevertheless served the purpose of defining the U.S. position more precisely, making clear what we would and would not fight for or talk about. By stressing that his essential objectives were carefully limited, Kennedy thereby stressed that his commitment to defend them was unlimited. . . .

But even in 1963, after the Cuban missile crisis and the nuclear Test Ban Treaty had helped change the bargaining atmosphere, no agreement was reached or in sight. Khrushchev did, however, remove his pressure and halt his threats; and the President believed that our demonstrated willingness to talk—by holding out the possibility of a reasonable settlement, by treating the Soviet Union as a great power and by making clear to the world that the intransigence was not on our side—had contributed in its own way to the peaceful defense of West Berlin. "Jaw, jaw" for its own sake had been helpful and effective, and Kennedy was not pushing for any new solutions now that the pressure was off.

In 1963 the Wall was still there, but the East Germans had initiated proposals for openings in exchange for trade. West Berlin was still a city in danger, an island of freedom and prosperity deep within imprisoned East Germany. And incidents still occurred—including an unseemly squabble in the fall of 1963 over whether Western troops at the *Autobahn* checkpoints needed to dismount or lower their truck tailgates to be counted. But access to West Berlin remained free—West Berlin remained free—and neither a devastating nuclear war, nor a collapse of the Western Alliance, nor a one-sided treaty of peace had taken place as once feared. "I

---

1. Aleksei Adzhubei, Khrushchev's son-in-law, editor of *Izvestia* (Russian newspaper), and member of the Central Committee

think [the Communists] realize," said President Kennedy, "that West Berlin is a vital interest to us . . . and that we are going to stay there."

KENNEDY GOES TO WEST BERLIN

The West Berliners also realized it. They gave John Kennedy the most overwhelming reception of his career on the twenty-sixth of June, 1963. The size of the crowd, their shouts and the look of hope and gratitude in their eyes moved some in our party to tears—even before we surveyed the Wall. The President—who would later remark that his trip had given him a far deeper understanding of the necessity of ultimate reunification—was moved to extemporaneous eloquence. "When I leave tonight," he told a trade union conference, "the United States stays." "You are now their hostages," he said to the American troops stationed in the city, "you are . . . the arrowhead." And at a luncheon given by Mayor Brandt at Berlin City Hall, he offered a toast "to the German people on both sides of the Wall [and] to the cause of freedom on both sides of the Wall."

It was on the platform outside that City Hall—from where I could see only a sea of human faces chanting "Kenne-dy," "Kenne-dy" as far as my vision could reach—that he delivered one of his most inspired and inspiring talks:

> Two thousand years ago the proudest boast was "Civis Romanus sum."[2] Today, in the world of freedom, the proudest boast is "Ich bin ein Berliner."[3]

> There are many people in the world who really don't understand, or say they don't, what is the great issue between the free world and the Communist world. Let them come to Berlin. There are some who say that Communism is the wave of the future. Let them come to Berlin. . . . And there are even a few who say that it is true that Communism is an evil system, but it permits us to make economic progress. "Lasst sie nach Berlin kommen."[4]

> Freedom has many difficulties and democracy is not perfect, but we have never had to put a wall up to keep our people in. . . .

> We . . . look forward to that day when this city will be joined as one—and this country, and this great continent of Europe—in a peaceful and hopeful globe. When that day finally comes, as it will, the people of West Berlin can take sober satisfaction in the fact that they were in the front lines for almost two decades.

2. I am a citizen of Rome.   3. I am a Berliner.   4. Let them come to Berlin.

All free men, wherever they may live, are citizens of Berlin, and, therefore, as a free man, I take pride in the words "Ich bin ein Berliner."

As we departed that evening to fly over East Germany to Ireland, the President was glowing from his reception. It would make all Americans recognize that their efforts and risks had been appreciated, he said. He would leave a note to his successor, "to be opened at a time of some discouragement," and in it he would write three words: "Go to Germany."

He came into the cabin of "Air Force One" with a look of pride and pleasure that reflected more, I believe, than that day's tributes. It reflected satisfaction that he had done what had to be done, despite dangers and detractors, to keep that city free. As he sat down across from me, weary but happy, he said, "We'll never have another day like this one as long as we live."

An Overview of the Cuban Missile Crisis

Raymond L. Garthoff

Raymond L. Garthoff traces the essential events surrounding the Cuban missile crisis of 1962. Knowing that Americans had plans for covert actions against Cuban president Fidel Castro, Nikita Khrushchev decided to place missiles and troops in Cuba. American intelligence detected Soviet military movements on the island, and Kennedy ordered a blockade to stop Soviet ships from further deployment. According to Garthoff, Khrushchev agreed to a settlement when he realized that Kennedy was determined that no Soviet missiles would reside close to American cities. Raymond L. Garthoff, a senior U.S. foreign service officer and senior fellow at the Brookings Institute, has been deputy director of political military affairs and ambassador to Bulgaria. He was active in the Cuban missile crisis decision-making process.

On a spring day in 1962, Soviet Party leader Nikita Khrushchev, vacationing at a dacha[1] in the Crimea, was visited by Defense Minister Rodion Malinovsky. As they were conversing, the marshal gestured toward the horizon to the south and remarked on the fact that medium-range nuclear missiles the United States was installing across the Black Sea in Turkey were just becoming operational. So far as we know, that is all the marshal said, and the next step was Khrushchev's reaction: Why, he mused, should the Americans have the right to put missiles on our doorstep, and we not have a comparable right? A few weeks later, while in Bulgaria, he carried the point one fateful step further: Why not station Soviet medium-range missiles in Cuba?

Khrushchev had long rankled at what he regarded as

1. a Russian country house or villa

American flaunting of its political and military superiority, and successful cultivation of a double standard. Why shouldn't the Soviet Union be able to assert the prerogatives of a global power? One reason, of course, was that the United States *did* have superiority in global political, economic, and military power. Moreover, while the Soviet Union had enjoyed some spectacular successes—in particular, its primacy in space with the first earth satellite and first test of an intercontinental ballistic missile (ICBM)—in the four years or so since that time, there had been reverses. In particular, after riding an inflated world impression of Soviet missile strength during American self-flagellation over a "missile gap," improved intelligence had now persuaded the American leaders—and the world—that the *real* missile gap, and a growing one, favored the United States.

Since Khrushchev personally had overplayed the Soviet hand on missiles, he had particular reason to want to offset the new, and to him, adverse gap. Indeed, if he wanted to carry forward his still-unsuccessful campaign on West Berlin, or even to prevent American exploitation of missile superiority in other political contests, some way had to be found to overcome the growing American superiority. Available Soviet ICBMs were not satisfactory; he needed several years to await the next generation. But the Soviet Union did have plenty of medium-range missiles (a category in Soviet usage that embraced both the Western categories of "medium-range" and "intermediate-range" ballistic missiles, MRBMs and IRBMs). It would certainly help deal with the problem of Soviet strategic missile weakness if the Soviet Union could create ersatz[2] ICBMs by deploying MRBMs and IRBMs near the United States, comparable to what the United States was doing in Turkey.

The second ingredient in concocting the decision to put Soviet missiles in Cuba was the interaction of Soviet and American relations with Castro's Cuba. By the spring of 1962, Cuba had become highly dependent on the Soviet Union, economically and politically. In turn, it was a declared socialist state and Castro was in the process of merging the old-line Cuban Communist party and his own 26th of July Movement, the former providing organizing ability and a structured ideology, the latter the leaders and the popular following.

2. being an imitation or substitute, usually inferior

AMERICA'S COVERT ACTION PROGRAM AGAINST CASTRO

Meanwhile, Cuban-American relations were precarious. The United States, frustrated by the defeat at the Bay of Pigs of the Cuban émigré invasion it had sponsored, had by no means lessened its hostility or given up its efforts to unseat Castro's regime. By the fall of 1961, the president had authorized a broad covert action program, Operation Mongoose, aimed at harassing, undermining, and optimally overthrowing the Castro regime. This effort included repeated and continuing attempts to assassinate Castro himself. While the Cuban and Soviet leaders did not (so far as it has been possible to ascertain) then know about high-level deliberations in Washington and planning papers on Operation Mongoose, they did know in considerable detail about the CIA operations in Miami sending reconnaissance and later sabotage teams into Cuba, and they knew about at least some of the assassination attempts.

Also, the United States, by February 1962, had extended its economic sanctions to a complete embargo against trade with Cuba, and had engaged in diplomatic efforts to get other countries to curtail trade. In January 1962, at Punta del Este, the United States had succeeded in getting the majority necessary to suspend Cuban participation in the Organization of American States (OAS). By the spring of 1962 the United States had also persuaded fifteen Latin American states to follow its lead and break diplomatic relations with Havana. In short, the United States was conducting a concerted political, economic, propaganda, and covert campaign against Cuba.

On the military side as well, the president had in October 1961 secretly instructed the Defense Department to prepare contingency plans for war with Cuba, with air attack and invasion alternatives. While secret, elements of these plans were tested in subsequent military exercises, and elements of the military forces needed to implement them were built up. Between April 9 and 24, when Khrushchev was brooding in the Crimea, a U.S. Marine air-ground task force carried out a major amphibious exercise, with an assault on the island of Vieques near Puerto Rico. Another exercise conducted from April 19 to May 11 on the southeastern coast of the United States involved more than 40,000 troops, 79 ships, and over 300 aircraft. While the exercise was publicly announced, the fact that it was designed to test an actual Commander in Chief, Atlantic (CINCLANT) contingency plan against Cuba was of course not disclosed. But the Cubans and Soviets assumed, correctly, that it was.

Under the circumstances, it was not surprising that Cuban and Soviet leaders feared an American attack on Cuba. There had been no decision in Washington to attack. But there were programs underway directed toward overthrowing the Cuban regime, and military contingency planning and preparation if the president decided to attack. The United States had the capabilities to attack, and its overall intentions were clearly hostile; any prudent political or military planner would have had to consider at least the threat of attack.

The Cubans sought Soviet commitments and assistance to ward off or meet an American attack. The Soviet leaders had given general, but not ironclad, public assurances of support. They were not, however, prepared to extend their own commitment so far as to take Cuba into the Warsaw Pact.[3]

THE SOVIETS PLAN MISSILE DEPLOYMENT IN CUBA

Khrushchev first raised the idea of deploying Soviet missiles in Cuba with a few close colleagues in May. Khrushchev's plan was to deploy in Cuba a small force of medium-range missiles capable of striking the United States, both to bolster the sagging Soviet side of the strategic military balance, and to serve as a deterrent to American attack on Cuba. The missiles would be shipped to Cuba and installed there rapidly in secrecy. Then, the Soviet Union would suddenly confront the United States with a fait accompli[4] and a new, more favorable status quo. The impact of the move, and perforce American acceptance of it, would bolster the Soviet stance (probably in particular in a new round of negotiation on the status of Berlin, although no concrete information is available on that point).

Anastas Mikoyan, a veteran Politburo[5] member and close friend, expressed strong reservations on at least two points: Castro's receptivity to the idea, and the practicality of surreptitiously installing the missiles without American detection. Khrushchev readily agreed to drop the idea if Castro

---

3. the organization of Communist countries, the counterpart of NATO, the organization of democratic European states and the U.S.   4. an accomplished fact or deed, presumably irreversible   5. the chief political and executive committee of the Communist Party

objected, but his sense of Castro's reaction was better than
Mikoyan's. On the question of practicality, it was decided to
send a small expert team headed by Marshal Sergei Biryuzov, the new commander in chief of the Strategic Missile
Forces, incognito (as "Engineer Petrov"), to check out the
terrain and conditions and advise on the practicality of secret deployment. The military, represented by Malinovsky
and Biryuzov, favored the scheme because of what it would
do to help redress Soviet strategic inferiority.

Khrushchev apparently brought the full Party Presidium
(as the Politburo was then known), or rather its members
available in Moscow at the time, into the decision-making
process only in late May when the mission was about to de-
part for Havana to ascertain Castro's response and evaluate
feasibility. . . .

Castro readily agreed to the Soviet offer of missiles, believing that he was serving the broader interests of the socialist camp as well as enhancing Cuban security. Biryuzov,
who evidently saw his task as fulfilling an assigned mission
rather than providing input to evaluation of a proposal, reported that they could secretly install the missile system.

Formal orders were given to the Ministry of Defense on
June 10, 1962, to proceed with the deployment, even though
many details remained to be decided. In early July 1962,
Cuban Defense Minister Raúl Castro visited Moscow, and he
and Marshal Malinovsky drafted a five-year renewable
agreement to cover the missile deployment. . . .

AMERICAN REACTION TO THE SOVIETS' ACTIONS

The "Cuban missile crisis" derives its name (in the United
States; in the Soviet Union, with the accent on American
hostility toward Cuba, it is called "the Caribbean Crisis")
from the central role played by the Soviet missiles. As President Kennedy had warned on September 4, 1962, shortly before the first missiles actually arrived in Cuba, if such Soviet
offensive missiles were introduced "the gravest issues would
arise," and nine days later, he stressed that in that case "this
country will do whatever must be done to protect its own security and that of its allies." It was, of course, too late to affect Soviet decisions long made and then reaching final im-
plementation.

President Kennedy's declaration included another element, rarely recalled, to which he applied the same warning

of "gravest" consequences: if, apart from missiles, the Soviet Union sent to Cuba "any organized combat force.". . . . What has not been appreciated until now is that the Soviets in fact *did* send such a combat force *in addition to* the missiles. The Ministry of Defense in Moscow on June 10 received orders not only on the dispatch of a mixed division of Strategic Missile Force troops, comprising three regiments of R-12 (SS-4) and two regiments of R-14 (SS-5) medium-range missiles; but also a Soviet combat contingent including an integrated air defense component with a radar system, 24 surface-to-air missile battalions with 144 launchers, a regiment of 42 MiG-21 interceptors; a coastal defense component comprising 8 cruise missile launchers with 32 missiles, 12 Komar missile patrol boats, and a separate squadron as well as a regiment totalling 42 IL-28 jet light bombers for attacking any invasion force. In addition, a ground force of division size comprised four reinforced motorized rifle regiments, each with over 3,000 men, and 35 tanks. In addition, 6 short-range tactical rocket launchers, and 18 army cruise missile launchers were part of the contingent. This force was seen as a "plate glass" deterrent to U.S. invasion, and reassurance to Castro as an alternative to Cuban membership in the Warsaw Pact.

While most of the weaponry was discovered by American aerial reconnaissance during the crisis, even afterward the number of Soviet military personnel was underestimated by nearly half—22,000 instead of 42,000. The United States failed to discover that a major Soviet expeditionary contingent, under the overall command of a four-star general, General of the Army Issa Pliyev, was in Cuba in October–November 1962.

Recently, former Soviet General of the Army Anatoly Gribkov, who was responsible for planning the Soviet dispatch of forces to Cuba in 1962, has declared that 9 tactical nuclear weapons were sent for the ground force tactical rocket launchers, and with authorization for their use delegated to General Pliyev in case of an American land invasion. If true, this was one of the most dangerous aspects of the entire deployment, and this was not known in Washington.

The medium-range missiles capable of striking the United States, in contrast, were placed under strict control by Moscow: General Pliyev was not authorized to fire them under any circumstances, even an American attack, without explicit authorization by Khrushchev.

SOVIETS SURPRISED BY AMERICAN INTELLIGENCE

Ambassador Anatoly Dobrynin arrived at the State Department at 6:00 P.M. On October 22, 1962, at the request of Secretary of State Dean Rusk. His demeanor was relaxed and cheerful; a short time later, he was observed leaving "ashen-faced" and "visibly shaken." A few hours earlier, Foreign Minister Gromyko had departed from New York for Moscow at the end of his visit in the United States, making routine departure remarks to the press and evidently with no premonition of what the president would be saying while he [Gromyko] was airborne. Incredibly, the Soviet leadership was caught by surprise by the American disclosure that the missiles had been discovered a week earlier and by the American "first step" action of imposing a quarantine, coupled with a demand that the missiles be removed.

Khrushchev has been reported to have initially in anger wanted to challenge the quarantine-blockade, but whether that is correct the actual Soviet response was cautious. The blockade was not challenged, and no counter-pressures were mounted elsewhere, such as Berlin (as had been feared in Washington). Even the Soviet response to the unparalleled American alert of its strategic forces and most forces worldwide was an announced, but actually hollow, Soviet and Warsaw Pact alert.

Khrushchev continued for a few days to believe that the United States might accept at least the partial Soviet missile deployment already in Cuba. But by October 26, it had become clear that the United States was determined. Moreover, the United States had rapidly prepared a substantial air attack and land invasion force. The tactical air combat force of 579 aircraft was ready, with the plan calling for 1,190 strike sorties on the first day. More than 100,000 Army and 40,000 Marine troops were ready to strike. An airborne paratroop force as large as that used on Normandy in 1944 was included in the preparation for an assault on the island. American military casualties were estimated at 18,500 in ten days of combat.

Soviet intelligence indicated on October 26 that a U.S. air attack and invasion of Cuba were expected at any time. Khrushchev then hurriedly offered a deal: An American pledge not to invade Cuba would obviate the need for Soviet missiles in Cuba and, by implication, they could be withdrawn. A truncated Soviet Presidium group (a Moscow "Ex-Comm") had been meeting since October 23. We still know almost nothing about its deliberations, but it is clear that Khrushchev was fully in control. Later on October 26, a new intelligence assessment in Moscow indicated that while U.S. invasion preparations continued, it was now less clear that an attack was imminent. Thus there might be some time for bargaining on terms for a settlement.

SOVIET AND AMERICAN LEADERS WORK OUT A SETTLEMENT

Meanwhile, Ambassador Dobrynin reported that Robert Kennedy had informed him that the United States was planning to phase out its missiles in Turkey and Italy; there might be opportunity to include that in a settlement. Moreover, the Soviet Embassy in Washington had reported that in a discussion between the KGB[6] station chief, Aleksandr Fomin, and an American television correspondent with good State Department contacts, John Scali, the American—after checking with Secretary Rusk—had indicated that an American assurance against attacking Cuba in exchange for withdrawal of the Soviet missiles in Cuba could provide the basis for a deal, but that time was short.

A new message from Khrushchev to Kennedy was sent that night, October 26, proposing a reciprocal withdrawal of missiles from Cuba and Turkey, as well as the American assurances against invasion of Cuba. But on October 27, later called "Black Saturday" in Washington, an ominous chain of events, including the stiffened Soviet terms, intensified concern. In Moscow, Soviet intelligence again reported signs of American preparations for possible attack on Cuba on October 29 or 30. A very alarmed message was also received from Fidel Castro expressing—for the first time—Castro's belief that an attack was imminent (within 24 to 72 hours), and urging Khrushchev in case of an invasion, to preemptively attack the United States. The effect of this call was to reinforce a decision by Khrushchev that Castro did not expect or want: prompt conclusion of a deal to remove the missiles in exchange for an American verbal assurance against attacking Cuba.

Other developments also contributed to moving Khrush-

6. the intelligence and internal security agency of the Soviet Union

chev, by October 28, to act on the basis he had first outlined on October 26. One was Castro's action on October 27 in ordering Cuban antiaircraft artillery to open fire on low-flying American reconnaissance aircraft. None were shot down, but the action clearly raised the risk of hostilities. Far more dangerous was the completely unexpected action of local *Soviet* air defense commanders in actually shooting down a U-2 with a Soviet surface-to-air missile. Khrushchev at first assumed that Cubans had shot the plane down, but at some point learned that even his own troops were not under full control. Although the much more restrictive instructions and other constraints still seemed to rule out any unauthorized firing (or even preparation for firing) of the medium-range missiles, the situation was getting out of control.

Kennedy's proposal on the evening of October 27 to exchange American assurances against invasion of Cuba for Soviet withdrawal of its missiles coupled with a virtual ultimatum, was thus promptly accepted. Khrushchev did not risk taking the time to clarify a number of unclear issues, including what the Americans considered to be "offensive weapons." He accepted the president's terms and sent his reply openly over Radio Moscow, as well as via diplomatic communication.

The Russian View of the Cuban Missile Crisis, and Kennedy's Response

Nikita Khrushchev and John F. Kennedy

In a speech delivered to the Supreme Soviet, the legislature of the Soviet Union, Nikita Khrushchev explains the reason for placing missiles in Cuba. This view, repeated in an interview several years later, portrays American actions toward Cuba as dangerous and aggressive. Khrushchev argues that the Cubans were fearful of an American military attack and that the Soviet Union was helping their fellow Communists defend themselves for the sake of peace. Following Khrushchev's speech is Kennedy's response delivered at a news conference five days later. Nikita Khrushchev, a Soviet politician, was appointed first secretary of the Communist Party and later served as Soviet premier from 1958 to 1964.

Cuba is terrible to the imperialists because of her ideas. The imperialists do not want to reconcile themselves to the idea that little Cuba dared to live and develop independently as her people want to and not in the way which would please the American monopolies. But the question of how people are to live, what road they are to take, is an internal matter for each people!

Flouting generally accepted standards of international relations, the United States reactionary forces have been doing everything from the first day of the victory of the Cuban revolution to overthrow Cuba's revolutionary Government and to restore their domination there. They broke off diplomatic relations with Cuba, were and are conducting subversive activity, established an economic blockade of Cuba. Threaten-

Excerpted from "In Defense of Cuba," by Nikita Khrushchev, *The Worker Supplement*, December 23, 1962 and *Public Papers of the Presidents, 1962* (Washington, DC, 1963).

ing to apply sanctions, the United States began pressing its allies not only to stop trading with Cuba but even not to make available ships for carrying food to Cuba from the socialist countries which came to the assistance of their brothers. This is an inhuman policy—a desire to starve a whole nation. But even this seemed little to them. Assuming the functions of a policeman, they decided to take the road of the military suppression of the Cuban revolution. In other words, they wanted to usurp the right to the export of counterrevolution.

United States policy in relation to Cuba is the most unbridled, reactionary policy. To declare that Cuba allegedly threatens America or any other country and to usurp on this plea a special right to act against Cuba is just monstrous.

Seeking to justify its aggressive actions, American reaction is repeating that the crisis in the Caribbean was created by Cuba herself, adding that blame rests also with the Soviet Union which shipped there rockets and IL-28 bombers.

JUSTIFICATION FOR SOVIET ACTIONS

But is this so? It is true that we carried weapons there at the request of the Cuban government. But what motives guided us in doing that? Exclusively humanitarian motives—Cuba needed weapons as a means of containing the aggressors, and not as a means of attack. For Cuba was under a real threat of invasion. Piratical attacks were repeatedly made on her coasts, Havana was shelled, and airborne groups were dropped from planes to carry out sabotage.

A large-scale military invasion of Cuba by counterrevolutionary mercenaries was launched in Cuba in April of last year. This invasion was prepared and carried out with full support on the part of the United States.

Further events have shown that the failure of the invasion did not discourage the United States imperialists in their desire to strangle Cuba. They began preparing another attack. In the autumn of this year a very alarming situation was created. Everything indicated that the United States was preparing to attack the Cuban Republic with its own armed forces.

Revolutionary Cuba was compelled to take all measures to strengthen her defense. The Soviet Union helped her to build up a strong army standing guard over the achievements of the Cuban people. In view of the mounting threat from the United States, the Government of Cuba in the summer of this year requested the Soviet Government to render further assistance.

Agreement was reached on a number of new measures, including the stationing of several score Soviet IRBM's [intermediate-range ballistic missiles] in Cuba. These weapons were to be in the hands of Soviet military.

EXPLANATION OF SOVIET AIMS

What were the aims behind this decision? Naturally, neither we nor our Cuban friends had in mind that this small number of IRBM's, sent to Cuba, would be used for an attack on the United States or any other country.

Our aim was only to defend Cuba. We all saw how the American imperialists were sharpening knives, threatening Cuba with a massed attack. We could not remain impartial observers in face of this bandit-like policy, which is contrary to all standards of relations between states and the United Nations Charter. We decided to extend a helping hand to Cuba. We saw a possibility of protecting the freedom-loving people of Cuba by installing rockets there so that the American imperialists, if they really decided to invade, would realize that the war which they threatened to start stood at their own borders, so that they would realize more realistically the dangers of thermonuclear war.

Such was the step we took because of the serious aggravation of the situation. We were confident that this step would bring the aggressors to their senses and that they—realizing that Cuba was not defenseless and that American imperialism was [not] all powerful—would be compelled to change their plans. Then the need for retaining rockets in Cuba would naturally disappear.

Indeed, had there been no threat of an invasion and had we had assurances that the United States would not invade Cuba, and would restrain its allies from this, had the United States guided itself by this course, there would have been no need for the stationing of our rockets in Cuba.

Some people pretend that the rockets were supplied by us for an attack on the United States. This, of course, is not wise reasoning. Why should we station rockets in Cuba for this purpose when we were and are able to strike from our own territory, possessing as we do the necessary number of intercontinental missiles of the required range and power?

We do not, in general, need military bases on foreign territories. It is known that we have dismantled all our bases abroad. All people who have any understanding of military matters know that in the age of intercontinental and global rockets, Cuba—this small, far-away island, which is only fifty kilometers wide in some places—is of no strategic importance for the defense of the Soviet Union. We stationed rockets in Cuba only for the defense of the Cuban Republic and not for an attack on the United States. Such a small country as Cuba cannot, naturally, build up such forces as could launch an offensive against such a big country as the United States.

Only those who are not "all there" in the head can claim that the Soviet Union chose Cuba as a springboard for an invasion of the American continent—the U.S. or countries of Latin America. If we wanted to start war against the U.S., we would not have agreed to dismantle the rockets installed in Cuba, which were ready for launching, for battle. We would have used them. But we did not because we did not pursue such aims.

Thus, all talk that Cuba was being converted into a base for an attack on the United States of America was a vicious lie. The purpose of this lie was to cover up the plans of aggression against Cuba. We are loyal to Lenin's principles of peaceful coexistence and hold that all disputes among states should be settled by peaceful means, by way of negotiations. . . .

SOVIET EFFORTS TO RESOLVE THE CRISIS

On October 23, immediately after the United States proclaimed the blockade of Cuba, the Soviet government, besides taking defensive measures, issued a Statement resolutely warning that the United States Government assumes a grave responsibility for the destinies of the peace and is recklessly playing with fire. We frankly told the United States President that we would not tolerate piratical actions by United States ships on the high seas and that we would take appropriate measures with this object in view.

At the same time, the Soviet government urged all peoples to bar the road to the aggressors. Simultaneously it took certain steps in the United Nations. The peaceful initiative of the Soviet government in settling the Cuban crisis met with full support by the socialist countries and the peoples of most other United Nations member states.

However, the government of the United States of America continued to aggravate the situation. United States militarist forces were pushing developments toward an attack on

Cuba. On the morning of October 27, we received information from the Cuban comrades and from other sources which bluntly said that the invasion would be effected within the next two or three days. We assessed the messages received as a signal of utmost alarm. And this was a well-founded alarm.

Immediate actions were needed to prevent an invasion of Cuba and to maintain peace. A message prompting a mutually acceptable solution was sent to the United States President. At that moment, it was not yet too late to put out the fuse of war which had already been lighted. Forwarding this message we took into consideration that the messages of the President himself expressed anxiety and the desire to find a way out of the obtaining situation. We declared that if the United States undertook not to invade Cuba and also would restrain other states allied with it from aggression against Cuba, the Soviet Union would be willing to remove from Cuba the weapons which the United States call "offensive."

The United States President replied by declaring that if the Soviet government agreed to remove these weapons from Cuba the American government would lift the quarantine, i.e., the blockade, and would give an assurance on renunciation of the invasion of Cuba both by the United States itself and other countries of the Western Hemisphere. The President declared quite definitely, and this is known to the whole world, that the United States will not attack Cuba and will restrain also its allies from such actions.

But we shipped our weapons to Cuba precisely for the prevention of aggression against her! That is why the Soviet government reaffirmed its agreement to the removal of the ballistic rockets from Cuba.

From the above follow some evident results of the beginning of normalization of the situation over Cuba.

First, it has been possible to avert an invasion which threatened the Republic of Cuba from day to day, and, therefore, to avert an armed conflict, to overcome a crisis which was fraught with the danger of universal thermonuclear war.

Second, the United States publicly, before the entire world, pledged not to attack the Republic of Cuba, and to restrain its allies from doing so.

Third, the most rabid imperialists who staked on starting a world thermonuclear war over Cuba have not been able to do so. The Soviet Union, the forces of peace and socialism, proved that they are in a position to impose peace on the exponents of war.

Which side triumphed? Who won? In this respect one may say that it was sanity, the cause of peace and security of peoples, that won. Both sides displayed a sober approach and took into account that unless such steps are taken as could help overcome the dangerous development of events, a World War III might break out. . . .

KENNEDY'S PERSPECTIVE ON KHRUSHCHEV'S SPEECH

THE PRESIDENT: I think in that speech this week he showed his awareness of the nuclear age. But of course, the Cuban effort has made it more difficult for us to carry out any successful negotiations, because this was an effort to materially change the balance of power, it was done in secret, steps were taken really to deceive us by every means they could, and they were planning in November to open to the world the fact that they had these missiles so close to the United States; not that they were intending to fire them, because if they were going to get into a nuclear struggle, they have their own missiles in the Soviet Union. But it would have politically changed the balance of power. It would have appeared to, and appearances contribute to reality. So it is going to be some time before it is possible for us to come to any real understanding with Mr. Khrushchev. But I do think his speech shows that he realizes how dangerous a world we live in.

The real problem is the Soviet desire to expand their power and influence. If Mr. Khrushchev would concern himself with the real interests of the people of the Soviet Union, that they have a higher standard of living, to protect his own security, there is no real reason why the United States and the Soviet Union, separated by so many thousands of miles of land and water, both rich countries, both with very energetic people, should not be able to live in peace. But it is this constant determination which the Chinese show in the most militant form, and which the Soviets also have shown, that they will not settle for that kind of a peaceful world, but must settle for a Communist world. That is what makes the real danger, the combination of these two systems in conflict around the world in a nuclear age is what makes the sixties so dangerous. . . .

THE DANGER OF MISJUDGMENTS

Well, now, if you look at the history of this century, where World War I really came through a series of misjudgments of the intentions of others, certainly World War II, where Hitler thought that he could seize Poland, that the British might not fight, and if they fought, after the defeat of Poland they might not continue to fight, Korea, where obviously the North Koreans did not think we were going to come in, and Korea, when we did not think the Chinese were going to come in, when you look at all those misjudgments which brought on war, and then you see the Soviet Union and the United States so far separated in their beliefs, we believing in a world of independent sovereign and different diverse nations, they believing in a monolithic Communist world, and you put the nuclear equation into that struggle, that is what makes this, as I said before, such a dangerous time, and that we must proceed with firmness and also with the best information we can get, and also with care. There is nothing—one mistake can make this whole thing blow up. So that—one major mistake either by Mr. Khrushchev or by us here—so that is why it is much easier to make speeches about some of the things which we ought to be doing, but I think that anybody who looks at the fatality lists on atomic weapons, and realizes that the Communists have a completely twisted view of the United States, and that we don't comprehend them, that is what makes life in the sixties hazardous.

CHAPTER 6

Assessing John F. Kennedy

An Assessment of Kennedy's Policies and Programs

William G. Carleton

In 1964, less than a year after Kennedy's death, William G. Carleton assesses Kennedy's goals, successes, and failures. He identifies two important ways Kennedy affected presidential campaigns, and he credits Kennedy with achievement in civil rights and national defense. However, he gives Kennedy little credit for achievement in domestic policies because, he says, Kennedy exerted too little effort to influence Congress. Carleton suggests that in foreign policy during a difficult time, Kennedy lacked clear direction during his first two years in office, but succeeded in the Cuban missile crisis. William G. Carleton has taught at the University of Florida in Gainesville. He is the author of *The Revolution in American Foreign Policy* and *Technology and Humanism: Some Exploratory Essays for Our Time* and has contributed to *American Scholar* and *Yale Review*.

Although John F. Kennedy has been dead less than a year, it is not too early to assess his place in history. Judgments about historical figures never come finally to rest. Reputations fluctuate through the centuries, for they must constantly do battle with oblivion and compete with the shifting interests and values of subsequent generations. Even so, contemporary estimates are sometimes not markedly changed by later ones.

The career of a public man, the key events of his life, most of his record, the questions he confronted, the problems he tackled, the social forces at work in his time are largely open to scrutiny when he leaves public life. . . .

Excerpted from "Kennedy in History: An Early Appraisal," by William Carleton, *Antioch Review*, vol. 24, no. 3 (Fall 1964). Copyright ©1964 by the Antioch Review, Inc. Reprinted by permission of the editors.

THE 1960 KENNEDY CAMPAIGN

Of 1960's 'issues', only the religious one will loom large in history. It was the religious implication which gave Kennedy the victory. Democratic gains in the pivotal Catholic cities in the states with the largest electoral votes were greater than Democratic losses in the Protestant rural areas. It was the Democrats, not the Republicans, who actively exploited the religious aspect. In the Protestant areas, citizens were made to feel they were bigots if they voted against Kennedy. But Catholics were appealed to on the grounds of their Catholicism. Any evidence of Protestant intolerance was widely publicized to stimulate Catholics and Jews to go to the polls to rebuke the bigots. But history will treat these Democratic tactics—a kind of bigotry in reverse—with kindness. The means may have been objectionable, but the good achieved was enormous. For the first time in American history a non-Protestant was elected President. The old barriers were downed. Now that an Irish-Catholic had been elected president, the way was opened for the election of an Italian Catholic, a Polish Catholic, a Jew, eventually a Negro. A basic American ideal had at last been implemented at the very pinnacle of American society. . . .

The second permanent contribution of the 1960 election lies in its underscoring the large degree to which presidential pre-convention campaigns and election campaigns have been geared to democratic mass behavior. Kennedy and his team wisely recognized that a mere pursuit of the politicians and delegates was not enough, that beginning with 1928, conventions had nominated the outstanding national favorite as indicated by the primaries and the polls. In Kennedy's case, winning the primaries and the polls was especially necessary to convince the doubters that a young man and a Catholic could be elected President. Hence Kennedy organization, money, and high-level experts were directed not merely to bagging delegates but even more to winning mass support, primaries, and high ratings in the polls. In this they succeeded marvelously well. In effect, the Democratic convention merely ratified the choice already made by the primaries, the polls, and the mass media. The revolution in the presidential nominating process had been in the making for over three decades, but it took the Kennedy campaign to make the public and even the pundits aware of it. . . .

Other party leaders were dwarfed as never before. The TV debates further spotlighted the nominees. Again, as in the pre-convention campaign, the Kennedy team did not create the trend to a personalized campaign, to glamorous celebrity politics. The trend and the techniques to make it work had been on the way for decades. Basically these emerged from the increasingly mass nature of American society. But Kennedy exploited the trend and the techniques in conspicuously successful fashion; he widened, intensified, and accelerated them; he made the nation aware of them; he did much to institutionalize them.

Thus the Kennedy campaigns will always be remembered for the dramatic way they contributed to the personalized and plebiscitic[1] Presidency.

No administration in history staffed the executive departments and the White House offices with as many competent, dedicated, and brilliant men as did Kennedy's. Kennedy paid little attention to party qualifications at top level; the emphasis was on ability, drive, imagination, creativity. Politicians made way for specialists and technicians; but Kennedy was on the lookout for specialists *plus,* for men who had not only technical competence but intellectual verve. Kennedy himself was a generalist with a critical intelligence, and many of the most prized of his staff were men of like caliber—[Ted] Sorensen, [Richard] Goodwin, [McGeorge] Bundy. After the brilliance of the Kennedy team, and with the ever-growing complexity of government problems, no administration is ever likely to want to go back to the pedestrian personnel of earlier administrations, although few presidents are apt to have the Kennedy sensitivity and magnetism capable of gathering together so scintillating an administration as his. FDR [Franklin Delano Roosevelt] will be known as the founder of the presidential brains trust, but Kennedy will be known as the President who widened and institutionalized it.

KENNEDY'S POOR RELATIONS WITH CONGRESS

In contrast to his performance in the executive departments, Kennedy's relations with Congress can scarcely be said to have been successful. The dream of enacting a legislative program comparable to that of Wilson and FDR soon vanished. The one outstanding legislative achievement of Kennedy was

1. characterized by direct, rather than indirect, exercise of national self-determination

the Trade Expansion Act of 1962. All of Kennedy's other major goals—farm legislation, tax reform, a civil rights law, medicare, federal aid to schools—bogged down in Congress. Since 1938, major welfare legislation had repeatedly been smothered in Congress at the hands of a Republican-conservative-Southern Democratic coalition. . . . Kennedy will not escape all blame for his legislative failures, for despite his awareness of the stalemate since 1938, he had promised a 'strong' legislative leadership like that of Wilson and the second Roosevelt. Moreover, in various ways Kennedy contributed to the personalized and plebiscitic Presidency: by the manner in which he waged his 1960 campaign, by his assigning to key posts not party leaders but men personally chosen for their expertise and creative intelligence, and by his monopolizing of the limelight. Kennedy and his family naturally made exciting publicity, but the President seemed to go out of his way to get even more— holding televised press conferences, for example, and permitting TV cameras to capture the intimacies of decision-making in the executive offices and of private life in the White House. All of this further exalted the Presidency, further dwarfed politicians, party, and Congress, and added to Congress' growing inferiority complex.

Now, Kennedy was not unaware of the susceptibilities of Congress. He carefully cultivated individual congressmen and senators, frequently called them on the phone, had them up for chats, extended them an unusual number of social courtesies and parties in the White House. His legislative liaison team, headed by Kenneth O'Donnell and Lawrence O'Brien, was diplomatic and astute, pumped and twisted congressional arms, applied both the carrot and the stick. But Kennedy left too many of the congressional chores to his liaison team. He simply did not give this aspect of the Presidency enough attention. Foreign affairs interested him intellectually much more than domestic measures. Despite his years in Congress and his love of politics, Kennedy did not really like or feel at home with small-bore politicians and congressional 'types', and he was not skillful in his personal bargaining with them.

Moreover, Kennedy made no attempt to initiate and institutionalize new devices for easing presidential-congressional relations, nor did he even explore this problem intellectually. The breath of life to politicians is publicity, but no effort was made to share the presidential glory, of which there was a superabundance. . . .

KENNEDY AND CIVIL RIGHTS

Kennedy's Presidency will be known as the time of the Negro revolution, when Negro aspirations widened to include desegregation in the private sector and were spectacularly supported by sit-ins and street demonstrations. As President, Kennedy not only gave full executive backing to the enforcement of court decisions but personally identified himself with the goals of the Negro revolution and gave them the full moral support of the Presidency. . . .

But by 1963, it appeared that what had been a political advantage might turn into something of a political liability. 'The Kennedys' were denounced in the South, and the President faced the loss of much of that section in 1964. More serious, there were indications that the civil rights issue would cost Kennedy many votes in the North, where considerable opposition to the Negro drive had developed. However, by this time Kennedy had chosen his course, and while there might be temporary shifts in tactics, there could be no turning back. Robert Kennedy has stated that at this point the administration really did not have any choice and that, besides, the administration's course was the correct one. He reports the President as saying: 'If we're going to lose, let's lose on principle.'. . .

KENNEDY'S PRECARIOUS START IN FOREIGN POLICY

In foreign policy, the first two years of Kennedy were ambiguous. In the third year, there was a clearer sense of direction, one which promised to harmonize American policy with emerging new realities in the world. . . .

In short, Kennedy was confronted with a new fluidity, a necessity and an opportunity for a reappraisal of American foreign policy. How much of the old foreign policy was still applicable? What aspects required a new orientation? To what degree was it safe, realistic, and advantageous to strike out in new directions? . . .

The chief stumbling block to an American-Soviet *detente*[2] continued to be Berlin, the two Germanies, and the territor-

2. a relaxing or easing of tension between rivals making way for increased diplomatic, commercial, and cultural contact

ial arrangements in East and Central Europe. . . . After the Communists built the Berlin Wall, Kennedy resisted all pressures to use force to tear it down.

Nevertheless, during his first two years in office, Kennedy seems needlessly to have fanned the tensions of the dying Cold War. (It may be that 'needlessly' is too strong a word; perhaps Kennedy thought he needed to arouse the country to obtain a more balanced military program, more foreign economic aid, the Alliance for Progress[3]; perhaps he thought, too, that a truculent tone was necessary to convince Khrushchev that America would stand firm under duress for its rights in Berlin.) His inaugural address was alarmist, already historically off key, more suited to the Stalinist era than to 1961. His first State of the Union Message was even more alarmist. The nation was told that the world tide was favorable, that each day we were drawing near the maximum danger. His backing of the Cuban invasion in April, 1961, further fanned the Cold War. His statement to newspaper publishers and editors gathered at the White House in May—that the United States was in the most critical period of its history—increased the popular anxieties. He overreacted to Khrushchev's Vienna ultimatum[4] in June, for in recent years Khrushchev's repeated deadlines and backdowns over West Berlin had become a kind of pattern. But for Kennedy, Vienna seems to have been a traumatic experience. On his return home he appealed to Americans to build do-it-yourself bomb shelters, and this produced a war psychology in the country and all manner of frenetic behavior, caused right-wingism to soar (1961 was the year the membership and financial 'take' of the right-wing organizations reached their peak), and weakened confidence abroad in Kennedy's judgment. . . .

KENNEDY'S CONTRIBUTION TO NATIONAL DEFENSE

The Kennedy Administration's contributions to national defense were notable. It emphasized a balanced and diversified establishment—both strategic and tactical nuclear weapons, conventional arms, and guerrilla forces—so the nation would never have to make the choice between the ultimate weapons and no other adequate defense. It was real-

3. a cooperative effort to spread democracy and improve the lives of the poor in Latin America   4. regarding Berlin

istic in its shift from bombers to missiles as the chief nuclear carriers of the future, and in its dismantling of the intermediate missiles bases in Britain, Italy, and Turkey as the Polaris submarines and inter-continental missiles became increasingly operational. Its attempt to find a formula for a NATO multilateral nuclear force was a way of countering De Gaulle's blandishments to the West Germans and of balancing the possibility of a *detente* with Russia with reassurances to Bonn. Its experiments with massive air-lifts of ground troops was in part a response to the desires of many of America's NATO allies for less rigidity, less insistence on fixed ground quotas, and more flexibility. However, NATO was plainly in transition, and while the Polaris submarines and inter-continental missiles were making the United States less dependent on European bases, ways were not yet actually implemented to share America's nuclear weapons with European allies on a genuine multilateral basis and satisfy their desires for less centralized direction from the United States.

There was an honest facing up to the terrible responsibilities inherent in the nuclear deterrent. That deterrent was put under tighter control to guard against accident and mistake, and the 'hot line' between Washington and Moscow was set up. A much more determined effort was made to get arms-control agreements and a treaty banning nuclear-weapons testing than had ever been made by Kennedy's predecessors. Negotiations with the Soviet Union had been going on for years, but the Americans now so yielded in their former demands for strict international inspection as to put the Russians on the defensive, making world opinion for the first time believe that it was the Russians and not the Americans who were the obstructionists. Kennedy's administration believed that the United States and Russia had an enormous common interest in preventing the spread of nuclear weapons to other countries, that the Sino-Soviet rift gave Khrushchev a new freedom and a new urge to make agreements, and that the increasing accuracy of national detection systems made the possibility of cheating on a test-ban treaty, even one without international inspection, 'vanishingly small'.

Kennedy's regime also showed its international-mindedness in its firm support of the United Nations. It defended the Secretariat, the executive, from Soviet attacks, and in practice the activities of the Secretariat were widened. The organization was saved from bankruptcy by American financial aid. The operation of the United Nations military force in the Congo, backed by the United States, showed that the American government had no sympathy for 'neo-colonialism'. . . .

Foreign economic aid was increased. The Food-for-Peace program was expanded. The Peace Corps was launched. The Alliance for Progress, an ambitious economic-aid program in Latin America coupled with domestic reforms, an experiment in 'controlled revolution', was undertaken.

However, Kennedy, like his predecessors, did little to make the average American understand foreign economic aid—that it is not only an attempt to raise living standards, prevent Communism, and contribute to the world's economic well-being and stability, but is also a substitute for those obsolete ways in which the old colonialism supplied capital to the underdeveloped areas. Until an American president takes to television and in a series of fireside chats explains to Americans in simple terms the real meaning of the foreign-aid program, that program will be in jeopardy.

THE SUCCESS OF THE CUBAN MISSILE CRISIS

The Cuban crisis of October 1962, provoked by the discovery of secret Soviet intermediate missiles in Cuba, was the high point, the turning point, in the Kennedy Administration. . . .

When the crisis came, even neutralist opinion seemed to feel that Khrushchev's attempt to compensate for his own inter-continental-missiles lag and the open and avowed American intermediate missiles in Turkey did not justify the sneaky Soviet operation in Cuba. America's quiet, deliberate planning of counter-measures, both military and diplomatic, was masterly. America's prudent use of force, enough but not more than enough to achieve its objective, won worldwide acclaim. Khrushchev and Castro lost face. . . .

Thereafter Khrushchev spoke even more insistently about the need to avoid nuclear war and pursue a policy of peaceful but competitive co-existence. From then on Kennedy gave more public recognition to emerging new international realities, the world's escape from monolithic threats, the trend to pluralism and diversity. . . .

The new spirit in world affairs expressed itself concretely in the consummation of the limited nuclear test-ban treaty in the summer of 1963, the first real break in the American-Soviet deadlock. After this, Kennedy proposed a joint American-Soviet effort to explore the moon, and he agreed to permit the Soviet Union to purchase American wheat.

By 1963, then, Kennedy had come to much awareness that the post-war world was ending and to a determination to attempt more shifts in American foreign policy in harmony with the emerging fluidity. By this time, too, he had developed close personal relations with a large number of premiers and heads of state the world over. It was felt that after his re-election in 1964 he would be in an unusually strong position to give American foreign policy a new direction, that the test-ban treaty was but a foretaste of more significant measures yet to come, measures which might lead to an American-Soviet *detente*, eventually even to a *rapprochement*.[5] Thus the President's life ended in a tragic sense of incompleteness and unfulfillment.

5. reestablishing cordial relations between two countries

An Assessment of Kennedy's Character

Thomas C. Reeves

*Thomas C. Reeves states that John Kennedy's char-
acter was formed and directed by his father, Joseph
P. Kennedy, resulting in a pragmatic nature given to
winning at any cost. Reeves acknowledges Kennedy's
major policy accomplishments, but emphasizes the
gap between Kennedy's public image and the private
man. Reeves contends that Kennedy's affairs with
women and his association with people connected
with the Mafia would have left him vulnerable to
blackmail had he lived to run for a second term.
Thomas C. Reeves, an ordained Methodist minister,
served as a pastor before teaching at Federal City
College in Washington, D.C., and Mount St. Mary's
College in Emmitsburg, Maryland. He is the author
of* Freedom and the Foundation: The Fund for the
Republic in the Era of McCarthyism *and* The Life
and Times of Joe McCarthy: A Biography, *and is the
editor of* John F. Kennedy: The Man, the Politician,
the President.

The major figure in an account of the life of John F. Kennedy
must be Jack's father. The elder Kennedy, that autocratic and
exacting patriarch, largely formed the minds and hearts of
his children, and his teachings and example were assimi-
lated by all the youngsters, forming their essential core values. Rose Kennedy's principal contribution seems to have
been a ritualistic and demanding brand of Christianity she
passed on to her children, in which form mattered more
than substance, public performance more than private conviction. Rose's personal detachment from domestic life,
however understandable given the nature of her marriage,
and her frequent absences from the home also played a role

in creating an emotionally confusing environment in which intense claims of family solidarity and unswerving loyalty covered up underlying anxieties and tensions.

Instilled in the Kennedys, above all, was an intense self-centeredness, aggressiveness, and a passionate desire to win at any cost. The principal aim of life for the Kennedy youngsters—as defined by their father—was to achieve public success and prestige. For the male members of the family, the primary goal was the acquisition of political power and influence, and the eldest son was expected to reach the highest level of such power in America and perhaps the world—the White House.

At the death of Joe Junior, this responsibility fell on Jack—less aggressive, less obviously bright, clearly less healthy, and much less ambitious than his older brother. Until coerced into politics by his father, Jack had dreamed mostly about becoming a great athlete. Much of his energy was spent in sports and the pursuit of women. After the war, he was commanded to be the family's torchbearer. The quest for political office—essentially the desire to fulfill his father's mandate—would consume his life. . . .

It was the elder Kennedy who financed and directed Jack's political campaigns for House and Senate seats and for the presidency. It was he who originally created the image of JFK the hero; the intellectual, visionary leader; and the ideal family man. It was Joe Kennedy's iron will that compelled Jack to overcome continuous exhaustion, sickness, and pain in the pursuit of votes. Along the way, substantive political and moral issues were secondary; for the most part, one did and said what appealed at the ballot box. Jack was expected to win, and he obediently worked hard to do so. . . .

What kind of man was John F. Kennedy when he entered the White House? He was indeed, as his official biographers claimed, intelligent, politically experienced, eager for information, respectful of first-class minds, and willing to link the presidency with good taste and high culture. He communicated exceptionally well with the press and public. He was capable of inspiring vast audiences with his rhetoric. He had at times in his life shown considerable courage. Ideologically, Kennedy was at best a sort of centrist Democrat, interested in using the federal government to right a number of wrongs. He was militantly anti-Communist and committed to an aggressive foreign policy.

THE GAP BETWEEN IMAGE AND REALITY

Beneath the surface, however, Jack was pragmatic to the point of amorality; his sole standard seemed to be political expediency. Gifted with good looks, youth, and wealth, he was often, in his personal life, reckless, vain, selfish, petty, and lecherous. Jack's character, so much a reflection of his father's single-minded pursuit of political power and personal indulgence, lacked a moral center, a reference point that went beyond self-aggrandizement.

It is precisely on that question of character that the gap between the Kennedy image, perpetuated by the Camelot School of modern American history, and reality is most profound. Chief executives may draw upon their intelligence, experience, and ideology; they may seek advice from experts in every field; they may master the political arts. But ultimately the character of the individual, his essential values and priorities, his sense of right and wrong, will determine the ends to which these resources will be used. . . .

A president must play several roles, including administrative director, legislative leader, party head, commander in chief, number-one diplomat, spokesman for social justice, friend of business and labor, and molder of the federal judicial system. He is also a moral exemplar to his people, one whose office commands and enables him to set the standard of ethics and excellence for all. As James David Barber put it [in *The Presidential Character*], "The President is expected to personify our betterness in an inspiring way, to express in what he does and is (not just in what he says) a moral idealism which, in much of the public mind, is the very opposite of 'politics.'" Michael Novak has observed [in *Choosing Our King: Powerful Symbols in Presidential Politics*]: "Every four years Americans elect a king—but not only a king, also a high priest and prophet." Harry Truman reflected late in life: "I've said before, the President is the only person in the government who represents the whole people . . . and when there's a moral issue involved, the President has to be the moral leader of the country."

The media largely shapes the public's perceptions of a President, and, during the Thousand Days and after his assassination, JFK was portrayed in large part as a saint and superman. However, we may now confidently conclude that Jack was not the man projected in the image. His attractiveness, easy confidence, wit, and charm were persuasive and seductive. He and his family were every reporter's dream and a nation's fantasy of what all families should look like and be. Jack's seeming energy, sincerity, and fidelity were congruent with America's self-image in the world. It all seemed glorious at the time and long after. But the sober truth, which readers of history seek when time has passed, was more complex and often much less flattering than the media of the moment would have had us believe.

A POINT-BY-POINT ASSESSMENT

As an administrator Kennedy was competent if unorthodox. He was more friendly to business than to labor. His judicial appointments, especially outside the South, seemed to reflect good judgment. Kennedy made little impact as a party leader; having usually worked outside the normal channels, he was not highly regarded within them.

As a legislative leader, Kennedy was relatively ineffective. Weak support in Congress was part of the problem. The president's lack of conviction and personal fervor for what he was advocating was partly responsible. His reluctant approach to civil rights, until quite late in his Thousand Days, is a case in point.

Jack was primarily interested in foreign affairs, and it was in his roles as commander in chief and diplomatic leader that he made his principal contributions. It is also in this area of presidential activity that Kennedy's character may be seen most vividly in the decision-making process.

In the Bay of Pigs fiasco, Jack rejected moral and legal objections to an invasion; he lied, exhibited an almost adolescent macho temperament, became involved with military operations just enough to make them worse, and then blamed others for the failure. He soon approved Operation Mongoose, the clandestine exercise in terrorism and murder. Determined to win in Cuba at any cost, Jack had secret dealings with one of the top mobsters involved in the assassination attempts. This reveals an irresponsibility and lack of judgment bordering on dereliction.

The administration's response to the crisis in Southeast Asia involved complex ideological, military, and political considerations. In Laos Jack approved a "secret war" that for years spread mayhem and death throughout the strife-torn nation. In Vietnam the president revealed an almost reckless posture and an intense determination to win. He approved the CIA's most aggressive operations, greatly increased the American presence in the conflict, and became involved in the overthrow of the government of South Vietnam. Moral and legal objections had little or no impact on Kennedy or his advisers as they assumed, by reason of American strength and power, the right to manipulate that country's affairs.

In the Berlin crisis, on the other hand, Kennedy's pugnacity in defense of free world rights was morally defensible, effective, and highly popular. The administration's diplomatic posture—drawing a line and daring the Soviets to cross it—was risky but, given the nature of Khrushchev's temperament and ambitions, probably inevitable. In retrospect the president's firm stand seems to merit the widespread praise it received at the time. And so does his postcrisis appeal to the United Nations for increased negotiations and a "peace race." Courage was an aspect of character which in Jack was almost always sufficient.

Similarly, in the Cuban Missile Crisis, Kennedy's courage in defending the nation and hemisphere from Khrushchev's appalling aggression continues to earn applause, and rightly so. One might well question ExCom's[1] diplomatic moves, which left far too much in the hands of the Soviets. At times Jack seemed overly bellicose, and yet he showed prudence and restraint at key moments in the struggle and quietly agreed even to risk his political career—sacred to a Kennedy—in the interest of peace. . . .

In assessing Kennedy's record as top diplomat and commander in chief, it is important to acknowledge his caution as well as courage. Against the recommendations of top advisers, he sharply limited America's role in the Bay of Pigs invasion and refused to send American troops into Laos and Vietnam. He elected not to attack East Germany when the Berlin Wall was constructed. During the missile crisis, he did what he reasonably could to avoid an invasion of Cuba, revealing a sensitivity about nuclear war that many others in Washington and elsewhere did not share.

Kennedy deserves credit for his efforts in 1963 to deintensify the Cold War and achieve meaningful disarmament. The American University speech and the test-ban treaty were significant achievements that signaled a measure of growth

---

1. ExCom: Executive Committee of the National Security Council

in such qualities as compassion and responsibility.

Due in part to a preoccupation with his own political agenda and an intense hostility toward reformers, Kennedy was a reluctant spokesman for social justice. As David Burner and Thomas R. West have concluded [in *The Torch Is Passed*], "The most loyal and affectionate liberal partisan of John Kennedy cannot make him into a dedicated, consistent, and impassioned champion of a leftward movement in American politics." Still, he could boast of several achievements, including the Area Redevelopment Act of 1961, which promoted public works in such economically crippled areas as West Virginia, and the civil rights legislation that occupied much of his attention in 1963. He also worked persistently, if unsuccessfully, on behalf of legislation to aid education. If Kennedy lacked a grand vision of what America might be, there were nonetheless a few programs he did feel strongly about. . . .

PERSONAL MISCONDUCT

If Kennedy was far from a moral crusader, what may be said in summary about his personal misconduct as it related to the presidency? Given the facts now available, it is clear that Kennedy abused his high position for personal self-gratification. His reckless liaisons with women and mobsters were irresponsible, dangerous, and demeaning to the office of the chief executive. They were irresponsible because of the enormous potential for scandal and blackmail they posed. Any number of women, gangsters, intelligence agents, and journalists might have used their knowledge of Kennedy's sexual meandering to force concessions from the office of the president. The Kennedys had purchased silence in the past, but the stakes were far higher now that Jack was in the White House, and money might well have been inadequate. Had Kennedy lived to see a second term, the realities of his lechery and his dealings with Sam Giancana[2] might have leaked out while he was still in office, gravely damaging the presidency, debilitating his administration, and severely disillusioning a populace which, no matter how jaded it seems, looks to a president with hope for reassurance and leadership. Impeachment might well have followed such public disclosure.

2. a leader in the Chicago mafia

194   *John F. Kennedy*

Kennedy's personal foibles were also dangerous to the welfare of this country and the free world. While we know of only one specific case in which the president was separated from the official who carries the secret information vital to the nation's nuclear defense, and is supposed to be near the chief executive at all times, such incidents surely happened often in the course of Jack's clandestine prowlings. When the president, for example, was roaming through the tunnels beneath New York's Carlyle Hotel to evade reporters and reach intimate friends, was he prepared to handle national security matters?

Kennedy's adultery also demeaned the presidency. Many people in Washington, Hollywood, and elsewhere made the man the butt of jokes and gossip which surely lowered their, and others', respect for the nation's highest office. Subsequent revelations have no doubt contributed further to the widespread public cynicism about the ability of politicians to sacrifice their personal indulgences in the service of national purpose and priorities. . . .

The real Kennedy—as opposed to the celebrated hero espoused by the Kennedy family, the media, and the Camelot School—lacked greatness in large part because he lacked the qualities inherent in good character. While he had ample courage and at times showed considerable prudence, he was deficient in integrity, compassion, and temperance. He was not a crusading reformer, especially early in his administration, because such idealism was low on his agenda of personal priorities. He backed unwise and clandestine activities in Cuba, Laos, and Vietnam largely because he was oblivious to the moral content of arguments against them. He failed to be a true moral leader of the American people because he lacked the conviction and commitment that create such exemplars of character for all to emulate. . . .

LESSONS FOR THE FUTURE

A major lesson that emerges from a careful look at Jack Kennedy's life concerns the moral responsibility of our presidents. From the nation's beginnings, in the exemplary George Washington, who thought about such things, there has been an implicit contract between the chief executive and the American people, an understanding that the nation's highest public official should exhibit such virtues as dignity, moderation, disinterestedness, self-mastery, resoluteness, strength of will, and personal integrity. Washington indeed was regarded as an "exemplification of moral values," a president widely perceived to be great because he was good. The public later attributed the same virtues to Abraham Lincoln. . . .

During the Thousand Days, Kennedy arrogantly and irresponsibly violated his covenant with the people. While saying and doing the appropriate things in the public light, he acted covertly in ways that seriously demeaned himself and his office. He got away with it at the time, and the cover-up that followed kept the truth hidden for decades. That this could happen again makes it imperative that we search for presidential candidates who can, by example, elevate and inspire the American people, restoring confidence in their institutions and in themselves. Kennedy's political skills are desirable, to be sure: the charisma, the inspiring oratory, the wit, the intelligence, the courage. But all of these qualities must be connected to an effort to live and lead by those values, known and declared for centuries, that link good character with effective leadership. The United States—and now the world—cannot settle for less.

Kennedy's Liberal Legacy

David Burner

David Burner argues that President Kennedy shifted the national political focus to the left, toward liberalism, during his years in office. Burner suggests that Kennedy's style in the White House and his appointment of liberal intellectuals to administrative posts set the stage for more liberal policies. Burner cites decisions surrounding the Bay of Pigs incident, the Berlin crisis, the Green Berets, the Peace Corps, the Cuban missile crisis, and the Nuclear Test Ban Treaty to make his case. David Burner has taught history at Colby College in Waterville, Maine, and the State University of New York at Stony Brook. He is the editor and author of many books, among them *A Giant's Strength: America in the 1960s* (with Robert Marcus and Thomas R. West), *The Torch Is Passed: The Kennedy Brothers and American Liberalism* (with Thomas R. West), and *John F. Kennedy and a New Generation.*

An aching-cold sunlight etched the public figures who performed the inaugural rites. It blinded the poet Robert Frost as he tried to read the poem he had composed for the ceremony. Thereupon he discarded it in favor of another poem he spoke from memory. But the words remembered today from January 20, 1961, are those that the speechwriter Theodore Sorensen had composed and the forty-two-year-old John Kennedy delivered to set the tone of his presidency. The country, Kennedy proclaimed in his clean harsh New England twang, was ready to "pay any price, bear any burden, meet any hardship." That the prices and the hardships, along with their objectives, were unspecified does not diminish the appropriateness of the address. . . .

Kennedy in 1960 won a substantial victory in the electoral college but a thin popular margin, probably aided by some vote manipulation in Chicago and Texas. Many Catholic voters favored his election, particularly in the large states where their votes were concentrated. But despite his successful attempt to conduct a campaign different from the parochial contest waged by Al Smith[1] over a generation earlier, the candidate, according to social scientists, lost more votes on account of his religion than he gained. His was the final triumph, nonetheless, for an Irish-American Catholic, the vindication of a heritage and an escape from its burdens. That election night also had powerful meaning for fellow Catholics of varying ethnic strains and for other minority groups—Jews, blacks, Hispanics, Asians. Kennedy's achievement represented the fulfillment of a national promise that Americans even of definably immigrant background might aspire to wealth, homes, education for their children, national leadership, or an ideal of justice.

A TONE OF INTELLECT AND CULTURE

Among the sectors of the public most satisfied with the new President were liberal academicians. The inaugural address had impressed them. A time would come of falling respect for the address, which has as its best-remembered line a contrived play of opposites: "Ask not what your country can do for you—ask what you can do for your country." But it is a rare speech on a ceremonial occasion that is taken seriously enough to receive continued reviews of any kind. The address is noteworthy for the somberness with which the new President chose to lecture his compatriots. He appeared actually to be thinking about his subject, in this respect breaking with political convention. During Kennedy's occupancy of the White House, and for a short time thereafter, much was made of the culture that the administration was supposed to represent, manifesting itself especially in Jacqueline Kennedy, whose attractiveness and social finish lent so much to the Kennedys' public image. That the First Lady spoke French impressed intellectuals in a nation where people do not customarily learn foreign languages well enough to use them. All this bespoke a hope that intellect allied to Democratic liberalism had entered the White

---

1. a candidate in the 1928 presidential election, defeated by Herbert Hoover

House. That hope attended a sense of confidence that in the West ideological conflict was no longer relevant, that science, technology, and civilization had advanced to the point that problems were now solvable by the application of intelligence and impersonal knowledge. Kennedy seemed the right leader to preside over the severe but ultimately benign technical forces of the age.

The administration's new appointments must have displayed to liberals a fitting polish. Robert McNamara, the cost-conscious president of Ford Motors with a mind as clean as a statistical table, became Secretary of Defense. . . . The President appointed the imperturbable Dean Rusk [as Secretary of State]—a Rhodes Scholar who had been a peace advocate before World War II, an open opponent of McCarthyism,[2] and a supporter of Adlai Stevenson[3] even in 1960. Rusk belonged to an almost forgotten company of old-line liberals. . . . A prime adviser who became chair of the Joint Chiefs of Staff was Maxwell Taylor. A scholar who could speak several languages and write serious books, Taylor was a liberal's general. Others on the staff—McGeorge Bundy, Walt Rostow, Chester Bowles, and Arthur Schlesinger, Jr.—constituted virtually a university faculty headed by a President whom [novelist] Norman Mailer once described as resembling a detached young professor.

THE BAY OF PIGS: KENNEDY'S FIRST MAJOR TEST

JFK's first major test occurred during April 1961 in the attempted invasion of Cuba, ending in disaster at the Bay of Pigs. The effort had its origins in the Eisenhower years, when the Central Intelligence Agency had done every bit of the planning for the invasion. Yet the scheme was much in the spirit of the liberalism that attached itself to Kennedy's presidency. Fidel Castro represented the type of leftist regime—repressive, speaking and thinking in slogans, instilling a militant ideological conformity—that liberals despised as a travesty of the idea of social and economic democracy. . . .

Yet the Bay of Pigs invasion looked like the work of amateurs. The planners had picked a landing site inadequate for defense or advance into the interior. The invading force, us-

2. Wisconsin senator Joseph McCarthy investigated public people and accused them of being communists during the early 1950s.   3. the Democratic nominee for President in 1952 and 1956

ing old freighters supplied by the United Fruit Company, was badly equipped and poorly supported. Promised air cover proved inadequate and untimely (the airplanes were operating on Eastern instead of Caribbean time); the boats' hulls ripped apart on coral reefs. . . .

His [Kennedy's] refusal in the final instance to use force conformed to the liberal idea of force exactly measured, stripped of any motives of self-gratifying belligerence. And this would be the rule throughout his presidency. Behind the language of confrontation, he and his lieutenants brought to foreign policy a large degree of caution and temperance. . . .

THE BERLIN CRISIS: A TREATY AND A WALL

The Cold War had begun out of an understandable fear of the Soviet Union, after a world war against a state[4] that the Stalinist monstrosity closely resembled. From the early and limited programs for protecting the Western European democracies, the confrontation with Moscow spread by its own moral and strategic logic to the rest of the world, growing hazier in its definition of the enemy. . . .

A crisis in Berlin brought the Cold War back to the continent of its origin. The Berlin airlift of 1948—when President Truman kept intact the Western presence there despite Stalin's attempts to choke the city by cutting off all land routes—had been the first head-to-head confrontation between the allies and the Soviet Union. It had been the West's clearest triumph. In 1961, Soviet Premier Nikita Khrushchev revived the threat to the city. He announced that unless the Western powers entered an agreement favorable to East Germany, Moscow was going to sign a separate peace treaty with its satellite power, whose status from the first days of Soviet occupation had been considered to be in suspension until the reunifying of all of Germany under free elections. What Khrushchev was proposing, in effect, was to make East Germany a (nominally) sovereign republic surrounding and endangering the freedom of West Berlin, the part of the city not under Soviet occupation. Khrushchev suggested that West Berlin become a free city under United Nations guarantees. But the allies did not relish making the city hostage to the good intentions of East Germany or that prospective nation's Soviet overlord. . . .

4. Germany under Hitler

The USSR had serious and legitimate concerns. Germany had won against Russia, Czarist and Bolshevik, the Eastern phase of World War I, extracting a favorable peace before suffering its own defeat on the Western front. That Germany in the Second World War had proved a monumental and unspeakable threat to the Soviet Union needs no argument. Now, under postwar conditions, a greater Germany would become an instrument of Western power against the Soviet bloc. A separate Eastern German nation would preclude that danger. A more immediate problem for the Soviet Union was the accelerating exodus to the West, through the border between East and West Berlin, of Germans whose education and skills were essential to the economy of eastern Germany and implicitly to the social stability of Moscow's other European satellite nations. As part of his scheme for Germany, Khrushchev insisted that the communists have authority to prevent exit through the border within Berlin. . . .

The Western allies believed they had a commitment to defend the freedom of the West Berliners, who having lived under freedom would suffer its loss more grievously than East Germans suffered its absence. Khrushchev's plan was to establish East Germany permanently as a separate republic. It would therefore have none of the obligations that bound the Soviet Union, as one of the postwar occupiers of Germany, to act in concert with her wartime Western allies in any future governance and disposition of Berlin. . . .

It was unpredictable what Khrushchev would do if, as observers at the time believed, a continued flow of refugees brought that collapse[5] nearer. To allow the communists to prevent passage into a freer society was ugly. But even uglier might be the reaction in Moscow to the possibility of economic and social disaster in Eastern Europe.

Resolution, then, had to balance against compromise, the needs of Berliners against the needs of peace. The adversary force was too powerful, and its wants too urgent, to make possible any satisfyingly easy use of Western force. At the same time the rights of Berliners were too important to be accorded a merely rhetorical heroism as their defense. The problem was of the kind that could not accommodate the palpitating emotions of the right.[6]

---

5. the economic collapse of Eastern Germany   6. the conservative right-wing politicians in America

Much of the Kennedy administration's response was an increase in belligerency, and not merely of words but of actions. The President called for an extensive civil defense program and on July 25, proposing an increase in military spending and in the armed forces, announced a doubling of draft calls and a mobilization of some fifty-one thousand army reserve troops. . . .

[In August 1961], the communists began restricting egress through the Berlin border and started construction of the infamous wall. That the act was ostensibly an East German rather than a Soviet initiative constituted in itself something of a challenge to the West. Although the German Democratic Republic had not yet signed a treaty with the USSR, it was acting like a sovereign power, precisely the status that Moscow wanted to force the West to acknowledge. But such technicalities did not preoccupy Western public opinion. The clearest result was that East Germans seeking freedom or opportunity in the West were now sealed up, unless they should find a means of escape. And then there was the added fear that construction of the wall might be the prelude to some attempt to swallow up West Berlin within East Germany.

KENNEDY'S STRATEGY: FUSING CONFRONTATION WITH RESTRAINT

Kennedy's reaction had the appearance of resoluteness. Denouncing the Berlin Wall as an outrage, he called up more military reservists and sent fifteen hundred troops to West Berlin along the Autobahn through communist Germany (former Secretary of State Dean Acheson advised sending a division, but he hailed from a more primitive stage of the Cold War). Vice President Lyndon Johnson visited West Berlin to affirm an American pledge to defend it. As his representative to Berlin, Kennedy appointed General Lucius Clay, who had conducted the airlift of 1948 that ended in a triumph of Western skill and resolve. . . . In October at the border between the two Berlins, there was at General Clay's initiative a moment's face-off of tanks snout to snout that ended only when the Russians pulled theirs back.

If the Kennedy administration had previously been sending hints to the Soviet Union that shutting off East Berlin would be understandable and acceptable, then why the militancy of the American response once the communists had acted? The President may have reflected that although he could not prevent Khrushchev from fencing in the East Germans, he could still rally the allies to the defense of West Berlin. . . .

As Kennedy was piecing out his confrontation with Khrushchev, the two men began a lengthy correspondence. Early in September the Premier told the *New York Times* of his willingness to meet with the President as he had inconclusively in Vienna the previous June, suggesting the solution of a dispute in Laos in return for a solution of the Berlin question. On September 25 Kennedy made a conciliatory address before the United Nations. To General Clay, who wanted authority to take quick unilateral action in Berlin as occasion demanded, Kennedy recommended instead cautious determination and coolness. . . .

The administration's response to the Berlin crisis was, in sum, a carefully managed fusion of confrontation and restraint, the general strategy of liberalism in its argument with the right. The confrontational element was not in itself the sending of military reinforcements to West Berlin—the minimal action required to make clear the will to sustain the enclave—but rather the original decision to preserve it. The Cold War policies crafted by liberals had committed the United States to Berlin as a symbol of its solidarity with West Germany and beyond with Western Europe. Here the nation probably went far beyond the actual frontiers of its self-interest. In the fantasy world of the right, on the other hand, the sacred mission of the United States was to drive communism back, preferably to the borders of the Soviet Union, and more preferably to oblivion. . . .

A PRAGMATIC SOLUTION FOR BERLIN

The Kennedy administration did not encourage the Western alliance to undertake the destruction of the Berlin Wall. Washington indicated its willingness to accept the wall, its determination to protect West Berlin, and its desire to do both as economically as possible. Its policy was spare and well calculated to those ends, an instance of the prudent statesmanship that qualified the somber militancy of the inaugural address.

In contrast to the way he had embarked on the Bay of Pigs invasion, then, Kennedy's behavior during the Berlin crisis reflected the very essence of the liberal cold warrior: measured, exact, cool, and patient. His hard line adviser on Latin America, Adolf Berle, did not like the performance: "The evidence coming in now," he wrote in his diary, "suggests that a little nerve would have stopped the [wall]."

THE INDIRECT BATTLE AGAINST COMMUNISM: THE GREEN BERETS AND THE PEACE CORPS

While restrained, carefully calibrated military confrontations were defining in part the Kennedy presidency, his administration was shaping other programs that added to the definition. The Peace Corps and the Green Berets, a new version of the special military unit of the 1950s, had a number of things in common. Both were intended as instruments of the war against communism. Each was, at least according to its original intellectual architects, to convert that war as far as possible into a project for social reform and technocratic economic progress. The Special Forces warriors and the Peace Corps volunteers must be elites of purpose, intelligence, and technical sophistication.

The Green Berets, whose official title was the Special Forces, were in the same tradition of a mobile, autonomous elite to which the PT-boat officers of World War II had belonged. Kennedy, along with Secretary of Defense Robert McNamara, included them in the administration's design for the renovation of the country's arms. The Secretary had an appetite for efficiency and a reliance on modern methods of gathering information. Our need, the administration reasoned, was for a more versatile and flexible defense than the existing city-killing nuclear weapons, for if an emergency should arise, they would limit us to choosing between doing nothing and incinerating the globe. Kennedy and McNamara developed a system that targeted Soviet missile sites rather than cities. Troops of the Special Forces as the administration imagined them looked something like a human equivalent of this projected missile force. They were supposed to be independent, skilled in individual combat, sensitive and knowledgeable in working with civilians. Any Special Forces personnel parachuted into Hungary, it was suggested, ought to be familiar with the major Hungarian poets.

The idea for a Peace Corps had in fact been around for some years before Kennedy's presidency. The notion, which Kennedy took up in the 1960 campaign, stood in counterpoint to an unflattering image that many Americans had come to have of their compatriots abroad—an image to which a novel published in 1958 by William J. Lederer and

Eugene Burdick had notably contributed.

The figure from whom their book *The Ugly American*[7] takes its name is physically ugly, a sign of plain moral character, and he is committed in a blunt earnest way to service and good work. He is an engineer whose ideas of appropriate technology, shaped to the needs and resources of traditional impoverished communities, have no appeal for the American, French, and Asian officials he encounters. . . .

The title, though not the argument, of the novel was quickly misconstrued. "Ugly American" soon came in common parlance to designate Americans who were the opposite of the novel's virtuously homely figure: Americans who flaunted their money, made loud demands for American standards of comfort, disdained knowledge of the language and culture of the country they were invading, and in general insulted their host population and embarrassed their homeland. The point of the Peace Corps was to field American teachers, agronomists, road surveyors, and the like who would be rewarded only by pride and commitment to the work: "Ugly Americans" in the original meaning of the book title.

No program advanced during Kennedy's presidency so perfectly fitted his call as did the Peace Corps to "ask what you can do for your country.". . . The program was, to be sure, meant to be an arm of the battle against communist infiltration of the Third World, and participants had to take a loyalty oath. But the designers of the Peace Corps sincerely intended the lessening of illiteracy and poverty as goods in themselves and perceived economic and social justice as integral to democratic pluralism. The condensed training was rigorous; Americans were actually required to learn to speak foreign languages; volunteers prepared to serve in the outlands, far distant from any access to exported American luxuries. The liberals of Kennedy's time shared in the continuing American preoccupation with the nation's character and ethos. . . .

The administration was moving toward articulating a persuasive alternative, and counter, to communist ideology. Previously the democratic West had offered little as an answer to communism: either mere anticommunism, which is no more

---

7. The expression had two meanings. As a book title, it referred to a physically unattractive man with good will and a good heart; as a phrase in the common culture, it referred to attractive Americans who acted with arrogance and poor manners and made unreasonable demands.

than definition by opposition and therefore devoid of substance; or militant capitalism, which has little that is convincing to say to the world's poor and excluded. Kennedy, for example, seems to have intended so to distribute Alliance for Progress funds as to lessen somewhat the structural inequalities of power and wealth in recipient countries. . . .

But the war with Third-World movements allied to Moscow or Beijing dictated that American policy would do business with repressive regimes of entrenched privilege claiming to be a bulwark against communist revolution, as has been the case in Washington's dealings with Latin America. And as long as extremes of structural inequality remained—and structural inequality was exactly what such regimes were determined to protect—even the best-intentioned programs of economic relief could offer no more than relief. . . .

THE CUBAN MISSILE CRISIS: KENNEDY'S MOST DANGEROUS TEST

The Kennedy administration had yet to face its most dangerous moment. That moment could not have been predicted. Its origins lay in considerations that in 1962 led Nikita Khrushchev secretly to begin installing missiles in Cuba, some of them supplied with nuclear warheads. . . .

In the early autumn of 1962 air photographs confirmed the existence of Cuban missile sites, and without revealing the findings to the public, the administration quietly prepared a response. Kennedy had learned from the disaster at the Bay of Pigs. He wanted counsel more balanced and thoroughly debated than a single group of advisers could give him. For the purpose he drew together from the National Security Council and elsewhere an executive committee, or ExComm, as it became called, in crisp alignment with the cold, swift decisions that the moment demanded. ExComm was an assemblage of the government's highest civilian and military officials, and they ranged in persuasion from the dovish Ambassador to the United Nations, Adlai Stevenson, to the Joint Chiefs of Staff, who, like former President Eisenhower, wished to take out the missile sites with an air strike. . . .

Not until Monday, October 12, did the public learn that the world was in a grave crisis. On television that evening the President revealed the presence of the missiles and the decision to impose a quarantine. Some have retrospectively criticized him for bringing the matter to public attention, which very likely made it more embarrassing for the Soviet Union to withdraw. To that the response has usually been that diplomatic efforts were then under way and the purpose of the speech was to mobilize international opinion on the side of the United States. For about two days the world waited to see what its future was going to be. Then on Wednesday, after the navy allowed a tanker to pass through, a Soviet ship containing equipment that could be used for the missiles turned back. But it had been a close thing. Some 180 warheads, many with nuclear warheads installed in the missiles, were already being assembled in Cuba, and local Soviet commanders had discretion over whether to use them. Kennedy knew nothing of this. And some forty-five thousand Soviet troops were on the island, far more than Washington had estimated.

Privately, Moscow and Washington had meanwhile been negotiating their mutual preservation. Khrushchev, frightened by Castro's desire to launch a preemptive attack against the United States, sent a telegram proposing a removal of the missiles in return for a promise not to invade Cuba. Then he sent another asking for the removal of Jupiter missiles in Turkey, which the Department of Defense had not yet dismantled as Kennedy had long since ordered. . . .

Robert Kennedy suggested a tactful response: ignore the second telegram, publicly accept the substance of the first with a private agreement not to invade Cuba, and privately let Moscow know that dismantling the Cuban missiles would bring dismantlement of ours in Turkey. On Sunday morning, Americans awakened to learn that the Soviet Union had decided to withdraw the Cuban missiles. . . .

In the wake of the crisis, in fact, the two nations became more civil toward each other than they had been at any time since the beginning of the Cold War. Kennedy's June 1963 speech at American University warned against having "a desperate and distorted view of the other side." Teletype communication, which Khrushchev had proposed over a year earlier, was established between Moscow and Washington—the hot line it became popularly known as for use in times of danger. . . . The American public began to acquire something close to a liking for Khrushchev's earthy exuberance—at times he seemed the classic peasant of folklore—and for the happy resolution of the moment of high tension that he, his country, and the American people had gone through together. The warming of relations was both cause and effect of the successful negotiation of a treaty banning the atmospheric testing of nuclear weapons.

THE TEST BAN TREATY

Earlier, in the days of anger over Berlin, Khrushchev had resumed nuclear testing, and the United States had followed quickly in September 1961; the next spring the light from an American Starfish test brought false daylight to Hawaii and flashed the skies as far as Australia. But in the spirit of friendship, or of the discovery of the precariousness of peace, or of the simple giddy relief that followed the Cuban missile crisis, Soviet and American leaders negotiated in late 1963 a treaty banning testing above ground.

Americans on the right, of course, denounced the treaty as appeasement. A later and opposite accusation has been that the treaty, rather than embodying a sense of equity on the part of the administration, merely halted the process of testing at a state of weaponry favorable to the United States. But partly in reaction to Herman Kahn's controversial *On Thermonuclear War* (1960), even the notion of nuclear superiority was becoming obsolete by the early 1960s. It was generally understood that in a nuclear exchange, no matter which side might have the slight advantage of instigating it, the results would be intolerable devastation to both sides. . . .

Right-wing critics at the time, who saw the treaty as an act of self-interest on the part of the Soviet Union, and later American critics on the left who labeled it an act of self-interest on the part of the United States, were both quite obviously correct: otherwise there would have been no treaty. . . .

The treaty's victory in the Senate in September 1963, by a vote of eighty to nineteen, represented in foreign policy what the victory of civil rights legislation was to signify on the race issue. It meant that a consensus was forming to the left of where American ultranationalists had for a time believed and hoped that it had fixed itself—in the case of the treaty, that unremitting hostility to the Soviet Union as a transcendent evil was giving way to a posture of armed watchfulness. Part of the story of the decades to follow lies in the right's attempt to reestablish the anticommunist certainties of an earlier day. . . .

In Kennedy's time the stretch of conflict and conciliation between the two powers surpassed the range during any other presidency. What more particularly qualified the conflicts of the time, on both sides, was a character of measure and meticulousness in the actions that accompanied and in some degree resolved them. It is as though the liberal idea, expounded against the jangled nerves of the right, of how to wage a protracted though cold war had found an opportunity to take the stage in the intricate moves of Berlin and the Cuban missile crisis, in the Peace Corps, the Green Berets, the test-ban treaty. And for that liberal idea to achieve the proper staging, it needed the unlikely cooperation of Nikita Khrushchev, who seemed to understand the motions of the dance.

DISCUSSION QUESTIONS AND RESEARCH PROJECTS

CHAPTER ONE

1. Rose Kennedy has been described as the most successful Kennedy campaigner. According to Gail Cameron's essay, what personal qualities and past experiences contributed to Rose Kennedy's success?

2. What does Richard J. Whalen mean by "toughness"? Provide examples from the first three generations of Kennedys that illustrate this quality.

3. Joseph Kennedy wanted to be identified as "American," not "Irish." Had he been accepted as American, do you think he would have become as rich? Would he have been as ambitious for his son John? Explain your answers.

CHAPTER TWO

1. Consider Gore Vidal's attitudes toward President Kennedy. Are these attitudes based on biased opinion, reasoned argument, or objective fact? Cite content and word choice to support your choices.

2. Compare and contrast Jack Kennedy's and Richard Nixon's preparation for the first live television debate.

3. What does Arthur Schlesinger mean by "the new frontiersmen"? Do you think this is a good model for a working staff? Why or why not?

CHAPTER THREE

1. How does the initial purpose of the Peace Corps compare with the domestic and foreign benefits that resulted a year later?

2. Was Kennedy justified in taking the action he did with the steel industry? Why or why not?

3. Compare and contrast Henry Fairlie's and Allen Matusow's analyses of Kennedy's commitment to civil rights. How do the authors differ in their discussion of Kennedy's actions and in their use of language?

CHAPTER FOUR

1. What was Kennedy's idea behind the formation of the Alliance for Progress? Was Bruce Miroff a reliable source to evaluate its failure? Why or why not?
2. If Kennedy had not inherited previous commitments concerning Cuba and Vietnam, would his decisions have been the same or different? Use the authors' analysis to justify your conclusion.

CHAPTER FIVE

1. How does Kenneth P. O'Donnell's airplane conversation with Kennedy offer clues to Kennedy's future foreign-policy decisions regarding Nikita Khrushchev and the cold war?
2. Kennedy's strategy in response to Khrushchev's threat to eliminate the western presence in Berlin was to stand firm, neither attacking nor retreating. Why did this strategy work? What would have been the results had he chosen either of the other strategies?
3. Consider viewpoints three and four. Which leader, Kennedy or Khrushchev, had the better justification for his action? Consider the way each framed his argument even if you do not agree with it.

CHAPTER SIX

1. According to William G. Carleton, was Kennedy a good president? Evaluate his opinion by considering his presentation of facts and reasons and any possible personal bias.
2. How does Thomas Reeves relate Kennedy's personal qualities and actions to the process of governing? Has the author used logical reasoning? Explain.
3. In the context of David Bruner's viewpoint, what does "liberal" mean? Provide examples of Kennedy's policies and actions that Bruner considers liberal.

GENERAL QUESTIONS

1. What do you think was Kennedy's most significant contribution to his country?
2. Why was Kennedy so popular and why has he remained popular after his death?

APPENDIX

EXCERPTS FROM ORIGINAL DOCUMENTS PERTAINING TO JOHN F. KENNEDY

DOCUMENT 1: THE COMPLEX MOTIVES OF POLITICIANS

In his book Profiles in Courage, *Kennedy describes the political lives of various American congressmen and senators. In the conclusion to his book, he reflects on the motives of the politicians he has profiled. He speculates on politicians' acting for their own good as opposed to acting for the good of the nation and concedes that his portraits of politicians "do not dispel the mysteries of politics."*

This has been a book about courage and politics. Politics furnished the situations, courage provided the theme. Courage, the universal virtue, is comprehended by us all—but these portraits of courage do not dispel the mysteries of politics.

For not a single one of the men whose stories appear in the preceding pages offers a simple, clear-cut picture of motivation and accomplishment. In each of them complexities, inconsistencies and doubts arise to plague us. However detailed may have been our study of his life, each man remains something of an enigma. However clear the effect of his courage, the cause is shadowed by a veil which cannot be torn away. We may confidently state the reasons why—yet something always seems to elude us. We think we hold the answer in our hands—yet somehow it slips through our fingers.

Motivation, as any psychiatrist will tell us, is always difficult to assess. It is particularly difficult to trace in the murky sea of politics. Those who abandoned their state and section for the national interest—men like Daniel Webster and Sam Houston, whose ambitions for higher office could not be hidden—laid themselves open to the charge that they sought only to satisfy their ambition for the Presidency. Those who broke with their party to fight for broader principles—men like John Quincy Adams and Edmund Ross— faced the accusation that they accepted office under one banner and yet deserted it in a moment of crisis for another.

But in the particular events set forth in the preceding chapters, I am persuaded after long study of the record that the national interest, rather than private or political gain, furnished the basic motiva-

212 John F. Kennedy

tion for the actions of those whose deeds are therein described. This does not mean that many of them did not seek, though rarely with success, to wring advantage out of the difficult course they had adopted. For as politicians—and it is surely no disparagement to term all of them politicians—they were clearly justified in doing so.

Of course, the acts of courage described in this book would be more inspiring and would shine more with the traditional luster of hero-worship if we assumed that each man forgot wholly about himself in his dedication to higher principles. But it may be that President John Adams, surely as disinterested as well as wise a public servant as we ever had, came much nearer to the truth when he wrote in his *Defense of the Constitutions of the United States:* "It is not true, in fact, that any people ever existed who love the public better than themselves."

If this be true, what then caused the statesmen mentioned in the preceding pages to act as they did? It was not because they "loved the public better than themselves." On the contrary it was precisely because they did *love themselves*—because each one's need to maintain his own respect for himself was more important to him than his popularity with others—because his desire to win or maintain a reputation for integrity and courage was stronger than his desire to maintain his office—because his conscience, his personal standard of ethics, his integrity or morality, call it what you will—was stronger than the pressures of public disapproval—because his faith that *his* course was the best one, and would ultimately be vindicated, outweighed his fear of public reprisal.

Although the public good was the indirect beneficiary of his sacrifice, it was not that vague and general concept, but one or a combination of these pressures of self-love that pushed him along the course of action that resulted in the slings and arrows previously described. It is when the politician loves neither the public good nor himself, or when his love for himself is limited and is satisfied by the trappings of office, that the public interest is badly served. And it is when his regard for himself is so high that his own self-respect demands he follow the path of courage and conscience that all benefit. It is then that his belief in the rightness of his own course enables him to say with John C. Calhoun:

> I never know what South Carolina thinks of a measure. I never consult her. I act to the best of my judgment and according to my conscience. If she approves, well and good. If she does not and wishes anyone to take my place, I am ready to vacate. We are even.

John F. Kennedy, *Profiles in Courage.* New York: Pocket Books, 1963. First published by Harper & Row, 1956.

DOCUMENT 2: PRESIDENT KENNEDY'S INAUGURAL ADDRESS

The Inaugural address of a newly elected president reveals the vision and timber of the man who will lead the nation. Kennedy's inau-

I *gural address, eloquently crafted, conveys a tone of sacrifice and hope, warning and assurance, and invites American citizens and the world to work together for peace and freedom.*

We observe today not a victory of a party but a celebration of freedom—symbolizing an end as well as a beginning—signifying renewal as well as change. For I have sworn before you and Almighty God the same solemn oath our forebears prescribed nearly a century and three-quarters ago.

The world is very different now. For man holds in his mortal hands the power to abolish all forms of human poverty and all forms of human life. And yet the same revolutionary beliefs for which our forebears fought are still at issue around the globe—the belief that the rights of man come not from the generosity of the state but from the hand of God.

We dare not forget today that we are the heirs of that first revolution. Let the word go forth from this time and place, to friend and foe alike, that the torch has been passed to a new generation of Americans—born in this century, tempered by war, disciplined by a hard and bitter peace, proud of our ancient heritage—and unwilling to witness or permit the slow undoing of those human rights to which this Nation has always been committed, and to which we are committed today at home and around the world.

Let every nation know, whether it wishes us well or ill, that we shall pay any price, bear any burden, meet any hardship, support any friend, oppose any foe to assure the survival and success of liberty.

This much we pledge—and more.

To those old allies whose cultural and spiritual origins we share, we pledge the loyalty of faithful friends. United, there is little we cannot do in a host of co-operative ventures. Divided, there is little we can do—for we dare not meet a powerful challenge at odds and split asunder.

To those new states whom we welcome to the ranks of the free, we pledge our word that one form of colonial control shall not have passed away merely to be replaced by a far more iron tyranny. We shall not always expect to find them supporting our view. But we shall always hope to find them strongly supporting their own freedom—and to remember that, in the past, those who foolishly sought power by riding the back of the tiger ended up inside.

To those peoples in the huts and villages of half the globe struggling to break the bonds of mass misery, we pledge our best efforts to help them help themselves, for whatever period is required—not because the Communists may be doing it, not because we seek their votes, but because it is right. If a free society cannot help the many who are poor, it cannot save the few who are rich.

To our sister [Latin American] republics south of our border, we offer a special pledge—to convert our good words into good deeds—

in a new alliance for progress—to assist free men and free governments in casting off the chains of poverty. But this peaceful revolution
of hope cannot become the prey of hostile powers. Let all our neighbors know that we shall join with them to oppose aggression or sub-
version anywhere in the Americas. And let every other power know
that this hemisphere intends to remain the master of its own house.

To that world assembly of sovereign states, the United Nations,
our last best hope in an age where the instruments of war have far
outpaced the instruments of peace, we renew our pledge of support—to prevent it from becoming merely a forum for invective—
to strengthen its shield of the new and the weak—and to enlarge
the area in which its writ may run.

Finally, to those nations who would make themselves our adversary, we offer not a pledge but a request: that both sides begin
anew the quest for peace, before the dark powers of destruction un-
leashed by science engulf all humanity in planned or accidental
self-destruction.

We dare not tempt them with weakness. For only when our
arms are sufficient beyond doubt can we be certain beyond doubt
that they will never be employed.

But neither can two great and powerful groups of nations take
comfort from our present course—both sides overburdened by the
cost of modern weapons, both rightly alarmed by the steady spread
of the deadly atom, yet both racing to alter that uncertain balance
of terror that stays the hand of mankind's final war.

So let us begin anew—remembering on both sides that civility is
not a sign of weakness, and sincerity is always subject to proof. Let
us never negotiate out of fear. But let us never fear to negotiate.

Let both sides explore what problems unite us instead of bela-
boring those problems which divide us. Let both sides, for the first
time, formulate serious and precise proposals for the inspection
and control of arms—and bring the absolute power to destroy other
nations under the absolute control of all nations.

Let both sides seek to invoke the wonders of science instead of
its terrors. Together let us explore the stars, conquer the deserts,
eradicate disease, tap the ocean depths and encourage the arts and
commerce.

Let both sides unite to heed in all corners of the earth the command of Isaiah—to 'undo the heavy burdens . . . [and] let the op-
pressed go free.'

And if a beachhead of co-operation may push back the jungle of
suspicion, let both sides join in a new endeavor, not a new balance
of power, but a new world of law, where the strong are just and the
weak secure and the peace preserved.

All this will not be finished in the first one hundred days. Nor
will it be finished in the first thousand days, nor in the life of this
Administration, nor even perhaps in our lifetime on this planet. But
let us begin.

In your hands, my fellow citizens, more than mine, will rest the final success or failure of our course. Since this country was founded, each generation of Americans has been summoned to give testimony to its national loyalty. The graves of young Americans who answered the call to service surround the globe.

Now the trumpet summons us again—not as a call to bear arms, though arms we need—not as a call to battle, though embattled we are—but a call to bear the burden of a long twilight struggle, year in and year out, 'rejoicing in hope, patient in tribulation'—a struggle against the common enemies of man: tyranny, poverty, disease and war itself.

Can we forge against these enemies a grand and global alliance, North and South, East and West, that can assure a more fruitful life for all mankind? Will you join in that historic effort?

In the long history of the world, only a few generations have been granted the role of defending freedom in its hour of maximum danger. I do not shrink from this responsibility—I welcome it. I do not believe that any of us would exchange places with any other people or any other generation. The energy, the faith, the devotion which we bring to this endeavor will light our country and all who serve it—and the glow from that fire can truly light the world.

And so, my fellow Americans: Ask not what your country can do for you—ask what you can do for your country.

My fellow citizens of the world, ask not what America will do for you, but what together we can do for the freedom of man.

Finally, whether you are citizens of America or citizens of the world, ask of us here the same high standards of strength and sacrifice which we ask of you. With a good conscience our only sure reward, with history the final judge of our deeds, let us go forth to lead the land we love, asking His blessing and His help, but knowing that here on earth God's work must truly be our own.

John F. Kennedy, "Inaugural Address." Washington, D.C., January 21, 1961. In *The Politics of John F. Kennedy*, by Edmund S. Ions. New York: Barnes & Noble, 1967.

DOCUMENT 5: THE NEW FRONTIER

In a speech in Pennsylvania, Kennedy outlines the new frontier of the 1960s as a series of challenges Americans must face at home. The challenges are a growing population, an expanding elderly population, the need to educate large numbers of young people, scientific advancement, and increasing amounts of leisure time.

What are the new frontiers of the 1960s? We can foresee earthshaking revolutions abroad—new nations, new weapons, new shifts in the balance of power and new members of the nuclear club. But equally earthshaking, equally fraught with both danger and opportunity, are the new frontiers we face here at home.

First is the new frontier of population. Nineteen hundred and sixty will conclude the largest 10-year growth in the history of our country, a growth which equals the entire population of Poland or Spain. By 1970, our population will have grown to 208 million people, and to maintain an advancing standard of living for that many people, we will have to increase our gross national product to three-quarters of a trillion dollars. . . .

Second is the new frontier of longevity. Already nearly 10 per cent of our population is over the age of 65. . . . But will these extra years be a blessing or a curse? Will they be years of loneliness, poverty, high doctors' bills, and low income? Or will they be years of dignity and security and recognition? . . .

Third is the new frontier of education. Pouring into our schools in the next 10 years will be the nearly 51 million children who were born in this country between 1946 and 1958—a number greater than our entire population in 1880. . . .

Fourth is the new frontier of suburbia, the fastest growing sector of the American population. Most suburban areas have gained more residents in the last 10 years than in the previous century, and that growth will be increased in the sixties. But they are not prepared. . . .

Fifth are the new frontiers in science and space. We are already racing from the jet age to the space age before meeting the safety, airport development, and other problems of the former. Space exploration that unravels the secrets of our universe, reconnaissance satellites that can replace a hundred U-2 planes watching over all the world, civilian travel in space vehicles, and the rule of law and disarmament in space itself, all these lie ahead of this generation. . . .

Sixth is the new frontier of automation. In every kind of endeavor, in office work as well as industry, in skilled labor as well as common tasks, machines are replacing men, and men are looking for work. . . .

Seventh and finally is the new frontier of leisure time. The coming of automation, the expansion of labor force, the extension of the lifeline, and the speed of modern transportation, all contribute to the amount of time available to Americans outside of work. What will we do with that time? If we continue to ignore the polluting of our streams, the littering of our national parks, and the waste of our national forests, we will be denying to ourselves and our children a part of their rightful heritage. . . .

The new frontier of which I speak is not too hard for us, neither is it far off. No one need bring it to us; it is here, both its dangers and its opportunities, and we must meet its challenges here, in our hearts.

John F. Kennedy, Speech at Valley Forge, Pennsylvania, October 29, 1960. In *The Politics of John F. Kennedy*, by Edmund S. Ions. New York: Barnes & Noble, 1967.

DOCUMENT 4: ADDRESS TO THE NATION ON SOVIET MISSILES IN CUBA

On October 22, 1962, on radio and television, President Kennedy addressed the nation regarding the Soviet Union's installation of mis-

siles in Cuba. In this excerpt, the president speaks of grave danger as he outlines evidence of Soviet actions, the steps he has taken in response, and his clear call for restraint. But he also makes clear America's resolve that the missiles be removed.

My fellow-citizens—
This Government, as promised, has maintained the closest surveillance of the Soviet military buildup on the island of Cuba. Within the past week, unmistakable evidence has established the fact that a series of offensive missile sites is now in preparation on that imprisoned island. The purpose of these bases can be none other than to provide a nuclear strike capability against the Western hemisphere.

Upon receiving the first preliminary hard information of this nature last Tuesday morning at 9 a.m., I directed that our surveillance be stepped up. And having now confirmed and completed our evaluation of the evidence and our decision on a course of action, this Government feels obliged to report this new crisis to you in full detail.

The characteristics of these new missile sites indicate two distinct types of installations. Several of them include medium-range ballistic missiles, capable of carrying a nuclear warhead for a distance of more than 1,000 nautical miles. Each of these missiles, in short, is capable of striking Washington, D.C., the Panama Canal, Cape Canaveral, Mexico City, or any other city in the Eastern part of the United States, in Central America or in the Caribbean area.

Additional sites not yet completed appear to be designed for intermediate-range ballistic missiles—capable of travelling more than twice as far—and thus capable of striking most of the major cities in the Western hemisphere, ranging as far North as Hudson's Bay, Canada, and as far South as Lima, Peru. In addition, jet bombers, capable of carrying nuclear weapons, are now being uncrated and assembled on Cuba, while the necessary air bases are being prepared.

This urgent transformation of Cuba into an important strategic base—by the presence of these large, long-range and clearly offensive weapons of sudden mass destruction—constitutes an explicit threat to the peace and security of all the Americas, in flagrant and deliberate defiance of the Rio Pact of 1947, the traditions of this nation and hemisphere, the joint resolution of the 87th Congress, the Charter of the United Nations and my own public warnings to the Soviets on 4 and 13 September. This action also contradicts the repeated assurances of Soviet spokesmen, both publicly and privately delivered, that the arms buildup in Cuba would retain its original defensive character, and that the Soviet Union had no need or desire to station strategic missiles on the territory of any other nation. . . .

For many years, both the Soviet Union and the United States—recognizing this fact—have deployed strategic nuclear weapons with great care, never upsetting the precarious *status quo* which en- sured that these weapons would not be used in the absence of some vital challenge. Our own strategic missiles have never been trans- ferred to the territory of any other nation under a cloak of secrecy and deception; and our history—unlike that of the Soviets since World War II—demonstrates that we have no desire to dominate or conquer any other nation or impose our system upon its people.

Nevertheless, American citizens have become adjusted to living daily on the bull's-eye of Soviet missiles located inside the USSR or in submarines. In that sense, missiles in Cuba add to an already clear and present danger—although, it should be noted, the nations of Latin America have never previously been subjected to a poten- tial nuclear threat.

But this secret, swift and extraordinary buildup of Communist missiles—in an area well-known to have a special and historical relationship to the United States and the nations of the Western hemisphere, in violation of Soviet assurances, and in defiance of American and hemispheric policy—this sudden decision to station strategic weapons for the first time outside of Soviet soil—is a de- liberately provocative and unjustified change in the *status quo* which cannot be accepted by this country, if our courage and our commitments are ever to be trusted again by either friend or foe....

Acting, therefore, in the defense of our own security and that of the entire Western hemisphere, and under the authority entrusted to me by the Constitution as endorsed by the resolution of the Congress, I have directed that the following initial steps be taken immediately:

First: to halt this offensive buildup, a strict quarantine on all of- fensive military equipment under shipment to Cuba is being initi- ated. All ships of any kind bound for Cuba, from whatever nation or port, will, if found to contain cargoes of offensive weapons, be turned back. This quarantine will be extended, if needed, to other types of cargo and carriers. We are not at this time, however, deny- ing the necessities of life as the Soviets attempted to do in their Berlin blockade of 1948.

Second: I have directed the continued and increased close sur- veillance of Cuba and its military buildup.... I have directed the Armed Forces to prepare for any eventualities; and I trust that, in the interest of both the Cuban people and the Soviet technicians at these sites, the hazards to all concerned of continuing this threat will be recognized.

Third: It shall be the policy of this nation to regard any nuclear missile launched from Cuba against any nation in the Western hemisphere as an attack by the Soviet Union on the United States requiring a full retaliatory response upon the Soviet Union.

Fourth: As a necessary military precaution, I have reinforced our base at Guantanamo, evacuated today the dependents of our personnel there and ordered additional military units to be on a standby alert basis.

Fifth: We are calling tonight for an immediate meeting of the Organ of Consultation under the Organisation of American States, to consider this threat to hemispheric security and to invoke Articles 6 and 8 of the Rio Treaty in support of all necessary action. The United Nations Charter allows for regional security arrangements, and the nations of this hemisphere decided long ago against the military presence of outside powers. Our other Allies around the world have also been alerted.

Sixth: Under the Charter of the United Nations, we are asking tonight that an emergency meeting of the Security Council be convoked without delay to take action against this latest Soviet threat to world peace. Our resolution will call for the prompt dismantling and withdrawal of all offensive weapons in Cuba, under the supervision of U.N. observers, before the quarantine can be lifted.

Seventh, and finally: I call upon Chairman Khrushchev to halt and eliminate this clandestine, reckless and provocative threat to world peace and to stable relations between our two nations. I call upon him further to abandon this course of world domination, and to join in an historic effort to end the perilous arms race and transform the history of man. He has an opportunity now to move the world back from the abyss of destruction—by returning to his Government's own words that it had no need to station missiles outside its own territory, and withdrawing these weapons from Cuba—by refraining from any action which will widen or deepen the present crisis—and then by participating in a search for peaceful and permanent solutions. . . .

We are prepared to discuss new proposals for the removal of tensions on both sides—including the possibilities of a genuinely independent Cuba, free to determine its own destiny. We have no wish to war with the Soviet Union—for we are a peaceful people who desire to live in peace with all other peoples. . . .

Finally, I want to say a few words to the captive people of Cuba, to whom this speech is being directly carried by special radio facilities. I speak to you as a friend, as one who knows of your deep attachment to your fatherland, as one who shares your aspirations for liberty and justice for all. And I have watched with deep sorrow how your nationalist revolution was betrayed and how your fatherland fell under foreign domination. . . .

My fellow citizens: let no one doubt that this is a difficult and dangerous effort on which we have set out. No one can foresee precisely what course it will take or what costs or casualties will be incurred. Many months of sacrifice and self-discipline lie ahead—months in which both our will and our patience will be tested—months in which many threats and denunciations will keep us aware of our danger. But the greatest danger of all would be to do nothing.

The path we have chosen for the present is full of hazards, as all paths are—but it is the one most consistent with our character and courage as a nation and our commitments around the world. The cost of freedom is always high—but Americans have always paid it. And one path we shall never choose is the path of surrender or submission.

Our goal is not the victory of might but the vindication of right; not peace at the expense of freedom, but both peace and freedom, here in this hemisphere, and, we hope, around the world. God willing, that goal will be achieved.

John F. Kennedy, Radio and Television Address to the Nation. Washington, D.C., October 22, 1962. In *The Politics of John F. Kennedy*, by Edmund S. Ions. New York: Barnes & Noble, 1967.

DOCUMENT 5: SPEECH TO THE NATION ON THE NUCLEAR TEST BAN TREATY

In a televised speech on July 26, 1963, President Kennedy explains the newly concluded treaty with the Soviet Union to ban nuclear testing in the atmosphere, in outer space, and under water. Though he refers to the treaty as a small ray of light, he sees hope in a first step toward curbing nuclear danger.

I speak to you tonight in a spirit of hope. Eighteen years ago the advent of nuclear weapons changed the course of the world as well as the war. Since that time, all mankind has been struggling to escape from the darkening prospect of mass destruction on earth. In an age when both sides have come to possess enough nuclear power to destroy the human race several times over, the world of Communism and the world of free choice have been caught up in a vicious circle of conflicting ideology and interest. Each increase of tension has produced an increase of arms; each increase of arms has produced an increase of tension.

In these years the United States and the Soviet Union have frequently communicated suspicion and warnings to each other, but very rarely hope. Our representatives have met at the summit and at the brink; they have met in Washington and in Moscow, in Geneva and at the United Nations. But too often these meetings have produced only darkness, discord or disillusion.

Yesterday a shaft of light cut into the darkness. Negotiations were concluded in Moscow on a treaty to ban all nuclear tests in the atmosphere, in outer space and under water. For the first time, an agreement has been reached on bringing the forces of nuclear destruction under international control. . . .

That plan and many subsequent disarmament plans, large and small, have all been blocked by those opposed to international inspection. A ban on nuclear tests, however, requires on-the-spot inspection only for underground tests. This nation now possesses a variety of techniques to detect the nuclear tests of other nations which are conducted in the air or under water. For such tests produce unmistakable signs which our modern instruments can pick up.

The treaty initialed yesterday, therefore, is a limited treaty which permits continued underground testing and prohibits only those tests that we ourselves can police. It requires no control posts, no on-site inspection, no international body. We should also understand that it has other limits as well. Any nation which signs the treaty will have an opportunity to withdraw if it finds that extraordinary events related to the subject matter of the treaty have jeopardized its supreme interests; and no nation's right of self-defense will in any way be impaired. Nor does this treaty mean an end to the threat of nuclear war. It will not reduce nuclear stockpiles; it will not halt the production of nuclear weapons; it will not restrict their use in time of war.

Nevertheless, this limited treaty will radically reduce the nuclear testing which would otherwise be conducted on both sides; it will prohibit the United States, the United Kingdom, the Soviet Union and all others who sign it from engaging in the atmospheric tests which have so alarmed mankind; and it offers to all the world a welcome sign of hope.

For this is not a unilateral moratorium, but a specific and solemn legal obligation. While it will not prevent this nation from testing underground, or from being ready to conduct atmospheric tests if the acts of others so require, it gives us a concrete opportunity to extend its coverage to other nations and later to other forms of nuclear tests.

This treaty is in part the product of Western patience and vigilance. We have made clear, most recently in Berlin and Cuba, our deep resolve to protect our security and our freedom against any form of aggression. We have also made clear our steadfast determination to limit the arms race. In three administrations our soldiers and diplomats have worked together to this end, always supported by Great Britain. Prime Minister Macmillan joined with President Eisenhower in proposing a limited test ban in 1959, and again with me in 1961 and 1962.

But the achievement of this goal is not a victory for one side; it is a victory for mankind. It reflects no concessions either to or by the Soviet Union. It reflects simply our common recognition of the dangers in further testing.

This treaty is not the millennium. It will not resolve all conflicts, or cause the Communists to forgo their ambitions, or eliminate the danger of war. It will not reduce our need for arms or allies or programs of assistance to others. But it is an important first step—a step toward peace, a step toward reason, a step away from war.

John F. Kennedy, Television Speech to the Nation. Washington, D.C., July 26, 1963. In *The Politics of John F. Kennedy* by Edmund S. Ions. New York: Barnes & Noble, 1967.

DOCUMENT 6: CONSERVATION AND THE ENVIRONMENT

To Congress, to university audiences, and to citizens throughout the country, Kennedy warned against pollution and waste and spoke about conserving America's environment and using resources wisely.

It is not always the other person who pollutes our streams, or litters our highways, or throws away a match in a forest, or wipes out game, or wipes out our fishing reserves.

Pinchot Institute for Conservation Studies,
Milford, Pennsylvania, Sept. 24, 1963

Our primary task now is to increase our understanding of our environment, to a point where we can enjoy it without defacing it, use its bounty without detracting permanently from its value, and, above all, maintain a living balance between man's actions and nature's reactions, for this nation's great resource is as elastic and productive as our ingenuity can make it.

University of Wyoming, Laramie, Wyoming, Sept. 25, 1963

. . . We are reaching the limits of our fundamental needs—of water to drink, of fresh air to breathe, of open space to enjoy, of abundant sources of energy to make life easier.

Pinchot Institute for Conservation Studies,
Milford, Pennsylvania, Sept. 24, 1963

Our national conservation effort must include the complete spectrum of resources: air, water and land; fuels, energy and minerals; soils, forests and forage; fish and wildlife. Together they make up the world of nature which surrounds us—a vital part of the American heritage.

Message to Congress, Washington, D.C., March 1, 1962

One of the great resources which we are going to find in the next 40 years is not going to be the land; it will be the ocean. We are going to find untold wealth in the oceans of the world which will be used to make a better life for our people. Science is changing all of our natural environment. It can change it for good; it can change it for bad.

University of Wyoming, Laramie, Wyoming, Sept. 25, 1963

Our nation's progress is reflected in the history of our great river systems. The water that courses through our rivers and streams holds the key to full national development. Uncontrolled, it wipes out homes, lives and dreams, bringing disaster in the form of floods; controlled, it is an effective artery of transportation, a boon to industrial development, a source of beauty and recreation and the means for turning arid areas into rich and versatile cropland. In no resource field are conservation principles more applicable. By 1980, it is estimated, our national water needs will nearly double—by the end of the century they will triple. But the quantity of water which nature supplies will remain almost constant.

Message to Congress, Washington, D.C., March 1, 1962

Lake Superior, the Apostle Islands, the Bad River area, are all unique. They are worth improving for the benefit of sportsmen and tourists. In an area of congestion and pollution, men make noise and dirt. Lake Superior has a beauty that millions can enjoy. These islands are part of our American heritage. In a very real sense they tell the story of the development of this country. The vast marshes of the Bad River are a rich resource providing a home for a tremendous number and varied number of wild animals. In fact, the entire northern Great Lakes area, with its vast inland sea, its 27,000 lakes and thousands of streams, is a central and significant part of the fresh water assets of this country, and we must act to preserve these assets.

Ashland, Wisconsin, Sept. 24, 1963

You cannot farm this valley without realizing that there are problems in this valley which can be solved by the united action of all our people, in developing the natural resources. . . . It isn't enough to concern ourselves with what happens in this valley. The United States must also be concerned with what happens in Colombia and the Congo and Indonesia.

One hundred years ago, when this state was founded, the people who came here worried about their farms. Now we have to concern ourselves with the whole globe around us. . . . In the American Revolution, Thomas Paine said, "The cause of America is the cause of all mankind." I think in 1960 the cause of all mankind is the cause of America.

Merced, California, Sept. 9, 1960

John F. Kennedy, Excerpts from several speeches. In *America the Beautiful: In the Words of John F. Kennedy.* Ed. by Robert L. Polley. Elm Grove, WI: Country Beautiful Foundation, 1964.

DOCUMENT 7: ART AND EDUCATION IN A DEMOCRACY
Kennedy used platforms at universities, social occasions in the White House, dedication ceremonies, and television programs to reiterate his belief that an educated person learns from across the disciplines—art, philosophy, history, and science; therefore, all are important.

Thomas Jefferson once said that if you expect a people to be ignorant and free you expect what never was and never will be.

Washington, D.C., Feb. 16, 1962

Democracy is a difficult kind of government. It requires the highest qualities of self-discipline, restraint, a willingness to make commitments and sacrifices for the general interest, and also it requires knowledge.

Dublin, Ireland, June 28, 1963

. . . As the world presses in and knowledge presses out, the role of the interpreter grows. Men can no longer know everything themselves; the 20th century has no universal man. All men today must learn to know through one another—to judge across their own ignorance—to comprehend at second hand. These arts are not easily learned. Those who would practice them must develop intensity of perception, variety of mental activity and the habit of open concern for truth in all its forms. Where can we expect to find a training ground for this modern maturity, if not in our universities?

Boston College, Newton, Massachusetts, April 20, 1963

Education, quite rightly, is the responsibility of the state and the local community, but from the beginning of our country's history, from the time of the Northwest Ordinance, as John Adams and Thomas Jefferson recognized, from the time of the Morrill Act at the height of the Civil War, when the land-grant college system was set up under the Administration of President Lincoln, from the beginning it has been recognized that there must be a national commitment and that the national Government must play its role in stimulating a system of excellence which can serve the great national purpose of a free society. . . .

San Diego State College, San Diego, California, June 6, 1963

Federal aid to education is not merely of importance to those with children in school. . . . We live under majority rule and if that majority is not well educated in its responsibilities, the whole nation suffers.

East Los Angeles College, Los Angeles, California, Nov. 1, 1960

. . .This university and others like it across the country, and its graduates, have recognized that these schools are not maintained by the people of the various states in order to merely give the graduates of these schools an economic advantage in the life struggle. Rather, these schools are supported by our people because our people realize that this country has needed in the past, and needs today as never before, educated men and women who are committed to the cause of freedom.

University of Washington, Seattle, Washington, Nov. 16, 1961

Too often in the past, we have thought of the artist as an idler and dilettante and of the lover of arts as somehow sissy or effete. We have done both an injustice. The life of the artist is, in relation to his work, stern and lonely. He has labored hard, often amid deprivation, to perfect his skill. He has turned aside from quick success in order to strip his vision of everything secondary or cheapening. His working life is marked by intense application and intense discipline. As for the lover of arts, it is he who, by subjecting himself to the sometimes disturbing experience of art, sustains the artist—and seeks only the reward that his life will, in consequence, be the more fully lived.

"The Arts in America" (From the book, *Creative America*, The Ridge Press, 1963)

. . . The life of the arts, far from being an interruption, a distraction, in the life of a nation, is very close to the center of a nation's purpose—and is a test of the quality of a nation's civilization.

"The Arts in America" (From the book,
Creative America, The Ridge Press, 1963)

I think politicians and poets share at least one thing, and that is that their greatness depends upon the courage with which they face the challenges of life. There are many kinds of courage—bravery under fire, courage to risk reputation and friendship and career for convictions which are deeply held. Perhaps the rarest courage of all—for the skill to pursue it is given to very few men—is the courage to wage a silent battle to illuminate the nature of man and the world in which he lives. . . .

Robert Frost is often characterized as an American poet—or a New England poet. And he is, of course, all of these things, for the temper of his region and of his nation has provided a good deal of the meter and the tone in which he has dealt. But he is not a poet bounded by geography. He will live as a poet of the life of man, of the darkness and despair, as well as of the hope—which is, in his case, limited by a certain skepticism—and also for his wit and understanding of man's limitations which lie behind all of man's profoundest statements.

Recorded for the television program, "Robert Frost: American Poet." (CBS) Feb. 26, 1961

. . . Today, as always, art knows no national boundaries.

Genius can speak at any time, and the entire world will hear it and listen. Behind the storm of daily conflict and crisis, the dramatic confrontations, the tumult of political struggle, the poet, the artist, the musician, continue the quiet work of centuries, building bridges of experience between peoples, reminding man of the universality of his feelings and desires and despairs, and reminding him that the forces that unite are deeper than those that divide.

Thus, art and the encouragement of art is political in the most profound sense, not as a weapon in the struggle, but as an instrument of understanding of the futility of struggle between those who share man's faith. Aeschylus and Plato are remembered today long after the triumphs of imperial Athens are gone. Dante outlived the ambitions of 13th-century Florence. Goethe stands serenely above the politics of Germany, and I am certain that after the dust of centuries has passed over our cities, we, too, will be remembered not for victories or defeats in battle or in politics, but for our contribution to the human spirit.

It was Pericles' proudest boast that, politically, Athens was the school of Hellas. If we can make our country one of the great schools of civilization, then on that achievement will surely rest our claim to the ultimate gratitude of mankind. Moreover, as a great democratic society, we have a special responsibility to the arts, for art is the great democrat calling forth creative genius from every sector of society, disregarding race or religion or wealth or

color. The mere accumulation of wealth and power is available to
the dictator and the democrat alike. What freedom alone can bring
is the liberation of the human mind and spirit which finds its greatest flowering in the free society.

Thus, in our fulfillment of these responsibilities toward the arts
lies our unique achievement as a free society.

> Closed-circuit television broadcast on behalf of the National
> Cultural Center, Washington, D.C., Nov. 29, 1962

I want to tell you how welcome you are to the White House. I
think this is the most extraordinary collection of talent, of human
knowledge, that has ever been gathered together at the White
House, with the possible exception of when Thomas Jefferson
dined alone.

Someone once said that Thomas Jefferson was a gentleman of
32 who could calculate an eclipse, survey an estate, tie an artery,
plan an edifice, try a cause, break a horse and dance the minuet.
Whatever he may have lacked, if we could have had his former colleague, Mr. Franklin, here we all would have been impressed.

> Dinner honoring Nobel Prize winners of the Western
> Hemisphere, Washington, D.C., April 29, 1962

John F. Kennedy, Excerpts from various sources. In *America the Beautiful: In the Words
of John F. Kennedy.* Ed. by Robert L. Polley. Elm Grove, WI: Country Beautiful Foundation, 1964.

DOCUMENT 8: SPACE EXPLORATION

*Kennedy saw space exploration not only as an end in itself, but also
as an opportunity to gain useful scientific knowledge and as a challenge to work cooperatively with other nations for common human
good.*

Our aim is not simply to be first on the moon, any more than
Charles Lindbergh's real aim was to be the first to Paris. His aim
was to develop the techniques of our own country and other countries in the field of air and the atmosphere, and our objective in
making this effort, which we hope will place one of our citizens on
the moon, is to develop in a new frontier of science, commerce and
cooperation, the position of the United States and the free world.

> State of the Union Address to Congress,
> Washington, D.C., Jan. 11, 1962

Frank O'Connor, the Irish writer, tells in one of his books how, as
a boy, he and his friends would make their way across the countryside and when they came to an orchard wall that seemed too high
and too doubtful to try and too difficult to permit their voyage to continue, they took off their hats and tossed them over the wall—and
then they had no choice but to follow them. This nation has tossed
its cap over the wall of space, and we have no choice but to follow it.
Whatever the difficulties, they will be overcome; whatever the haz-

ards, they must be guarded against. With the . . . help of all those who labor in the space endeavor, with the help and support of all Americans, we will climb this wall with safety and speed, and we shall then explore the wonders on the other side.

Dedication of Aero-Space Medical Health Center,
Brooks Air Force Base, Texas, Nov. 21, 1963

We choose to go to the moon in this decade and do the other things, not because they are easy, but because they are hard, because that goal will serve to organize and measure the best of our energies and skills, because that challenge is one that we are willing to accept, one we are unwilling to postpone, and one which we intend to win, and the others, too.

Rice University, Houston, Texas, Sept. 12, 1962

We set sail on this new sea because there is new knowledge to be gained, and new rights to be won, and they must be won and used for the progress of all people. For space science, like nuclear science and all technology, has no conscience of its own. Whether it will become a force for good or ill depends on man, and only if the United States occupies a position of pre-eminence can we help decide whether this new ocean will be a sea of peace or a new terrifying theater of war. I do not say that we should or will go unprotected against the hostile misuse of space any more than we go unprotected against the hostile use of land or sea, but I do say that space can be explored and mastered without feeding the fires of war, without repeating the mistakes that man has made in extending his writ around this globe of ours.

There is no strife, no prejudice, no national conflict in outer space as yet. Its hazards are hostile to us all. Its conquest deserves the best of all mankind, and its opportunity for peaceful cooperation may never come again. But why, some say, the moon? Why choose this as our goal? And they may well ask why climb the highest mountain? Why, 35 years ago, fly the Atlantic? Why does Rice play Texas?

Rice University, Houston, Texas, Sept. 12, 1962

John F. Kennedy, Excerpts from various sources. In *America the Beautiful: In the Words of John F. Kennedy.* Ed. by Robert L. Polley. Elm Grove, WI: Country Beautiful Foundation, 1964.

Chronology

1917

United States entered World War I on April 6; John Fitzgerald Kennedy is born on May 29.

1918

World War I ends.

1920

League of Nations is organized.

1929

The American Stock Market crashes; the Kennedy family moves to Bronxville, New York, and purchases a summer home at Hyannis Port, Massachusetts.

1930

Enters Canterbury School.

1931

Enters Choate School.

1933

Franklin Delano Roosevelt becomes the thirty-second president; Hitler is voted into power in Germany.

1933–1936

Severe drought creates the "Dust Bowl" on the American plains.

1935

Graduates from Choate; studies in Europe during the summer; enters Princeton in the fall.

1936

Enters Harvard.

1938

Joseph Kennedy is appointed ambassador to Great Britain.

1939

Germany invades Poland, starting World War II.

1940

Graduates from Harvard; *Why England Slept* is published; joins the navy; Joseph Kennedy resigns as ambassador to England.

1941

Japan bombs Pearl Harbor; United States declares war on Japan, Germany, and Italy.

1944

Franklin Roosevelt dies; Harry S. Truman becomes the thirty-third president.

1945

Is discharged from navy; works as correspondent for Hearst newspapers; Germany surrenders; United States drops atomic bombs on Hiroshima and Nagasaki; Japan surrenders, ending World War II.

1946

Defeats nine other candidates in the Democratic Party for the Massachusetts Eleventh Congressional District; wins the general election for Congress in the fall.

1950

Korean War begins.

1952

Defeats Henry Cabot Lodge Jr. for a Senate seat.

1953

Marries Jacqueline Bouvier; Korean War ends.

1955

Writes *Profiles in Courage.*

1956

Tries to win Democratic nomination for vice-president, but fails.

1957

Receives Pulitzer Prize in Biography for *Profiles in Courage*; Soviet Union launches Sputnik, the first satellite in space; daughter Caroline is born.

1958

Wins election to second Senate term by large margin; Castro ousts Batista in Cuba and sets up his own regime.

1960

Announces candidacy for presidency and runs in primaries; is victorious in West Virginia primary; Democrats nominate Kennedy as presidential candidate; debates Nixon in first live television debate; wins the presidential election by small margin; son John Fitzgerald Jr. is born.

1961

Is inaugurated as thirty-fifth President of the United States; creates Peace Corps by executive order; proposes Alliance for Progress between United States and Latin America; assumes responsibility for failed Bay of Pigs invasion; proposes putting American space team on the moon within the decade; meets with French president Charles de Gaulle in Paris; meets Nikita Khrushchev in Vienna; Soviets build the Berlin Wall; reaffirms U.S. commitment to West Berlin; enlarges advisory force in Vietnam; Congress defeats Kennedy legislation on education, medical care for the aged; Alan Shepard becomes America's first man in space; Pablo Casals entertains in the White House.

1962

Forces United States Steel Company to rescind its price increase; James Meredith enters the University of Mississippi protected by federal troops; astronaut John Glenn flies first U.S. space flight around Earth; announces naval quarantine to halt the Soviet missile buildup in Cuba; Khrushchev removes the missiles; signs executive order barring segregation in federally funded housing facilities.

1963

Calls for massive tax reduction and tax reform to help the economy; delivers speech at American University proposing talks on a nuclear arms test ban treaty; mobilizes the Alabama National Guard to admit two black students to the University of Alabama; proposes sweeping civil rights legislation; travels to Berlin, Ireland, and Italy; signs the Limited Nuclear Test Ban Treaty; son Patrick Bouvier dies two days after premature birth; is assassinated by Lee Harvey Oswald in Dallas, Texas, on November 22; is buried in Arlington National Cemetery following a state funeral on November 25.

For Further Research

About John F. Kennedy

Letitia Baldrige, *In the Kennedy Style*. New York: Doubleday, 1998.

Jim Bishop, *A Day in the Life of President Kennedy*. New York: Franklin Watts, 1962.

David Bruner, *John F. Kennedy and a New Generation*, ed. by Oscar Handlin. Boston: Little, Brown, 1988.

Robert Donovan, *PT 109: John F. Kennedy in World War II*. Greenwich, CT: Fawcett, 1961

C. David Heymann, *A Woman Named Jackie*. New York: Penguin, 1990.

Victor Lasky, *J.F.K.: The Man and the Myth*. New York: Macmillan, 1963.

I.E. Levine, *The Young Man in the White House: John Fitzgerald Kennedy*. New York: Julian Messner, 1964.

William Manchester, *The Death of a President*. New York: Harper and Row, 1967.

Jude Mills, *John F. Kennedy*. New York: Franklin Watts, 1962.

The New York Times, The Kennedy Years. Harold Faber, ed. New York: Viking, 1964.

Kenneth P. O'Donnell and David Powers, with Joe McCarthy, *"Johnny, We Hardly Knew Ye": Memories of John Fitzgerald Kennedy*. Boston: Little, Brown, 1970.

Peter Schwab and J. Lee Shnudman, *John F. Kennedy*. Boston: Twayne, 1974.

Hugh Sidney, *John F. Kennedy, President*. New York: Atheneum, 1964.

ABOUT KENNEDY'S TIMES

Jules Archer, *The Incredible Sixties: The Stormy Years that Changed America.* San Diego: Harcourt Brace Jovanovich, 1986.

Benjamin C. Bradlee, *Conversations with Kennedy.* New York: W.W. Norton, 1975.

Philip B. Kunhardt Jr., ed., *Life in Camelot: The Kennedy Years.* Boston: Little, Brown, 1988.

Karal Ann Marling, *As Seen on TV: The Visual Culture of Everyday Life in the 1950s.* Cambridge: Harvard University Press, 1994.

Douglas T. Miller and Marion Nowak, *The Fifties: The Way We Really Were.* Garden City, NY: Doubleday, 1977.

Allan Nevins and Henry Steele Commager with Jeffrey Morris, *A Pocket History of the United States.* 9th rev. ed. New York: Pocket Books, 1986.

Ronald Oakley, *God's Country: America in the Fifties.* New York: Dembner Books, 1986.

Norman L. Rosenberg, Emily S. Rosenberg, and James R. Moore, *In Our Times: America Since World War II.* Englewood Cliffs, NJ: Prentice-Hall, 1976.

I.F. Stone, *The Haunted Fifties,* Boston: Little, Brown, 1963.

Robert Weisbrat, *Marching Toward Freedom, 1957–1965: From the Founding of the Southern Leadership Conference to the Assassination of Malcolm X.* New York: Chelsea, 1994.

BY KENNEDY

John F. Kennedy, *Profiles in Courage.* New York: Harper & Brothers, 1955.

_____, *Why England Slept.* New York: Wilfred Funk, 1961.

INTERNET

John Fitzgerald Kennedy Library and Museum website. Online. Available at http://www.cs.umb.edu/jfklibrary.

INDEX

Abram, Morris B., 126
Adams, Arthur S., 124, 126
Addison's disease, 13
adultery, 194
African Americans
  university admittance denied for, 106
  see also civil rights
Alabama National Guard, 105, 106
Albert, Carl, 74
Alliance for Progress, 24, 132, 186, 205
  and Bay of Pigs, 134–35
  conference on, 135–36
  failure of, 137–39
  furthered American imperialism,
    139–40
  goals of, 133–34, 136
Alte Hofburg, 143
Ambassador East Hotel, 64
American University, 206
*And the Crooked Places Made
  Straight: The Struggle for Social
  Change in the 1960's* (Chalmers), 81
Area Redevelopment Act of 1961, 193
Argentina, 136
Armco Steel, 93
Aronson, Arnold, 95
Assumption School, 51

Baez, Joan, 109
Baldwin, James, 98, 106
Barber, James David, 190
Barnett, Ross, 99
Bayley, Edwin R., 126
Bay of Pigs, 164, 191, 192
  and Alliance for Progress, 134–35
  as a disaster, 24–25
  liberal policy used in, 198–99
  mission, 117–19
  possibilities in success of, 122–23
  reasons for failure of, 119–22
Belafonte, Harry, 106
Bergquist, Laura, 20
Berlin airlift of 1948, 199
Berlin crisis, 192, 199–200

attempted negotiations on, 151–52
Kennedy's response to, 147–48,
  201–203
Kennedy's television address on,
  153 54
and military build up, 151
Vienna talks on, 144–46
  see also Berlin Wall
Berlin Wall, 26, 149–50, 154–55
Kennedy's response to, 155, 157,
  183–84
tensions created from, 158
Bernstein, Irving, 87
Bethlehem Steel, 92, 93, 94
Birmingham, Alabama
  demonstrations in, 103–105
  riot in, 105–106
Biryuzov, Sergie, 166
Bissel, Richard, 119–20
Black Saturday, 170
Block, Joseph, 93
Blough, Roger M., 88, 90, 91, 94
Bodenheimer, Susanne, 137
Bohlen, Charles E., 122, 143
Bonsal, Philip, 115
Boston Latin School, 38, 51–52, 54–55
Bouvier, Jacqueline. *See* Kennedy,
  Jackie
Bowles, Chester, 122, 198
Boyce, Gordon, 126
Brazil, 124, 131
Britain, 124
Brogan, Sir Denis, 74
Bundy, McGeorge, 181, 198
  on Kennedy's speech in Berlin, 156
  personality of, 73
  and steel industry, 92
  and Ted Sorensen, 72
  on U.S. relations with Cuba, 117
  war experience of, 76
Bunting, Mary, 126
Burdick, Eugene, 203–204
Burner, David, 193, 196
Burns, James MacGregor, 54

business
  Kennedy's conflict with, 87–88
  in Latin America, 139–41

Cabot, Henry, 15
Cameron, Gail, 36
campaigns
  for House Representative, 15
  1960 presidential, 20–22, 180–81
    primaries, 18–20
  for Senator, 15–16
  vice-presidential, 16–17
Caplin, Mortimer, 76
Cardona, José Miró, 118
Carleton, William G., 179
Casals, Pablo, 27
Castro, Fidel, 18, 198
  and Alliance for Progress, 134
  assassination plot against, 115–16,
    120
  Eisenhower administration on, 115,
    116
  Kennedy on, 116
  on Soviet missiles in Cuba, 166
  U.S. effort to overthrow, 164–65
  on U.S. invasion, 169
  White Paper on, 118
  see also Bay of Pigs
Castro, Raúl, 166
Catholics, 180
  John Kennedy as, 21–22
  Rose Kennedy as, 59
Celler, Emanuel, 96, 110
Chalmers, David, 81
Charter of Punta del Este, 136
Chelsea Naval Hospital, 14
Chile, 131
China, 176
Choate, 13
*Choosing Our King: Powerful Symbols
  in Presidential Politics* (Novak), 190
CIA (Central Intelligence Agency), 18
  and Bay of Pigs, 118, 119–20
  and Cuba, 115–16, 164
civil rights, 17
  American public on, 110–11
  bill passed on, 113
  Birmingham campaign for, 103–105
    and riot, 105–106
  consensus politics on, 101
  influence of march on, 100
  Kennedy on, 102, 183
    bill proposed by, 107–108, 109–10
    in campaign, 29
    ignores demands on, 97–98
    inaction by, 95–96
    speech on, 107
    television address on, 99
  legislation on, 105–106
  Lyndon B. Johnson on, 111–12

  protests on, 98–99, 106–107, 108–109
  Washington march on, 108–109
Civil Rights Act, 113
Civil Rights Commission, 97, 102–103
Clark, Joseph, 96
Clark, Kenneth C., 98, 106
Clay, Lucius, 157, 201, 202
Cleveland, Harlan, 74
Clifford, Clark, 23, 93, 94
Cold War. *See* Berlin crisis;
  communism; Cuban missile crisis
Colombia, 131
Colorado Fuel & Iron, 93
Columbia Trust Company, 49
communism, 176, 177
  and Alliance for Progress, 134
  American fear of, 17–18
  Kennedy's war against, 203–205
Congress
  on civil rights bill, 108, 109–10, 112
  Kennedy's relations with, 181–83
  see also Kennedy administration
Connor, Eugene T., 99, 103–104
Cordiner, Ralph J., 88
Coriolanus (Shakespeare), 82
Cox, Archibald, 64, 93
Cuba, 18, 132
  and Soviet Union, 163
  U.S. campaign against, 164–65
  Khrushchev on, 171–72
  U.S. relations with
    under Eisenhower, 115–16
    under Kennedy, 117
  see also Bay of Pigs; Castro, Fidel;
    Cuban missile crisis
Cuban missile crisis, 28, 192
  deployment of missiles, 165–66,
    167–68
  events leading to, 162–65
  Kennedy's response to, 166–67
  Kennedy's success in, 186–87
  Khrushchev's explanation of, 172–74
  missile withdrawal, 169
  Soviet Union's efforts to resolve,
    174–75
  and U.S. imperialism, 171–72
Cuban Revolutionary Council, 118
Curley, Jim, 14–15
Cushing, Cardinal Robert Richard, 23

Dallas Trade Mart, 30
Daughters of the American
  Revolution, 125
Day, Edward, 76
debate, Nixon-Kennedy, 21
  importance of images in, 70
  Kennedy's preparation for, 64
  Kennedy's strategies, 67–68
  Nixon's errors in, 69–70
  Nixon's preparation for, 65

in studio before, 65–67
DeGaulle, Charles, 25–26
Democratic Convention, 1960, 19
demonstrations, civil rights, 103–104, 106
see also marches, civil rights
Dennis, Lawrence, 126
Diem, Ngo Dinh, 18
Dillon, Douglas, 76, 94, 135
Dirksen, Everett McKinley, 112
Dobrynin, Anatoly, 159, 168, 169
domestic policy. *See* Alliance for Progress; civil rights; Peace Corps
Dominican Republic, 136
domino theory, 18
Donovan, Robert, 14
Douglas, Paul, 89–90
Dulles, Allen, 18, 118, 119–20
Dungan, Ralph, 72
Dutton, Fred, 72
Dylan, Bob, 109

East Germany. *See* Berlin crisis
economic sanctions, 164
Ecuador, 136
Eisenhower, Dwight D.
  and civil rights, 97
  contact with real world, 84–85
  Khrushchev on, 144
  on politics, 84
  as president, 17, 18
Eisenhower administration
  on Cuba, 115–16
  on Latin America, 133
  White House during, 79
elections, 1960 presidential, 22–23, 197
  polls on, 63
  see also campaigns
Evans, Rowland, Jr., 19
Evashevski, Forest, 126
Evers, Medgar, 107
executive committee (ExComm), 205

Fairlie, Henry, 95
Farber, David, 23
Farmer, James, 99
Fay, Paul, 76
Feldman, Mike, 64
Feldman, Myer, 72
Finch, Bob, 65, 67
Fisher, Bob, 53
Fiske, Arthur Irving, 51–52
Fitzgerald, Ellen Rosanna, 36
Fitzgerald, John F. (grandfather), 36
  childhood of, 37–38
  as mayor, 41
  in politics, 38–40
  relationship with daughter, 36–37, 39–40
Fitzgerald, Mary Ellen, 36

Fitzgerald, Rosanna (great-grandmother), 36
Fitzgerald, Rose. *See* Kennedy, Rose
Fitzgerald, Thomas (great-grandfather), 36, 37
Fomin, Aleksandr, 169
Food-for-Peace program, 186
foreign policy. *See* Berlin crisis; Cuban missile crisis
Freeman, Orville, 76
Frost, Robert, 23, 196
Fulbright, William, 74, 122

Galbraith, John Kenneth, 122
Gardner, Richard, 74
Garthoff, Raymond L., 162
Gavin, James, 76
Gearan, Mark, 129
General Electric, 88
Germany
  Khrushchev on, 144, 146
  as threat to Soviet Union, 200
  see also Berlin crisis; Berlin Wall; West Berlin
Giancana, Sam, 193
Goldberg, Arthur, 76, 89, 90, 94
Goodwin, Dick, 72, 181
  and Alliance for Progress, 133
  and Bay of Pigs, 122
Gordon, Kermit, 74
  and steel industry, 90, 92
Gordon, Lester, 126
Gore, Albert, 89–90
Grady, Ronan, 50
Green Berets, 27–28, 203
Greene, Marie, 40, 43
Gregory, Dick, 109
Gribkov, Anatoly, 167
Gromyko, Andrei, 159, 168
Guatemala, 136

Halle, Louis, 64, 119
Hansberry, Lorraine, 106
Harris, Louis, 110
Harris, Seymour, 74
Harvard University
  John Kennedy at, 13–14
  Joseph Kennedy at, 52–53
  and Kennedy administration, 74
  Medical School, 38
Hayden, Stone and Company, 56
Hershey, Lewis B., 129
Herter, Christian, 117
Hewitt, Don, 66
Hickey, Mary (grandmother), 49
Hilsman, Roger, 76
Hitch, Charles, 74
Hodges, Luther, 80, 87–88, 92–93
Honduras, 136
Horne, Lena, 106

House Rules Committee, 72
Hovde, Frederick, 95
Humphrey, Hubert, 125
Hyannisport, 60

I'm for Roosevelt, 57
inaugural address, 23, 196, 197
India, 131
Inland Steel, 93
Inter-American Economic and Social
    Council, 135
International Cooperative Alliance,
    127, 128-29
Ireland, 29, 48
    immigrants from, 37, 45-46, 47-49
Italy, 29, 169

Johnson, Lyndon B., 19
    and civil rights, 100, 111-12, 113
    and Peace Corps, 126
    on presidential debate, 70
    sworn in as president, 31
    visit to Berlin, 149-50, 157, 201
Jones & Laughlin (steel company), 93

Kahn, Herman, 207
Kaiser, Philip, 74
Kaiser Steel, 93
Katzenbach, Nicholas, 74, 76, 106
Keating, Kenneth B., 125
Kempton, Murray, 100
Kennedy, Bridget Murphy (great-
    grandmother), 46
Kennedy, Caroline (daughter), 17
Kennedy, Edward (brother), 12, 20
Kennedy, Eunice (sister), 12, 15
Kennedy, Jack. *See* Kennedy, John
    Fitzgerald
Kennedy, Jackie, 16-17
    admiration of, 32-33
    and campaigning, 20, 22
    cultural appeal of, 197
    international attention given to, 26
    at Kennedy's funeral, 30-31
    Khrushchev with, 145
    memorial to Kennedy, 33
    and space dog, 149
    and White House events, 27
Kennedy, Jean (sister), 12
Kennedy, Johanna (great aunt), 46
Kennedy, John Fitzgerald, 171
    achievements of, 192-93
    America's public image of, 32-33
    assassination of, 30-31
    back surgery, 16
    on Bay of Pigs, 119, 121, 122
        liberalism in, 198-99
    on Berlin crisis, 147-48, 152-54,
        201-203
        commitment to West Berlin,

151-52, 159-60
    Khrushchev's softened attitude
        toward, 148-49
    talks on, 143-44, 146-47, 158-59
    on Berlin Wall, 149-50, 183-84
    birth of, 12
    and campaign against Cuba, 164-65
    childhood illnesses of, 13
    on civil rights, 29, 95-96, 102-103,
        183
        bill proposed by, 107-108, 111
        consensus politics on, 99-101
        ignores protests on, 98-99
        King's criticism of, 96-98
        legislation as response to, 105-106
        response to Birmingham
            demonstrations, 104
        voter opinion on, 110-11
        and Washington march, 108-109
    and Cold War, 184
    conflict with Business Advisory
        Council, 87-88
    contact with real world, 84-85
    criticism of, 191-92
    and Cuban missile crisis, 28, 166-67,
        186-87
        response to Khrushchev's speech
            on, 176-77
        settlement by, 169-70
        success in, 186-87
        television address on, 205-206
    Cuba problem worsened under,
        116-17
    education of, 13-14
    election victory, 22-23
    as exemplary presidential figure,
        194-95
    family influences on, 188-89
    first year as president, 24-27
    foreign aid programs under, 186
    funeral of, 31-32
    as House Representative, 14-15
    image vs. reality of, 190-91
    inauguration of, 23, 196, 197
    intellectual/cultural appeal of,
        197-98
    on Latin America, 134-37
        and business community, 139-40
    legislative achievements of, 181-82
    marriage of, 16
    and national defense, 184-85
    on "New Frontier," 75
    and Peace Corps, 123, 129-30
    personality of, 82
    personal misconduct of, 193-94
    physical appearance of, 80-81
    politics of, 83-84
    and presidential debate, 64, 66, 67-68
        facial language in, 70
        Nixon's comments on, 69-70

and presidential election, 20–22,
180–81, 197
relationships of, 82–83
relationship with administration,
72–73
relationship with Congress, 182–83
relationship with Joe Junior, 43,
60–61
relationship with press, 80
as Senator, 15–16
and steel industry
fights U.S. Steel, 91–93
on price hikes, 89–91
victory over, 93–94
on test ban treaty, 145, 185, 207
on Third World problems, 132–33
on United Nations, 185–86
vice-presidential campaign, 16–17
on Vietnam, 27–28
visit to Berlin, 156, 160–61
visit to Europe, 27–29
visit to Ireland, 48
and war against communism,
203–205
in World War II, 14
see also Kennedy administration
Kennedy, John F., Jr. (son), 23, 32
Kennedy, Joseph, Jr. (brother), 12
death of, 189
family responsibilities of, 59
relationship with John Kennedy, 43,
60
Kennedy, Joseph Patrick (father),
54–55
birth of, 49
and campaigning, 18–19
childhood of, 50
death of, 14
education of, 51–53
fortune built by, 55–56
influence on John Kennedy, 188, 189
on money, 53
moneymaking during youth, 50–51
parenting of, 12–13, 58–59, 60, 61
political involvement of, 56–57
public's image of, 57–58
stroke of, 29–30
Kennedy, Kathleen (sister), 12, 15
Kennedy, Margaret (great aunt), 46
Kennedy, Mary (great aunt), 46
Kennedy, Patricia (sister), 12
Kennedy, Patrick (great-grandfather),
45, 46
Kennedy, Patrick Bouvier (son), 30
Kennedy, Patrick Joseph (grandfather)
business practices of, 49–50
as father, 51
and Kennedy's visit to Ireland, 48
marriage of, 49
in politics, 46, 48, 50

as saloon owner, 47
youth of, 46
Kennedy, Robert (brother), 12
on brother's illnesses, 13
on civil rights, 98–99, 106, 112, 183
and Cuban missile crisis, 169, 206
and Kennedy's campaign, 15, 18–19,
20
and steel industry, 92
Kennedy, Rose (mother)
influence of, 188–89
and Kennedy's campaign, 15–16
marriage of, 55
as mother, 12, 13, 42–44, 59
on politics, 40–42
relationship with father, 36–37,
39–40
Kennedy, Rosemary (sister), 12
Kennedy administration, 79–80, 181
criticism of, 77–78
intellectualism of, 74–75
liberalism of, 198
mood of, 71–72, 76–77
reform under, 73–74
staff of, 72–73
versatility of, 77
war experiences of, 75–76
Kennedy children, 12, 55
competition between, 58–59
upbringing of, 42–44
Khrushchev, Nikita, 67, 171
on Berlin, 146
and Berlin crisis, 158, 159
correspondence with Kennedy on,
202
Kennedy's thoughts on, 147–48
softened attitude with Kennedy on,
148–49
talks with Kennedy on, 142–44
and Cuban missile crisis, 168, 206
explanation of Soviet actions by,
172–74
settlement by, 169–70
on Soviet efforts to resolve, 174–76
on Germany, 144, 199–200
and Jackie Kennedy, 26
on Laos problem, 145
on nuclear testing, 207
on U.S. campaign against Cuba,
171–72
on U.S. superiority, 162–63
King, Martin Luther, Jr., 107–108
and campaign in Birmingham, 103
criticism of Kennedy, 96–98
Kennedy assisting, 22
speech by, 29, 100, 109
Klein, Herb, 65
Kohler, Foy, 143

Laos, 144–45, 191

Latin America
  Eisenhower on, 17
  U.S. aid to, 132
  see also Bay of Pigs; Castro, Fidel;
    Cuban missile crisis
Leadership Conference on Civil
  Rights, 95
Lederer, William J., 203–204
legislation
  civil rights, 29, 95–96, 102, 105–106,
    109–10, 111–13
  Kennedy's contribution in, 181–82,
    191
"Letter from the Birmingham Jail,"
  103
Lewis, John, 100, 109
liberalism, 207–208
  and Bay of Pigs, 198–99
  and Berlin crisis, 202–203
  in Kennedy's politics, 83–84
  and test ban treaty, 207
Lincoln, Abraham, 111, 195
Lincoln, Evelyn, 26, 72
Lincoln Memorial, 109
Lippmann, Walter, 99, 116
Livernash, Robert E., 89
Lodge, Henry Cabot, 15
Lukens (steel company), 92

MacGregor, James, 15
mafia, 193
Malcolm X, 105
Malinovsky, Rodion, 162, 166
Mansfield, Mike, 108
marches, civil rights, 29, 100, 108–109
  see also demonstrations, civil rights
Maritime Commission, 56–57
Markmann, Charles Lam, 123
Marshall, Burke, 104, 105
Martin, Louis E., 126
Martin, Ralph G., 21, 25, 156
Matthews, Christopher, 63
Matusow, Allen J., 102
Mazo, Earl, 63
McCarthy, Joseph, 142
McConnell, Grant, 94
McCulloch, William, 110
McDonald, David, 90
McDonald, Norman, 12–13
McGhee, George, 74
McLouth Steel, 93
McMurray, Joseph, 95
McNamara, Robert, 92, 198, 203
Meany, George, 124
media. *See* press, the; television
Meyers, Chuck, 129
Mikoyan, Anastas, 165
military
  in Cuba
    Soviet, 167–68

United States, 164–65, 168–69
  unauthorized firing by, 170
  in Germany, 150, 152, 155, 157, 201
Miller, Loreen, 98
Miroff, Bruce, 132
Mississippi, 103
Monnet, Jean, 74–75
Mutual Security Agency, 127

NAACP (National Association for the
  Advancement of Colored People), 96
Nation, The, 97, 98
National Advisory Council (Peace
  Corps), 126
National Student Conference, 124
NATO (North Atlantic Treaty
  Organization), 147, 185
New Deal, 57, 76
New Frontier, 75–76
New Frontiersmen, 23
  see also Kennedy administration
Newsweek, 99
New York Times
  Kennedy on businessmen in, 92
  story on Vienna talks in, 146–47
Nigeria, 124, 131
Nixon, Richard, 20
  in Gallup poll, 63
  in presidential debate, 21, 65–67,
    68–70
  on public's opinion of, 64
  on television's influence, 63
Noddle's Island, 45
Novak, Michael, 190
nuclear missiles, 116
  and Kennedy's administration,
    184–85
  and U.S. superiority over Soviet
    Union, 162–63
  see also Cuban missile crisis
nuclear war, 142, 151

O'Brian, Lawrence, 66–67, 72, 182
O'Donnell, Ken, 72, 76, 91, 142, 182
On Thermonuclear War (Kahn), 207
Operation Mongoose, 164, 191
Operation Zapata, 121
Organization of American States
  (OAS), 164
Oswald, Lee Harvey, 31
Oxford, 74

Pakistan, 131
Passman, Otto E., 125
Paterson, Thomas G., 115
Patterson, Bradley, 125–26
Peace Corps, 24, 132, 186
  administration of, 125–26
  financing/purpose of, 127, 129
  first volunteers for, 130–31

Kennedy on, 123, 129–30
popularity of, 131
preparing volunteers for, 128
strong support for, 124–25
volunteers living abroad for, 128–29
as war against communism,
203–204
Peru, 136
Philippines, 131
Pliyev, Issa, 167
Pollock, Henry, 124
polls, 1960 election, 63
potato famine, 37
Powers, David F., 25, 142
Presidential Character, The (Barber),
190
press, the
Kennedy's image through, 190–91
Kennedy's relationship with, 26–27,
80
Princeton University, 13
Profiles in Courage (Kennedy), 16
PT 109, 14
Punta del Este, 136–37, 164
Pushinka (space dog), 148–49

Quimby, Thomas H.E., 126

Radziwill, Princess Lee, 26
Rayburn, Sam, 23
Reed, James, 76
Reeves, Thomas C., 145, 188
Republic Steel, 93
Reston, James, 26–27
Reuss, Henry, 125
Rhodes Scholars, 74
riots. *See* demonstrations, civil rights
Robinson, James, 126
Rockefeller, John D., IV, 126
Rogers, William, 65
Roosevelt, Franklin D.
Joseph Kennedy's support for, 56, 57
Rostow, Walt, 157, 198
Rowen, Hobart, 88, 90
Ruby, Jack, 31
Rusk, Dean, 74, 76
and Bay of Pigs, 121–22
and Berlin crisis talks, 143, 159
and Cuban missile crisis, 168
as liberal, 198
on U.S.–Cuba relations, 117
Rusk, Howard A., 126
Russell, Richard B., 112
Rustin, Bayard, 100

Salinger, Pierre, 72, 76, 96
Saltonstall, Leverett, 38
Santamaria, Carlos Samz de, 124
scarlet fever, 13
Scharf, Adolf, 143

Schlesinger, Arthur, Jr., 71, 198
and anti-Castroism, 118
and Bay of Pigs, 122
on Latin America, 139–40
and steel industry, 94
Schonbrunn Palace, 145
Seali, John, 169
Securities and Exchange Commission,
56
segregation. *See* civil rights
Senior Citizens Committee, 104
Sherwin, Mark, 123
Shriver, Sargent, 24
and Peace Corps, 125, 131
on presidential debate, 70
Sims, Albert G., 126
Smith, Al, 21
Smith, Earl, 82
Smith, Howard K., 67
Smith, Jerome, 98–99
Smith, Merriman, 77–78
Sorenson, Ted, 16, 72, 73, 151, 181
during campaigns, 21
and civil rights legislation, 96
and inaugural address, 196
and presidential debate, 64
and *Profiles in Courage*, 16
speech on civil rights, 107
and steel industry, 92
South Vietnam, 132, 191–92
U.S. aid to, 27–28
Soviet Union
and Cuba, 18, 116, 163, 165
and Cuban missile crisis, 28
efforts to resolve, 174–76
Khrushchev's explanation of,
172–74
knowledge of U.S. actions on, 164
missile deployment by, 165–66,
167–68
Germany as threat to, 200
and nuclear test ban treaty, 185
space program, 18, 25
U.S. nuclear missile superiority over,
162–63
space programs, 18, 25
Special Forces, 203
Sputnik, 18, 25
dog in, 149
Stahr, Elvis, 74
Stanton, Frank, 66
State of the Union Message, 25, 184
Steel, Ronald, 134
steel industry
price increases in, 88–91
see also U.S. Steel
Stevenson, Adlai, 19, 122
and Cuban missile crisis, 205
and Peace Corps, 127
presidential campaign by, 16–17

St. Matthew's Cathedral, 31
Stone, Galen, 56
Stone, I.F., 99
Stravinsky, Igor, 27
strikes, steel industry, 88–89
Suffolk Coal Company, 49
Sumner Savings Bank, 49
Szulc, Tad, 138

Tanganyika (Africa), 130–31
Taylor, Maxwell, 198
television
    Kennedy's address on Berlin crisis
        on, 153–54
    Kennedy's address on Cuban missile
        crisis on, 205–206
    Kennedy's address on discrimination
        on, 99–100
    and 1960 presidential campaign,
        20–21
    Nixon on influence of, 63
    Oswald's death on, 31
    possibilities through, 33
    and presidential debate, 65
    White House tour on, 27
test ban treaty, 145, 146–47, 159, 185,
    186–87, 207
Third World
    Kennedy's approach to, 132–33
    see also Alliance for Progress; Peace
        Corps
Thompson, Llewellyn, 143, 159
Timmons, Lane, 74
Tobin, Maurice, 92
Torch Is Passed, The (Burner and
    West), 193
Trade Expansion Act of 1962, 182
Triffin, Robert, 74
Truman, Harry, 190
    personality of, 81–82
    on presidency, 190
Turkey, 162, 163, 169, 186
Turnbow, Hartman, 113
Tyson, Robert, 93

Udall, Stewart, 76
Ugly American, The (Lederer and
    Burdick), 204
United Fruit Company, 118, 198–99
United Nations, 185–86
United States
    campaign against Cuba, 164–65
        Khrushchev on, 171–72
    and Cuban missile crisis, 166–67,
        168
        Khrushchev on, 173–74
    imperialism in Latin America,
        139–41
    in 1950s, 18
    nuclear missile superiority over

Soviet Union, 162–63
    relations with Cuba, 115–16, 117
    see also Congress
University of Alabama, 106
U.S. Steel
    defeat of, 93–94
    demands price increases, 91–92
    as price leader, 89
    at war with government, 92–93

Vesey, Ernest, 130
Vidal, Gore, 79
Vienna Boys' Choir, 145–46
Vienna talks, 143–46
Vieques (island), 164
Vietnam, 18, 191–92
Voluntary Overseas Services, 127

Wallace, George, 106
Walsh, Ed, 25
Warren, Earl, 17
Warren Commission, 31
Washington, George, 194–95
Watson, Thomas J., 126
West, Thomas R., 193
West Berlin
    after building of Berlin Wall, 159–60
    Johnson's visit to, 149–50, 157, 201
    Kennedy's commitment to, 151–52
    Kennedy's visit to, 156, 160–61
    military in, 155, 157
    refugee exodus to, 154–55, 200
    see also Berlin crisis; Berlin Wall
Whalen, Richard J., 45
White, Byron, 74, 76
White, Lee, 72
White House
    as "Camelot," 81
    cultural/intellectual endeavors in, 27
    during Eisenhower administration,
        79
    see also Kennedy administration
"White Paper," 92, 94, 118
Why England Slept (Kennedy), 13–14
Why We Can't Wait (King), 104
Wiggins, Warren W., 126
Wilkins, Roy, 95, 107
Williams, Robert F., 105
Wofford, Harris, 96
World Health Organization, 131
World War II
    and Kennedy administration, 75–76
    Kennedy's service in, 14

Xaverian School, 51

Yorkshire Post, The, 124
Young, John D., 126
Young, Whitney, 99
Youngstown Steel, 93